THE CROSS
UNDER THE
ACACIA TREE

The Story of David & Eunice Simonson's
Epic Mission in Africa

BY JIM KLOBUCHAR

KIRK HOUSE PUBLISHERS
MINNEAPOLIS, MINNESOTA

THE CROSS UNDER THE ACACIA TREE

The Story of David & Eunice Simonson's Epic Mission in Africa

Cover Design: Karen Walhof

Production of this book is partially funded with a grant from Lutheran Brotherhood.

Library of Congress Cataloging-in-Publication Data

Klobuchar, Jim
    The Cross under the acacia tree: the story of David and Eunice Simonson's epic mission in Africa / Jim Klobuchar
      p. cm.
    ISBN 1-886513-22-8
    1. Simonson, David. 2. Simonson, Eunice. 3. Missionaries—Tanzania—Biography. 4. Missionaries—United States—Biography. 5. Lutheran Church—Missions—Tanzania. 6. Maasai (African people)—Missions. I. Title.
    BV3625.T42S555   1999
    266'.41'0922—dc21
    [b]   98-55356
                                                                        CIP

Kirk House Publishers, PO Box 390759, Minneapolis, Minnesota 55439
Manufactured in the United States of America.

FOREWORD

An encounter of legendaries, this book is the outcome of the meeting of three characters who are each strong enough to have sought strength in others and to have given it freely, with a reckless self-abandon that makes them fascinating.

The first is Jim Klobuchar. A longtime columnist for the Minneapolis Star, then the StarTribune, his colorful, insightful writing has thrown life in the Twin Cities into oblique, so that it appeared in different angle. Whether it was an executive bathroom key that disappeared in a putsch at the Lutheran Brotherhood, some high-jinks with one of the old Viking players, an obscure ordinary caught in a tangle or a hilarious reminiscence from his days on Minnesota's iron range, Jim has always had an eye for the soft ironies and hard edges, the vacant stupidities and quiet heroics of the day.

But he hasn't spared himself. Wiry, tough to the core, he has pushed his own limits physically—on a bicycle, climbing in the Himalayas, hiking in the Serengeti or traveling to some remote corner. He has done the same emotionally. Without becoming maudlin or offering himself as a hero of moral self-reclamation, he has written directly of his family struggles or his difficulties passing an old watering hole like the Little Wagon after work. And he has taken on the good Lord, coming to faith without yielding the questions that form its dark background. Whether it's one of his columns, a book like this one or a passing conversation, Jim always gives at least as good as he gets—generally, far better.

The second legendary in these pages is Eunice Simonson. Once when she had returned from Tanzania alone, Carolyn, my wife, and I picked up Eunie to go and visit some other Tanzanian friends. They had asked that we also give a ride to a school psychologist in town over the weekend from Denver, a national consultant specializing in gifted and talented programs for public schools. The four of us rode together for an hour, visiting in the car, at the party and then on the way back again. After we dropped Eunie off and were on our way, the psychologist immediately started asking questions about her. As he got out of the car a little later, he said, "You know, I think that woman is the strongest person I ever met."

When she later heard the story, Eunie typically demurred. Girls from Norwegian-American families in towns like Portland and Mayville, N.D., weren't necessarily taught the coyness Yankee women have valued. But part of the immigrant culture, for both girls and boys, was not to put yourself forward. Eunie knows that as well as anyone.

But there is a different way of being forward that can hardly ever be treasured enough, and that is how Eunie's strength shows. Jim Klobuchar saw what I and hundreds of other house guests of the Simonson's have seen, a back door clinic, opening early in the morning as people from all over the mountainside showed up seeking Eunie's nursing skills. The lines are generally long, the conversations whispered in Kiswahili, the help tenderly and relentlessly given, whether it's a young mother carrying a sick child or an AIDS victim in the inevitable decline.

It was the same but of a different order when Eunie came back to care for her daughter, Becky, after surgery for a brain tumor. No bureaucratically imposed hospitalization stay limit could speed that recovery—it was more than 60 days worth. Word of the faith, the courage and love evident in that room spread into the nurses' network in the Twin Cities, so that nurses from other hospitals—strangers but friends—showed up to visit, see and hear for themselves. Eunie would say it was Becky they all came to see, but Becky was hardly ever alone in the room.

Finally, the third legendary is David Simonson. A pastor's son whose mother came from one of the great Norwegian immigrant Lutheran families in Canada and the US, Dave grew up in places like Scobey, Mont., and Sisseston, S.D., one of several brothers, all of them carrying their parents' strength.

Joseph L. Knutson, long time president of Concordia College, Moorhead, Minn., Dave and Eunie's alma mater, once described Dave as having the best of the Hauges. Now commonly condemned for the self-absorption and legalism that became characteristic of the movement as it degenerated, Haugeanism gets its name from a revival movement in 19th century Norway. At its best, it had an urgency to proclaim Christ directly to the heart and at the same time, a deep compassion for the sufferings of others. The Simonsons and the Stolees, joined in Dave's parents, were deeply aware of their roots in this heritage. But there were some wild seeds in those prairie towns where the Simonsons served, such as long remembered legends of the Sioux, which could take a boy's fancy. Disparate, far removed as they seem, the Haugean roots and the old Sioux seeds came together to shape a missionary dedicated to the gospel, eager to serve anyone caught in injustice. This missionary would become one of the elders of the Maasai, an African tribe not unlike the great American Indians of the northern forests and plains.

Some years ago, Dave and I went to Seattle for meetings with a small group of people particularly interested in world missions. The preacher was another legendary figure, R. Peder Waldum, one of David's closest friends who has since died of cancer. Pete preached on the promise God made to Abraham to give him and Sarah descendents as many as the stars. With his great gift with the language, Pete envisioned the contrast between Abraham and Sarah's long-term childlessness and that promise, setting out the quiet, laughable, seemingly hidden but finally starlike way in which it has been fulfilled.

A few months later, David, Eunie, my (at-that-time 13-year-old) son, Jacob, and I drove across the Serengeti to a town called Loliondo. Some years before, Dave and Eunie were living there, when they were banished and left without a vehicle following conflict with a church official. You will read of the conflict over David's loyalty to the Maasai. At that time he walked, just as he and Jim Klobuchar would walk through that territory some 20 years later, but this time with another mission. David worked his way from village to village, bearing witness, addressing people in their circumstances. With what time was left over, he caught rides out of the bush to scavenge parts for a Land Rover he put together.

But this time, in 1993, it was different. The four of us drove rutted prairie trails marked by barrels, traveling up the side of the Serengeti—zebras, gazelles, and wildebeest almost always in sight, sometimes ostriches and even hyenas, once a pride of lions—to that beautiful little town, not so far from the Kenyan border. We were going to that area for the baptisms of 350 Maasai people. After years of futility, when David and other missionaries—on foot and with wheels—found one convert here, another there, but hardly any numbers, all of a sudden the stars had come out. The mass baptisms had started the year before and would continue.

The first night out at Loliondo we slept in a tent; after that we moved into the church in town, spreading our sleeping bags on the cement floors. The last night, Dave and I went out into the early morning darkness to prepare for the long drive back to Arusha. The sky was black, the moon full and the stars so bright that the sky seemed to be radiating with them. We turned and went back into the church, kneeling together in the darkness, remembering Pete's sermon and the Maasai in all of their elegance and color now washed in the triune name. When David began to pray—for Peder and his wife, dear Grace; for Eunie and their family; for Jake and me and our family at home; for the Maasai, that the word would continue its course; for the Evangelical Lutheran Church in Tanzania; for our church; for the larger community—it was as though the roof had been lifted and the whole world opened.

There are any number of stories that could be told—of Jim, holding such gifts of observation and language together with a spirit to match; of Eunie, so relentlessly self giving; of David, tough and gentle—but for now, you have the three of them together, paged between the covers of this exciting volume. You're going to have a reading adventure. But then they wouldn't be satisfied if their stories didn't point away from themselves to the Story. That's just who they are, conundrums, contradictions not withstanding.

JAMES ARNE NESTINGEN
Luther Seminary, St. Paul, Minn.

THE AUTHOR

Jim Klobuchar is a longtime newspaperman and adventurer who wrote a popular column in the Minneapolis StarTribune for more than 30 years. He has traveled in Africa often, both as a writer and as the director of an adventure travel organization. Those travels introduced him to the work of David and Eunice Simonson and deepened his personal and professional explorations in Africa. He is the author of 17 books that reflect a range of interests that include mountaineering, spirituality, the human condition, the open road and athletics. In 1984, the National Society of Newspaper Columnists named him the country's outstanding columnist for newspapers over 100,000 circulation.

CHAPTER 1

The low cloud of the East African night sky scowled on the tossing savannah below it. To Simonson, sitting in a motionless Land Rover with a 16-bore shotgun in his lap, the sky looked hostile and perverse. He was waiting for the lion, and he rued the absence of moon and stars. When the night was normal here, they were spectacular ornaments in the equatorial sky above the Maasai Steppes of Tanganyika. They had another virtue. They made it easier to see a lion at night.

But this night was not normal. It had been a year since Simonson had come to Africa in 1956 to preach God according to Martin Luther. The wonder of staring up at its blazing sky at night still stirred him as it would a child. In starlight, the place was engulfing. Oceans of high grass and the random acacias stretched to the highlands. The hills lifted to the limitless sky and created a synergy that for the Rev. David Simonson fused heaven and earth. God had to be in there somewhere. The stars lit the scene with the power and mystery of an Africa that he'd idealized back in the seminary. It was there where he was aroused for the life of a missionary among those gaunt and elegant tribesman called the Maasai.

This night had no mystery or aesthetics for the young preacher from Minnesota. It did offer a man-killing, cattle-killing lion. From the Land Rover, Simonson could hear the lion's episodic grunting, but the black night gave him no illumination to see it. He tightened his grip on the stock of the shotgun. The preacher was trying to control his fear. It was not a grinding, unhinging fear. It was offset by an excitement he couldn't suppress. He told the village's Maasai warriors to lay back while he went after the lion. It was the sensible thing, in the interests of both the Maasai and the preacher, precluding an accident that might turn the night into a disaster. So he was secure in that decision. Still, the grunting and roaring rattled him. He knew it was not quite as near as it sounded, but God, it was near enough. The lion was somewhere out in the savannah beyond the village, whose warriors stood by behind the thornbush hedges of their boma (a Maasai settlement), holding their spears while they looked out in the direction of the Land Rover. Some of them wanted the honor or to assert the right to go after the lion themselves. But they also knew that this lion was a killer. Every few minutes they would hear simba's booming sounds out there near the wells. And they also knew that the shotgun was their best hope.

The Maasai scarcely knew this big young preacher with his black beard and wrestler's shoulders. He'd arrived in Naberera a few days before to get acquainted with the south Maasai district of the Lutheran Church of Tanganyika, where he was going to be the apprentice evangelist, replacing a pastor who almost got killed trying to climb Kilimanjaro and needed to be rehabilitated in the U.S.A.

The Maasai were aware that the new preacher had a shotgun. They also knew the lion was coming over the thornbush fence unless somebody stopped him. They had spears and, by the codes of their tribal culture, no fear of the lion. But by its behavior they were convinced this was a crazed animal, and their spears were not going to protect the boma. Two nights earlier, with its mane streaming in the village torchlight, the lion had entered the town and terrorized some school teachers near a shop, forcing them to flee into the church. The lion leaped through an open window of the church, routing the school teachers and temporarily staking out territory behind the organ of a now emphatically empty church. The lion, it was determined later, had worn away its long teeth on its hunts, exposing the nerves and leaving it deranged in pain, a rogue. In that state it had abandoned its normal predator habits, turning away from hunting wildebeest and zebra. The replacement prey were humans and cattle. Both escaped the lion's first night rampage and also the second, when the villagers had to take refuge in the school. On the third afternoon the Maasai sent a delegation of *murran*, the warriors, to the mission cottage on the outskirts of Naberera, where Simonson was eating his supper of goat meat.

These people were going to be his parishioners if he ever made it in Tanganyika. Simonson understood that and welcomed the prospect. Affably, he stood to greet them and offered what he could. The Maasai came to recruit, not to eat. They were tall and solemn. With a mix of Swahili and Maasai language that Simonson figured out quickly, they were asking a 28-year-old man of God—which is not quite the same as man of peace—to help them kill a bloodthirsty lion and save the village.

Simonson grew up in eastern Montana and South Dakota; he took his college education at Concordia College in Moorhead, Minn., and later at Luther Theological Seminary in St. Paul, Minn. He was a kind of voluntary roughneck in his grade school days. From adolescence to his young adulthood, he was an elbows-flying fullback and captain of the Concordia football team as well as a pheasant and duck hunter. When he came to Africa he brought as much of his artillery—rifle, shotgun and pistol—as the British customs agents would allow in Tanganyika, the country which later became independent as

Tanzania. He hunted wildebeest and warthog with the other missionaries in his early months of mission training in the Pare Mountains of eastern Tanganyika and around Marangu off the slopes of Kilimanjaro.

But a warthog is not a charging lion in the lonely bush surrounding a Maasai boma. On this night, the homicidal lion and nearly a hundred miles of roadless nothing separated the young man of God from the shelter of the diocese in Arusha.

Simonson sat back at his table to consider his options while the goat meat got cold. He did it briefly. The Maasai weren't there to socialize. Also, from some place in the distance, they could hear the first guttural "hoof-hoofs," the unmistakable descending grunts of the approaching lion. Simonson knew enough about the habits of lions stalking a village. They usually came twice to terrify whatever was in sight or earshot. Reconnoitering, military people would call it. The third night they came to kill. They preceded the assault with ferocious sound effects calculated to freeze the victims into paralysis.

"He will come straight down the road tonight," they said. "He's going to jump over the thornbushes and come into the boma. We're going out to hunt him. Maybe you can head him off with your gun."

The preacher weighed his choices and decided quickly: Go out and face the lion. If you kill it, you entrench yourself forever with the Maasai, or at least with this village tribe. You'd probably also save some lives.

It wasn't the way he planned to start spreading the word of God, but no manual existed that could guide him on a decision like this. He sorted through the odds. The second possible outcome of preacher vs. lion was that the preacher's gunshot missed, or he never unloaded, and the preacher died. It was a more likely possibility than the first one. Simonson was a hunter, but an amateur. The lore of East Africa was filled with sagas of the great white hunters who lost in a showdown with the lion and came back in a sack. Simonson thought about that. He thought about Eunice and the kids back at Marangu. He also thought about his other option: Tell the Maasai warriors he had a wife and three kids back at Marangu and couldn't meet the lion tonight.

Give them that answer, Simonson told himself, and you may as well pack up and go back to preach in South Dakota. You're finished as a missionary. No Maasai from Naberera to the Serengeti is going to take you seriously when you talk about the brave Jesus Christ facing death to save humanity.

Simonson told the Maasai he would take his shotgun and go out to meet the lion.

The animal's roars were getting closer. He was suddenly gripped by the conviction that he ought to finish that meal. Maybe his body was telling him he needed all the protein he could get. Maybe it was some quirky mind game about a last supper. He asked the Maasai to wait outside, and he'd join them in a few minutes. When the meat was gone, he loaded his gun, put on his jacket, prayed briefly and went outside.

I'll go alone, he told the Maasai. Although surprised, they respected his decision. The big preacher with his decisive movements and authoritative voice that filled up the house was something they hadn't expected. The Maasai aren't easily impressed by macho appearances. They are wary, tough and pretty well convinced that nobody can match the Maasai's personal discipline and fearlessness. But this man was standing there with his shotgun and telling them to stay home; he was going after the lion himself.

Simonson explained it to a village school teacher before he headed the Land Rover toward the village outskirts. "I don't want to get one of those guys shot if he gets into the line of fire."

The teacher nodded his understanding. A humanitarian, this preacher.

Well, yes and no. The preacher was that, but it wasn't the only reason Simonson was going out solo. If he did blunder into accidentally killing one of the warriors, he was finished as a missionary among the Maasai no less than if he had bugged out of their appeal for help. The more people around, the more people who could get hurt. If the Maasai were out there with their spears, and the lion jumped a warrior, and Simonson fired his 16-bore buckshot to save the warrior, he was probably going to hit them both.

There was another reason Simonson went after the lion alone. If he was honest, he had to admit it.

He was riding out to face a killer lion, and he was less scared than he was wired by the anticipation. Dave Simonson was a mixed personality. He was about spreading the gospel in East Africa, and about being a husband to Eunie and a father to Steven and Naomi and Nathan, and about someday bringing schools and medicine to these people. But he was also about risk. The allure of it lubricated some of his behavior and some of his attitudes. So here was a lion coming toward the village of a people he had vowed to befriend, to convert to Jesus Christ and to heal. More than incidentally, the lion was also coming toward David Simonson.

He checked the pump action of the shotgun. An old mission man back in Minnesota strenuously argued the case for the 16-bore. "Everybody out there hunts with a 12-gauge," he said. "If you go with that, they're going to be bumming shells off you until you go dry."

He wheeled slowly toward the tawny grass outside of town. If the lion was coming to kill, he wasn't going to be skulking in the grass or ducking behind trees. He was, as the Maasai had predicted, coming down the middle of the road, splitting the black night with his bellowing. The middle of the road outside Neberera wasn't any thoroughfare. It was defined by a couple of ancient wells that Simonson had heard were dug by the Phoenicians a few thousand years ago but were still useable. Near the wells was a trough from which the Maasai women would haul the water in buckets or gourds to care for the cattle. He steered slowly toward the wells, feeling his aloneness in the midst of the rising excitement, hearing the lion, knowing it was there.

The headlights picked out something amber and hairy and moving near the trough. The lights caught its eyes. The lion wasn't ducking. It was huge. It stood staring into the lights, throwing its head, snarling. God, it was close. Twenty feet at the most. Simonson felt a shiver inside. Freeing the gun's safety, he got out of the Land Rover and stood behind the headlights. For a moment, he was conscious of his sensations. He was scared and electrified, charged with adrenaline. It surged through him like floodwater, making him bigger and lusting to go one-on-one with this killer beast in front of him. He was a minister of God, but at this very moment he was indivisibly and gloriously a hunter, and this was the trial he'd never envisioned. How was he going to deny the thrill of it? The adrenaline was eating him up. Inwardly he was yelling at the lion as he put the stock to his shoulder. "All right, simba. Let's go." He'd never experienced this. It was almost out-of-body, the current of combat that propelled the movement of the gun to his shoulder.

He fired.

The charge hit the lion squarely and flung him backwards. He flashed his teeth, thundered his fury and pain and started to get up.

Simonson shot again. The lion slumped, dead. Simonson stared, speechless. Then he flung himself to his knees in the soft earth and bawled, "Thank you, Lord." And then he was crying and laughing, liberated from the domineering tension of this bizarre encounter. Within minutes he was surrounded by spear-waving Maasai warriors, declaring their gratitude and their respect—perhaps their amazement—for the black-bearded preacher who went out to face the lion alone, and brought him down.

He was a warrior, they said. He was one of them.

It was his initiation into a brotherhood that would last a lifetime. It was the beginning of a ministry—his and that of his wife, Eunice—that would heal thousands of Africans and build schools for thousands of children who until then had tried to read and write in the merciless sun or behind rocks or in the thornbushes. It was a ministry that brought the sacrifice and gospel of Jesus Christ into the lives of thousands of Africans. Some of them reacted to Christianity with exuberance and some with bafflement, in about the normal proportions of tribal converts. It was a ministry that would unite the Africans with huge numbers of Americans whose consciences were stung or wheedled by Simonson's relentless appeals for money to save the lives and educate the kids of people he now called his brothers and, considerably later, his sisters. Along the road his obsessions and commitments, his spasms of ego and his impatience, his raw visibility as a bigger-than-life character on the mission frontier, brought him into conflict with church authorities and peers. They got him into quarrels with accountants, got him exiled for four years by an African bishop, and ran him into the hospital with near fatal disorders.

He carried his faith—and it was unbreakable—wherever he went.

Whenever it was prudent, he also carried his shotgun.

God, he decided early in his stewardship, expected his preachers to be people of faith. God had no objection, he also decided, if they went eyeball-to-eyeball with a lion in a Maasai village. In that case, a steady hand on the shotgun might be worth as least as much as a citation from Luke as a tool of evangelism.

The next day, there were a few more Christians in the Maasai village.

CHAPTER 2

Sometime around the year 30 A.D., Jesus Christ of Nazareth was crucified near Jerusalem on a hill now called Calvary. The charge against him was blasphemy, for calling himself the Messiah. The disciples who had followed him, who believed that he was the Son of Man and the Son of God, who had listened to his prophecies of his approaching death, went into seclusion, frightened and bewildered. If he was truly the Messiah, the deliverer of Israel and the redeemer of sinners, why was Jesus Christ dying on a cross? Why was a King and their Master crying out in his final hour, "My God, why have you forsaken me?"

Yet, within a few weeks this demoralized gaggle of eleven was transformed with the fire of irreversible belief. It emboldened them for the rest of their lives to carry the gospel of the one they now called Savior. They said he had appeared to them as the risen Christ, resurrected from the tomb. Almost all of them went to their death because of their evangelism, joined by Paul, the former Christian-baiting Saul of Tarsus.

So began the Christian mission.

In its impact on humanity and the current of history, most scholars define it as one of the most powerful events in world civilization. In the fever of Christian evangelism, some of Jesus Christ's simple message, his call for sharing of wealth, humility and loving of enemies, got clouded in the Western obsession to remake the world by expanding its own. The advance of Christianity, first around the Mediterranean, then through Europe, and then beyond the seas into tribal lands, merged with the flowering of Europe's Renaissance, with its age of colonialism, the search for gold, and its enlistment of science. It was fueled by the industrial revolution and stirred into international power struggles and wars, with divisions of spoils. But Christianity also tapped into and fostered in the hearts of thousands of its followers an awareness of a need to serve. It created growing cadres of men and women of good will in the spreading age of enlightenment. They resolved: We can heal these people in their jungles and their mountains. We can call out for the end of the slave trade We can love them and teach them and befriend them and introduce them to the living God.

Invitations weren't necessary. Christian mission brought the message of Jesus Christ, of his sacrifice and the hope it created, into the lives of masses of what were then called primitive peoples. The military regiments that accompanied it also often brought subjugation into the lives of those same people, and the corporate engineers who weren't far behind brought their machines that hauled out the Africans' treasure—or what they learned later was their treasure. Christian mission collided with Islam, conflicts which inflicted bruises on both. It collided with the animistic belief of the natives, with the spirits that had ruled or demonized their religious lives. It brought a white man's god, which millions of the natives ultimately accepted but which disillusioned others. Christian mission not only survived the great waves of African nationalism that swept the continent in the middle of the 20th century, but it also flourished as never before. As it matured, it acquired a deeper understanding of African life and took a more conciliatory approach to its evangelism. It discovered that if Christian preachers were to make Christianity appealing to Africans, they had to learn something from the traditional African religions. Christian mission long ago had dropped some of its more naive and obtuse ideas about trying to westernize the Africans' minds—and dress—in the process of Christianizing their souls.

And almost from the beginning, the Christian missionary movement brought medicine and schools, which the great mass of people needed more than immediate salvation.

Thousands and then millions accepted Christianity as a revelation. Millions more did it for more practical reasons. If the church of Jesus Christ could make the sick healthy and teach children how to stay alive, why not listen to these white-cheeked preachers whose symbol was the cross and whose mission seemed to be to make lives better in the jungle and the mountains?

The primitive cultures were forever changed, some of them willingly, some of them not.

By the late 1800s, thousands of Christian missionaries were working the steaming river villages and the sub-Saharan steppes of Africa. The casual massacre of some of those missionaries by unimpressed Africans had pretty much dwindled into history, although not entirely. Conversions had been made on an unprecedented scale, and dioceses had organized. African preachers had been trained, slowly, and increasingly they became the glue of the Christian church in their countries. By the 1930s, hundreds of those Christian missionaries were Americans. Some of them were Lutherans. And some of those Lutheran missionaries would come back to the Midwest plains on furlough, to tell country congregations about their cause and their adventures. They asked for money to feed and clothe the Africans and, incidentally, to provide a few nickels for the underpaid missionaries. Local ministers offered their homes, bread and hospitality to the roaming preachers. Every now and then one of the missionaries would be welcomed into the home of the Rev. Rudolph and Gladys Simonson of Scobey, Mont., and later of Sisseton, S.D.

Their accounts of the faraway places inflamed little Buddy Simonson. They were his first exposure to a thrilling idea. He, Dave Simonson, would some day be a preacher like his father. Only he would preach to these dark-skinned people wearing beads and thongs and singing their mysterious and hypnotic songs, the ones the missionaries talked about. He would introduce them to his God on their island in the Pacific. Or in South America.

Or, if he and God could some day work it out, in Africa.

The Simonsons didn't have much largesse to offer the wandering shepherds who logged in from those remote places. From Fergus Falls, Minn., where the couple began their married life, Rudolph had answered his first call by the Lutheran church just as America was sinking into the Great Depression. In fact, David was born a month after the stock market crash in the fall of 1929. The Lutherans of Scobey needed a parson. Rudolph examined the map. Scobey didn't quite qualify as a pillar of American commerce. It was a town of a few hundred people in the corner of northeastern Montana, just north of the Fort Peck Indian Reservation. But there were Lutherans there who needed a preacher, and young Rudolph Simonson was a down-the-line, uncompromising, don't-mess-with-the-Bible Lutheran. He was tall and intense and persuasive and aching to sound out across the prairie with the good news of Jesus Christ. So they went to Scobey, where David was born in November of 1929, the second of the Simonson's four sons. Hardship didn't much intimidate them, and they weren't bogged down by the absence of money or the long hours. Problems of clothing their kids and managing on lean budgets were commonplace and nothing to whine about. Rudolph and Gladys both came from Norwegian immigrant stock and out of their families' pulpit tradition. You didn't go into the ministry to get rich or to be comfortable. You did it in the hardheaded realization that you were committing yourself to a lifetime of service to family and faith, to ailing parishioners and to a thousand potluck suppers.

But Gladys Simonson knew that something more would be needed. In the America of the Depression, preachers in the farm belt didn't count on monthly paychecks. Sometimes Rudolph Simonson's compensation came in the back of a small truck—half of a hog one of the parishioners had butchered, or a half-dozen tubs of butter.

The reverend offered his prayer of gratitude, but it didn't hurt to have a backup resource in the house. Gladys handled all jobs not connected with redemption. She was a short and spunky lady with a masters degree who baked the bread, made the clothes, washed the dishes and herded the kids to classes. She also taught school off and on for 25 years to help pay the bills and to put enough pork and potatoes on the table to turn four growing boys into the college football players they eventually became. In the Simonson house, it was the pastor who invoked God and the Golden Rule and from whom Dave Simonson probably acquired his eventual eloquence in the African pulpits and on the American podiums as pitchman for his schools and clinics. But it was Gladys who lit the sparks of the kids' ambitions. She was pungent with her familial advice, right up until her last years in a nursing home. By then her memory had slipped and, although Rudolph had died five years before, her mind had turned cloudy about that. She asked one of her sons, Paul, if anybody had seen dad lately. "Mom," he said, "Dad left to be with Jesus."

She grumped hearing the news. "Just like him," she said, "taking off without telling anybody."

Years later, when Dave Simonson assessed his life and tried to assemble all the interwoven cords that seemed to impel him into African mission life, he would remember the strongest of those: His parents and their daily gospel to their sons that they should serve God and serve humanity. He would remember the tales of the itinerant missionaries. They were stories that aroused in him a fervor to cross the same oceans, to mingle his life with those same tribes and to be fired by the sight of the same wild animals.

When he ultimately found himself in that land of his childhood fantasies, he remembered the Indian kids of the Montana and South Dakota plains.

He remembered them when he looked into the eyes of some of the Maasai or Sonjo kids in Tanzania, and saw the same hunger to break out into the free air of discovery of what they could be and who they were. The mischief in those dark eyes made the children of the two continents inseparable to Simonson—those he saw on the Dakota plains where the Sioux kids lived, and in the bomas of the Maasai kids. Somehow the world seemed to be leaving those kids behind—the world in its speed and its more privileged people in their thirst to live better, to get richer. The Indian kids back in northeastern South Dakota and the African kids who lived on the edge of the Serengeti Plain seemed to know that. They didn't express it in words, but what he saw in their faces molded for Dave Simonson a kinship between the Sioux Indian kids and the African kids.

When he began his work in Africa, he was shaken for a time by the presumption of it. Here he was trying to teach about God and about health, without the baldest understanding of how the Africans taught themselves. Then he recalled the years when as a boy he played with Indian kids. Sometimes he'd walk miles with one of them to the home of their parents or their grandparents. And sometimes it was the same home for all of them.

Was it so much different in Africa?

In his childhood he listened to the grandmother of his best Indian friend telling the boy about some episode out of the past. She was being the historian, the teacher of family and tribal history, orally passing it on to the boy.

Was it any different in Africa?

David Simonson as a kid somehow got himself acquainted with minority kids on the plains in the way most of the settlers' children didn't. Indians weren't the most popular inhabitants of Montana and South Dakota among the white folks with whom they lived. They looked and acted different, and some of the Indians got drunk and the Indians often looked disreputable. If you were forced into the concentration camp of reservation life, you might look that way yourself, Dave Simonson told his friends when he heard that kind of talk.

"They were pretty awful places, the reservations," he would say later. "We got their land and put them practically behind bars and made them despicable people in our eyes. Then we couldn't understand why they couldn't find a job and work and be respectable like the rest of us, like the ones who put them in their concentration camps."

A man who could see this as a kid growing up in Sisseton, S.D. was a man likely to find his way to a place like Africa when he entered the ministry. But as a kid, Dave Simonson was not quite the family's designated angel. He was, in fact, a self-appointed enforcer when that seemed to be the most useful way to achieve juvenile justice. In Sisseton, where the family moved after six years in Montana, he befriended a Chinese boy, Luey Lung Forn, whose family operated an Oriental cafe in town. The Chinese kid crossed the path of one of the town's juvenile thugs. The bully decided to beat up on the Chinese kid on a street corner one day for no special reason other than the kid's eyes didn't look straight and he didn't pronounce r's and l's the way everybody else did.

The Simonson kid stepped in. He was big for his age and he had thick arms and a glare in his eyes that did not escape the incumbent thug. "If you want to fight," the Simonson kid said, "try me."

No such attempt was made. The dispute ended. The strategy was different in Madison, Minn., not long afterward. There were four Simonson kids not far apart in age—Luther, the oldest, who also became an ordained minister; Dave; Paul, who became a businessman; and James, the youngest, who became a missionary doctor and served in Ethiopia. As youngsters, the four of them transferred temporarily to a country school in Madison, where their grandfather was a minister. On the first day at school they went through an initiation that was all but mandatory in country schools of the day. The four visiting yokels were roughed up by some of the hometown scholars, one by one, as they left the school. It was the usual testing ritual. You didn't have to pass it. What you were expected to do was to take it. The Simonson kids decided overnight that there had to be an option to that. So they got to school early the next day and, as the farm kids trooped in with their bib overalls and long shoulder straps, the Simonson kids cheerfully ambushed them and hung them up by their straps on the cloak hangers, one by one. No further tests were imposed on the visiting yokels.

Not surprisingly, all of the Simonson boys played high school football in South Dakota. And, not surprisingly, all earned scholarships to one of the fortresses of Lutheran learning on the prairie, Concordia College in Moorhead, Minn. There Jake Christianson, the football coach, appreciated the discipline of these pastors' kids almost as much as the width of their shoulders and their vigor at tackling in the open field.

It was at Concordia where Dave Simonson, in his last year of study and as the captain of the football team, met a young woman with traffic-stopping auburn hair and a smile to charm a mortgage forecloser. Simonson's skin was considerably less thick than the mortgage man's, and his eyesight was probably a lot better. He was captivated. He also, in his later years, was convinced that his meeting with Eunice and their marriage a year later was part of a plan for his life. He believed that his life and Eunice's were directed, and that it was God's will for the two of them to serve in Africa. He also believed, through all of those African years, it was God's will that they would survive an extraordinary chain of accidents and potentially fatal illnesses that confronted them in the more than 40 years they served. It was God's will, he and Eunice were both convinced, to put them in places and endow them with the energies and tenacity that would eventually reach into thousands of lives in Africa.

It may have been. If so, it was abetted by the impulse of Dave Simonson to knock down all fences that cluttered his road and the resourcefulness of Eunice Simonson as a healer and widely loved "mama" to the Africans who received her care and friendship.

The question is tantalizing: Does God have a design for our lives, a place where God wants us to go, a service to perform and a goal to reach? When theologians tackle it, they answer with more syllables than the amateurs in the Bible classes, but with outcomes just as murky. Does God really try to manage or direct lives? Is there any more to "God's design for our lives" than to give us choices of how to live? We can live generously and decently, for example, or selfishly and immorally. Is "God's will" simply giving us the light of knowing the difference? No, David and Eunice Simonson will argue, God actually moved their lives, brought them together, impelled them to Africa. It was reflected, they said, in the hundred things that happened to them that were beyond surface explanation.

Skeptics are permitted their predictable frowns here. But how do they then explain Gustav Otto Richard Reusch?

How do they explain the appearance of Gustav Otto Richard Reusch in the lives of a schoolgirl named Eunice Nordby and a seminary student named

David Simonson, years apart. Gustav Otto Richard Reusch was a native of Russia but a German by heritage, a Tsarist soldier as a young man during World War I and a Cossack rider. Later he was a Lutheran minister in exile from the Communists and a multilingual adventurer as a missionary. For a change of pace, he became a lion-slayer, mountain climber and one of the truly bizarre characters out of the carousel of bizarre characters in Africa during the early 20th century.

How do you explain the fulfillment of a prediction he made to both of them, in scenes imbedded in their minds for the rest of their lives? They would serve the Maasai in Africa, he said, and they would serve the Maasai because it was ordained that way.

In truth, not a whole lot about Richard Reusch is explainable.

He materialized on the campus of Gustavus Adolphus College in St. Peter, Minn., in 1954, as a professor of religion. He arrived with a store of adventure sagas that dazzled his students and stretched the minds of the stolid Scandinavian folk of southern Minnesota. Research suggested that most of his stories bore the essential elements of truth. Many of the others were too good not to believe. He told how he killed an elephant with a machete, creeping up on him and slicing the great gray beast from underneath before the elephant could trample him. It was not totally explained why he had to undertake this creative form of assault. He told of climbing Kilimanjaro so often the cartographers named a crater after him—which, in fact, they did. He told of hand-to-hand combat with Communist revolutionaries, of killing more than 20 lions in East Africa and of disguising himself as a Whirling Dervish and a Moslem holy man to talk his way through a potential ambush of angry Arabs. He also arrived in Minnesota with an enormous chest expansion, the result of daily weight-lifting in which he persisted for decades. His chest was so bulky, in fact, that it defeated the efforts of all St. Peter clothes merchants to find a winter overcoat wide enough to fit his chest without dragging a foot of fabric on the ground because of his 5-foot-3 height. These uneven dimensions gave him the look of a man whose squat body was in imminent danger of being toppled by his overhanging chest.

With him when he came to Minnesota, the Rev. Richard Reusch brought a collage of 18 languages which he said he spoke fluently. He also brought a saber and a scabbard. They were the apparent remnants of his military actions against the Bolsheviks or against the desert bandits of Arabia, whom he had encountered in his ramblings through the Middle East and Africa on his missions in behalf of Jesus Christ.

An Indiana Jones would not dare to conceive some of Reusch's epics, in fear of a jeering response from the movie critics. But in addition to his undeniable service on behalf of Jesus Christ and the East Africans in his 32 years of mission work, Richard Reusch was one of those zesty and melodramatic people who flowered in the intrigues of the Central Europe of World War I and later the African bush. He belonged with those personalities who so flavored the Africa of the 1920s, 30s and 40s. They were the ones who had engraved it for generations of book readers and film goers of the latter 20th century. He belonged with Karen Blixen, Ernest Hemingway, Beryl Markham, Denys Finch Hatton and all of the hunting guides and miscellaneous fortune hunters, mystics and drifters who now fill the rosters of a colonial Africa that disappeared in the aftermath of World War I. Richard Reusch came out of the sizable colony of Germans who were invited into Tsarist Russia in the 1800s to help modernize Russian agriculture and industry. At the time of the Communist Revolution he was a Russian citizen like the other German settlers, in his 20s and prepared to serve his tsar to the end. It was Reusch's good luck that the end of Nicholas II came long before Reusch's. He switched to the ministry after the war, studied in Estonia and then decamped for Tanganyika as a Lutheran missionary. There, the Christian mission in the early 1920s was in disarray because of Germany's defeat in World War I. When the European colonial powers carved up Africa, Germany was a relatively late arrival. But Tanganyika was one of the lands in which it was entrenched in the late 19th century, to the point where the German and English monarchies—as part of their cozy live-and-let-live colonial arrangements before Sarajevo in 1914—arrived at a boundary between the British province of Kenya and Germany's Tanganyika. Earlier cartographers would have placed Kilimanjaro, Africa's highest summit, within the boundaries of Kenya. But Germany's Kaiser Wilhelm I argued that because the mountain had been "discovered" by a German, Kilimanjaro morally ought to belong to Tanganyika. England's Queen Victoria headed off any wounded monarchial feelings with a novel piece of philanthropy. She made Kilimanjaro a birthday gift to her German grandson, who eventually became Kaiser Wilhelm II. The queen is alleged to have explained that her grandson "likes everything high and big." Kilimanjaro thus became part of the future Tanzania and undoubtedly ranks as the largest birthday gift in world history, nearly four miles high.

Advancing the banner of Lutheranism in Tanganyika was for years the charter of the Leipzig, Bethel and Berlin mission societies of Germany. But the German missions dissolved with the transfer of Tanganyika to the League of Nations and ultimately to British supervision. Yet the German tradition was still strong in Tanganyika in the 1920s, and Reusch naturally gravitated there with his Germanic history.

His style and personality attracted the early hostility of the Maasai he was trying to serve. But his verve and his clear commitment to Christian service warmed most of the Africans he met. It was there where he was introduced to a nurse named Elveda Bonander, a woman with Minnesota roots. They married and moved to St. Peter with their family when his work in Africa drew to a close. Not surprisingly, it took the blue-eyed scholars of St. Peter some time to understand this uncommon character who had descended on them from the banks of the Volga and the elephant grass of East Africa. He walked about campus bald, stumpy and looking marginally fierce. He wore no overcoat in the bitterest of Minnesota's winter windchills and yet in social events he was elaborately courtly in the continental tradition. Richard Bosch, one of his students in the early 1960s, remembers each meeting with Reusch as something of an event that deserved to be perpetuated. In the Gustavus archives, it is.

"The guy had a vagrant sense of humor which he usually tried to conceal behind that deadpan demeanor," Richard Bosch remembered. "But he didn't try too hard. He gave you the impression that he had a lot to keep hidden in his past life of adventure, but which he was dying to share if you gave him any kind of cue. Walking around campus, he was an irresistible figure. He looked super serious and even wary, as though he was momentarily anticipating a Bolshevik attack on Gustavus and he was going to defend the whole student body with his saber.

"But he'd come to a fraternity event and pass out cigars to all of the men in the style of a veteran of a thousand parties in the social centers of the world. He was attentive, of course, to the young women. When he'd see one with a carnation on her dress, he'd walk up to her with great solemnity, snap his heels, kiss her hand and say, "Does zis red flower mean that you have a red flame in your heart?"

She might have. But the poor young woman was so overwhelmed by the sheer weight of the professor's drawing room gallantry that her reply was lost in the density of the cigar smoke around her.

Bosch remembers Reusch also for the charismatic power with which he could persuade his listeners when he talked of his African experience, of his kinship with the Maasai and of the need for motivated young men and women to venture where he had. "In the classroom, he wasn't exactly a fireball. He read painstakingly from his notes, right down to the inclusion of his punctuation: Eet was time to bring Jesus Christ into the boma, comma. . . ."

Face to face, he could absolutely inspire those who wanted to be inspired to preach where Reusch had preached. These were the young people who wanted to befriend the warriors Reusch had befriended and, in the case of a young ex-football captain from Concordia in Moorhead, Minn., to face the lions Reusch had **and** to befriend the warriors Reusch had.

The ardor for mission abroad felt by ministerial students in the Midwest in the middle of the 20th century was nourished by Luther Seminary in St.Paul, the campus of Gustavus Adolphus and other similar Lutheran strongholds. Many of these students were returning veterans of World War II. They had experienced the world and were aroused by the prospect of bringing the Christian message and better education and health care into the lives of peoples in what we now call the Third World. Others, like David Simonson, had been moved to the mission idea as youngsters who had been exposed in their churches or homes to visiting evangelists. With America emerging as a world leader and as a wellspring of a better life for people battered by war and adrift spiritually, it was a time of high idealism for these young people. Nobody nourished that idealism with the panache of Richard Reusch on his visits to seminaries and in his classroom. Late in his studies at Luther Seminary in St. Paul, David Simonson was introduced to Richard Reusch. Any doubts about his future in the ministry dissolved irrevocably.

"I had just about made up my mind not long after I entered the seminary," he recalled years later. "The stories I'd heard, the outside reading I'd done, the meetings I had with the missionaries—all of these pointed me in the direction of Africa and what was then Tanganyika. But I think the final lift came from Reusch. He just seemed consumed by his African experience. He energized me in my goal to go to Africa as a missionary. He did it in a way that no one else had. He was such an extraordinary guy. He made you feel you were there, or that you should be there. I thought of no place else after that."

So was it stark coincidence that at Concordia in his final year as an undergraduate student that Dave Simonson should meet Eunice Marie Nordby of Portland, N.D.? This same Eunice Nordby years before as an eight-year-old attending a relative's wedding with her parents had met another wedding guest, a stumpy man with a powerful chest, penetrating eyes and a military bearing—Richard Reusch. Who else? The woman Reusch had married was related to one of Eunice's cousins, Stan Benson, who later became a missionary to Africa. Was it coincidence that this man with the bulging chest took Eunice Nordby's hand, snapped his heels and kissed it, and with elaborate courtesy asked her what she hoped to do with her life? The teenager gulped; she said she'd like to go into medical work and serve her church somehow.

Today, Eunice Nordby Simonson remembers their meeting with an amazement that has not dimmed in her hundreds of recitals of the story.

"He said he had spent years as a missionary in Africa, and he was in Minnesota on furlough. At first I wasn't sure what to make of him. Who could? He was a very dramatic man with those piercing eyes. Never in my young life or wildest imaginings had there been anyone like this man. He spoke with a soft and strange accent. He said, 'I am zo happy to meet you, Eunice.' He had a thin black mustache and a kind of egg-head. He looked a little like Inspector Poirot of the Agatha Christie movies I saw later. He was very solemn and intense. I learned later that he would grab the altar and hold it in a tight grip when he prayed, and that sometimes he would take a coin and bend it with his fingers to show his strength.

"After the wedding service when the younger people in the group clumped together to talk, I heard my name being spoken in that beautiful accent: 'Eunice, would you like to see some of the things I have from Africa?' I was surprised and excited. I followed Dr. Reusch into the study of the family house; it was like walking into another world. The room was lined with books, and it had a large working desk where Dr. Reusch sat in a swivel chair. He talked briefly and then began bringing out treasures. He showed me a lion's claw, an African elder's fly whisk made of ebony, a wildebeest tail, bright beaded necklaces and collars, earrings with dangling beads, carved ebony animals and sculptures of Maasai warriors. I'd seen collectors proud to show off their things, but this wasn't like that. This man wasn't showing them out of a sense of ownership. He was revealing what seemed to be a deep devotion to these icons of a past that few people had experienced. He talked of his approaching retirement from mission work. He seemed to recede into his private thoughts, and his faced softened. I was nearly in a trance. His stories about Africa had taken me out of myself and into a world even my imagination couldn't quite handle. As I talked a little more about wanting to go into something medical, he got very animated. Suddenly he reached across the desk and took both of my hands. He looked into my eyes as though he were making some kind of prophecy. He said very slowly, 'You, my child, will one day go to my Maasai.' The way he said it left no doubt that it was going to happen. And right at that very moment, I just stood with my mouth open and wondered how on earth I would ever get to Africa and see the Maasai."

In a few years the road suddenly opened, beginning with what might have been the zaniest wedding night in the history of the Red River Valley of Minnesota and North Dakota. What lay ahead in Africa for Dave and Eunice Simonson might have been foretold by their lives as children on the prairie. It may have been foretold by the horizons that stretched out for them then and, on one day, by a tragedy witnessed by Eunice Nordby, one which brought her a truth she would not forget.

CHAPTER 3

He was lying motionless with his face down in the middle of muddy road. The rainstorm was ending, but the gray-black clouds that brought it, streaked with lightning, were still rolling through the prairie sky as two school children approached the man in the road.

One of them, Delores, gasped and then screamed. "It's my father. It's Dad."

Her friend, Eunice Nordby, stopped and hugged the other girl. The man's skin had been blackened. They were afraid to go closer. Something repelled them.

They didn't know that it was the presence of death. A moment before they were two little girls, walking a familiar road home, skipping through its dirty rivulets of rainwater. They laughed their way through their splashings, getting their shoes wet. They had watched the storm's fireworks in the shelter of the school until the teacher said it was safe to go. Their lives were all about games and school and church and playing with their dogs. How could they recognize sudden death in the rain of the North Dakota farm country? It was a place where the rhythms of life almost never changed and almost every day was like yesterday.

Sometimes Delores couldn't understand her father. He was strict and moody. But she loved him. She was like most kids growing up in the farm country. Her father was strong and invincible. But now he was lying there in the mud, not moving while she cried out.

They ran to Delores' house to find her mother.

On that terrible day, Eunice Nordby at the age of eight learned something about human beings and about contrition. It would cling to her for the rest of her life and sensitize her in a way no other growing-up experience had. On that day she learned about the injustice that human beings, even children, can inflict on others when they are misled by appearances. Eunice Nordby had misjudged this man. The scene recurred to her time and again, in college, in the hospitals where she worked and in the more than 40 years of Africa. It recurred each time she saw ugliness or crudity in the behavior of people around her. When she did, she remembered the man lying in the road.

She'd been invited to her friend's house a few weeks before that and the father, John, had done something gross when he'd come in from the yard. Eunice thought she could sense a tension with John in the house. He was a man with large dark brows and an attitude that seemed unfriendly and repulsing. She hadn't seen him up close before, and she wished she hadn't. In the house he spat incessantly. He would lean back in his chair and loose a long, black, obnoxious stream of spit into the copper can five feet away. Eunice restrained her disgust. She made no sign, but she wanted to leave the house and this dreadful man. Delores and her mother must have seen her discomfort. They offered her some baked goods that Clara, the mother, had made. They were delicious, and Eunice was touched by their attempts to make her welcome. But this man! Eunice could not imagine this man being capable of one single act of human tenderness.

This man was the one lying in the road. They came across the field to tell Clara. She didn't understand immediately. "Didn't your dad walk you home?" she asked her daughter. "He was so worried about you walking home in the storm. He went out to find you."

They pulled her out across the field and onto the road and pointed to the man lying in the puddle of mud. Decades later, Eunice remembers the scene with all of the pain and guilt she experienced then.

"Clara screamed and ran to him and threw herself into a muddy rut next to her husband. The lightning had entered his head and burned its way through the soles of his feet and over the top of his boots. She tried to breathe life back into him. It was hopeless. She sobbed and hugged him, this man who had seemed so crude to me. He meant everything to her. She loved him. He'd gone out into the storm to bring his girl home. And he must have been much more than the man I had judged so badly."

The woman Eunice Nordby Simonson became in Africa was admired by the hundreds who knew her and depended on her. She was a woman of generous spirit, one that was reflected by a genuine welcome and invitation in her face and voice. Her devotion to healing seemed instinctive. She was a human being who seemed nourished by a rare grace, some of which may have sprung from that day of death in the country in North Dakota, when she'd learned a truth so painfully.

They were an uncommon pair when she and the big-shouldered young reverend got to Africa in 1956. Their ideals were an almost perfect mesh. They wanted to serve, and they wanted to make a difference. And although the personalities and attitudes they brought into this chancy new world were shaped both by their prairie experience and their Christian environment, those personalities were emphatically separate and distinct. Dave Simonson came with big goals and impetuosity, with the competitor's urges to make it happen and sometimes with the carnival hustler's wiles. He came to bring Africans into the family of God, to build schools and churches, to recruit doctors. He was going to cut the bureaucracies' corners and to Find a Way. He came equally energized by the urge to evangelize and the electricity of risk in doing it. If the door to a better way was locked, he'd make a key. If that didn't work, he'd break down the door.

He'd do it, Simonson would say, with God's permission.

He was an ordained swashbuckler who soon became familiar to thousands of Africans with his rolling walk, his bulky frame, his Bible, his Crocodile Dundee hat, his Texas boots and his beard, which started out coal black and got to be as white and dramatic as Ernest Hemingway's. If the African landscape excited him, it enthralled Eunice. Growing up in a preacher's household had given her the discipline to deal with the sickness and poverty around her. But from the very beginning on the prairie, she was a child filled with sensations. She responded to the allure of nature's caprices and its color. She was drawn by its innocence and its furies, by the loveliness of falling snow and by the wistful moments when she walked in the fallen leaves. Someplace in Eunice Nordby Simonson there was poetry she had to convey to herself and eventually to others. She was fascinated by how people behaved and why. From her first day in Tanganyika, she was captured by Africa's sounds and space. Africa was full of enigma and force. It was primitive and brutal, but it was also glorious. For Eunice there seemed something about Africa that evaded her, something inexpressible, a longing and a sadness that lingered above its beauty and its cruelty. After she gave medicine to an African child at the door of her house, the child's face would cling to her for hours—the child's pained yet trusting eyes and, behind the child, the mother, scared but thankful. When such a mother and child left her house, Eunice Nordby Simonson often just broke down and bawled, thanking God that she could join her world with that of the African child.

A day in Africa could put her in the midst of death or dusty roads, machines that broke down, dirty drinking water and the cries and fights of her own children trying to understand where they lived and who they were. Yet Eunice Simonson in Africa—no less than Eunice Nordby the farm girl—found her cup full each day with the wonder and unpredictability of the world around her, and her willingness to be educated to it each day.

Her father was a circuit riding parson in northeastern North Dakota, tending to the souls of three or four congregations from their country home near the town of Portland. Her life as a child was pretty much of a frolic, with the new friends and the nutty discoveries farm kids made in those years when the winters and the Depression and the remoteness of the North Dakota prairie put them in a world apart. She remembered it when she wrote to a friend many years later.

26

"I loved winter. I loved the snow and all the fun we could have in it and on it and with it. Winters in North Dakota could be dangerous as well as exciting. The part that was never too thrilling was having to wake up while it was still dark and very cold. The chimney of the potbellied stove downstairs passed through my room. Sometimes it was so cold outside I felt like hugging it. The stove gave us the only heat we had, but by morning it had nearly burned itself out. Mother would call us through the heat register—and while I'm at it I could never figure out why they called it a 'register.' When mom heard our feet on the floor she'd begin breakfast. Father would be filling the stove with lignite coal and listening to the first news on the radio. I can hear the newscaster's voice still, deep and dramatic: 'This is Alex Dreier for Skelly Oil.' How familiar that name became. I'd gather the clothes I picked out for the day and run downstairs to dress by the stove. Long underwear and heavy socks. I hated them, but I knew if we weren't going to freeze on the mile and a half to school, I had to wear them. After our cereal breakfast, my brother Harold and I were bundled into our snowsuits and helped with our skis. Yes, skis. That's the way we did it. For the first two years the teacher in our country school lived just across the road and made wonderful ski tracks for us to follow. Years later she told me how angry she'd get because we messed up her tracks with our funny little skis and it wasn't easy to ski home. There was a big hill half-way there. It looked like a mountain to us. Until we became good skiers, we flopped time after time and had to dig around in that deep snow for our lunch buckets. Mom and dad always cautioned me: 'Never let Harold lay down in the snow and sleep. He could freeze to death.' They were serious, and you could see they were worried. Going to school in the middle of winter in the North Dakota country was no lark. You could get hurt. And I was forever telling Harold, 'Don't lay down in the snow.'"

Harold didn't, and he grew up to become a renowned research scientist in the field of citrus foods. About those wintry bouts in Dakota, he and Eunice agree now that they weren't always scary. Kids and snow tend to get along. There were weeks when the snow reached to the telephone wires. "It was just perfect for digging caves and tunnels and sliding and tobogganing," Eunice remembers. "When Christmas came, we couldn't get enough of the snow, because snow belonged to Christmas and somehow made all of us family out there in the country. We had Christmas programs at school, and I was allowed to do the murals on the blackboard because they thought I had some talent as an artist. The Christmas trees must have come from faraway places, because we didn't have any pine trees within miles. We decorated them with paper chains, popcorn on strings and cut out stars and candy canes. In church we enacted the birth of Jesus. I thought it was beautiful. People cried."

But Eunice, the parson's girl, also ran into some strict family protocol and lost her chance for stardom. She wanted to play Mary in the Christmas story and probably would have done it well.

"But my parents thought as the preacher's daughter I ought to step aside and another girl should play the part." Lutheran decorum strikes on the prairie. But the snow. So much, so lovely and so great for the sleigh ride. Most of the settlers were Norwegian and brought the sentimental traditions of Christmas from the fjords. One of them was a kind of masquerade party in which the revelers would ride from house to house and come to the door wearing costumes and disguises. The hosts had to guess the identity of their alien guests. There usually wasn't much suspense. And when all of the disguises were seen through and sorted out, they all celebrated with hot cocoa and Christmas cookies, although some of the men might have preferred—and found—something stronger. When it came time for Eunice to enter disguised, she pranced into the host house wearing a mask and chirping out nonsensical words because it seemed like the thing to do. "I got the giggles and they guessed who I was on the spot, and I stumbled because it was hard to see through the mask. I leaned against what I thought was the wall, but it was the entrance to the pantry, and I fell and landed in a crock of buttermilk. Could anyone make a wilder exit than that?"

So as a kid she was something of an artist, something of an actress, a romper in the snow and an imaginer of faraway places. One thing was especially hard, though, for little girls growing up in North Dakota in the Depression. Boys might dream about being doctors or bankers or rich farmers or lawyers or missionaries. Not much was available to little girls.

And yet as she grew up to become a beautiful young woman with yens for life and a hundred friends and a dozen beaus, Eunice Nordby decided that a fruitful life should include first and foremost service to God and humanity. Adventure in exotic places was a close second. Two routes to that kind of life were available to a preacher's daughter from North Dakota, she thought. It was possible she could forge such a life with her own energies and commitment, but if she could find those same attributes in a handsome young man, her chances rose exponentially. What she needed at this point was a stroke of serendipity, sometimes known as destiny. Such an act materialized in a lab session in a biology class at Concordia over the prostrate form of a dead frog. The project was to dissect a frog, an undertaking Eunice Nordby found abhorrent despite her once strong ambitions to be a medical missionary. In the class with her was a robust fullback on the football team who moved in confidently on the frog. Eunice was impressed by Dave Simonson, but she was also involved with a congested social life. The fullback was not intimidated. In fact, part of campus lore that later grew up around the Simonson-Nordby romance included the story of a collision during one of the Concordia scrimmages. In it, the fullback crashed head-on into another player who happened to be his leading rival in the pursuit of Eunice Nordby. The medical report disqualified the leading rival from any further contention in the pursuit of Eunice Nordby, it being awkward to press a courtship with a broken leg.

No denials of this campus lore have ever been heard from Simonson.

The romance flowered one day when the fullback showed up at a church rally in Eunice's home of Portland, N.D., where her role in the entertainment was to play the piano on a flatbed truck. Simonson arrived in a striking black and white wool sweater that accentuated his powerful physique and drew long sighs from Eunice's girl friends. One of their earlier double dates was arranged by Chris Rotto, Eunice's closest confidante and one who still stakes out credit for bringing Dave and Eunice together. She later married Dick Hefte, a lawyer who became one of Simonson's closest associates in the monumental Operation Bootstrap project to build schools in Africa. J. David and Eunice were engaged not long after the church rally in Portland, and Eunice brought him home to meet her parents. Her mother, Olga, a gentlewoman of Swedish genes, nonetheless was appalled by the appearance of this young male giant from the labyrinths of the Concordia locker room.

"He's so . . . so big," Olga protested. "Eunice, he could do almost anything to you."

The daughter nodded agreeably.

"I hope he does," she said.

Olga went blank in raw mortification.

There was a time in their college careers when Eunice Nordby's longing to become a medical missionary burned deeper than Dave Simonson's intentions in the ministry. For awhile, Simonson drifted from God. Campus life graduated into a party. He was popular and a visible man on campus. God was sometimes an intrusion. His old goals of missionary life shifted. He considered medicine. A career in the ministry at this point didn't seem very electrifying. The pre-seminary students he observed at Concordia didn't strike him as being particularly towering mentalities or potential beacons of the church. He confided these impressions to the elder Simonson, who took note of his son's disapproval and offered a solution: "Why don't you do something about it? Get into those courses yourself."

In short, if you can do it better, forget about medicine and get serious about God.

To David Simonson, this sounded like a reasonable proposition. Quick motivation and impulse decisions were part of his field of action. He recruited six or seven of his locker room chums and enrolled in some of the school's pre-seminary classes. It was a decision he never second-guessed. He made his apologies to God for his temporary waywardness and renewed his fervor for mission work. "For me, it was only going to be mission life in my ministry. When my friends asked why, I told them I'd been in a preacher's family too long to go in any other direction. I'd seen most of the problems the church pastor had do deal with, and I wasn't burning up to get involved with those. Another thing I couldn't do temperamentally was spending the next 30 years facing weak coffee and Ladies Aid meetings on Thursday afternoon. Somebody had to do it, bless the pastors and the ladies, but it wasn't going to be me. I wasn't going to advance the cause of Christianity very far presiding over coffee klatches."

Eunice by then had pretty much abandoned the grail of being a medical missionary. As a bright and versatile high school student at Oak Grove in Fargo, N.D., and an engaging personality who quickly acquired friends of all ages, she clearly earned opportunities in college. Although her parents had limited means, she was able to attend Concordia with the financial assistance of a prosperous Red River Valley farmer, Hartwig Fugleberg, who was a friend of the family. But without the resources to go on to medical school, she decided to pursue nursing and entered nurses' training at Fairview Hospital in Minneapolis in 1951, at about the time Dave Simonson enrolled at Luther Seminary in St. Paul. They chose June 14 the following year as their wedding date, an event they announced to their parents with a mixture of joy and wariness. They were wary because it was reasonable to assume that the news was not going to be greeted with hallelujahs by the Nordby and Simonson elders. The first storm cloud was the relationship between the Rev. Edward Nordby and the Rev. Rudolph Simonson, a relationship coated with ice since their first days in the seminary. Warmer feelings have been exchanged between seal hunters and environmentalists.

To understand the uncanny beginnings of the connection between Dave Simonson and Eunice Nordby, you have your choice of explanations, starting with Dave Simonson's. It was Simonson's solemn belief, voiced repeatedly in later life, that the hand of God was in some form present in all of the events that brought them into missionary service in Africa. In other words, destiny. The less devout normally have trouble with that theory. Destiny always seems convenient when the events don't make sense otherwise. But if you don't buy Simonson's convictions about the hand of God, you have to wonder what else to call it. When Edward Nordby and Rudolph Simonson attended Luther Theological Seminary, fellow students would have been floored by the notion that their children would some day marry. The future reverends, Nordby and Simonson shared a room before their ordinations. They acquired a strong, working dislike for each other.

In their subsequent service in the name of the Lord, there is no evidence that those attitudes changed in any substantial way. What this means is that there are limits to love even among God's most determined servants. There might be even fewer limits to Scandinavian stubbornness. Moreover, Gladys Simonson herself was not red hot for the marriage, suspecting that Eunice Nordby was too flashy for her son and might not be worthy to be his life partner. And Olga Nordby's reservations about her new son-in-law were blunt and well-documented in the family councils.

But the younger members of the Simonson clan ignored the pouting and looked forward to a fruitful marriage. Why not? It was going to unite two people who shared ideals and values that would not only enrich their own lives but quite likely the lives of others they met in their calling. As a wedding day forecast, it couldn't have been closer to the truth.

But if this wedding was supposed to be the stuff of poetry, no floating swans or rainbows were in evidence. Neither were there any gowns from Fifth Avenue. Because of the meager family treasury, Eunice designed and sewed her own white satin gown. It was lovely, and it was also late. She was still hemming 30 minutes before the processional at her father's church in Portland, N.D. One of the reasons for the prenuptial panic was the late arrival of the flowers for all attendants. "We didn't have the money to afford to buy them," Eunice wrote in the wedding's postmortems years later. "So I went around to the neighbors' yards gathering peonies for all of the corsages."

The script for the event and the honeymoon gave the newlyweds the better part of a week together. David was attending the seminary at the time and had a part-time job as a carpenter in Eau Claire, Wis., from which he got four days off. Eunice received the necessary leave time from her training courses at Fairview. On the surface, it looked like a comfy if compact little idyll with which to begin married life. The groom on June 14 was massively handsome in a white dinner jacket. The bride fulfilled all of the storybook prescriptions in her satin gown. She was the picture of serenity and beauty and love, and never mind that she had loused up part of the hem in her haste.

Pastor Edward Nordby, the father of the bride, presided over the linkage at the altar with solemnity and pride. Pastor Rudolph Simonson served as his son's sponsor. If there was eye contact between the feuding reverends, it wasn't apparent to the congregation. But the music soared, the couple kissed, the congregation applauded and the marriage of Dave and Eunice Simonson was well and truly launched.

What happened in the hours thereafter owed less to the poets of bliss than to Edgar Allan Poe.

The newlyweds had made reservations to spend their wedding night at a hotel in Detroit Lakes, Minn. near the town of Audubon, where Rudolph and Gladys Simonson were now living. There, the Simonsons had invited all of the close relatives to attend their 25th wedding anniversary on Sunday, the day after the wedding of Dave and Eunice in North Dakota. Detroit Lakes is approximately 80 miles from Portland, N.D. Since Dave had no car of his own, his father offered the use of the Simonson family car for the drive from Portland to Detroit Lakes. After all of the ceremonies in Portland had subsided, Dave Simonson asked his father for the car keys.

The offer, his father said, had been withdrawn. The newlyweds couldn't use his car.

Rudolph Simonson went to his grave more than 40 years later without ever providing an explanation for this sudden removal of his car from the wedding night logistics. Young David, being his dutiful son, quickly forgave but later tried to figure it out. "I don't know. Dad was never crazy about this marriage. After his part in the wedding, he really didn't want anything to do with it. Maybe part of it was the business that I was his second son and was the first to get married. That might have offended his sense of family traditions and that sort of thing. All I know is that we had reservations at this hotel in Detroit Lakes and no idea how to get there."

David's brother, Paul, rallied to the emergency. Paul attended the wedding with his fiancee, Bonnie, who lived in Audubon near Detroit Lakes. And since they were driving to Audubon, Paul said, they could give the stranded honeymooners a lift to Detroit Lakes, and the crisis was solved.

It was, until they reached Hillsboro, N.D., where their little postwar Studebaker ran out of gas at night. Luckily, they were not far from the town gas station. The problem was the proprietor of the gas station. He was in Detroit Lakes himself, attending a dance. The station was closed. Nobody in town could open it.

"When do they expect him back from the dance?" David Simonson asked one of the townspeople.

"Six in the morning," the man said.

With waning enthusiasm, the bridegroom pondered the prospects of their wedding night. It had been raining, and now it was a prairie cloudburst. The four of them, David, Eunice, Paul and Bonnie settled into the little Studebaker—Eunice in her white satin wedding gown, David in his wilting white dinner jacket. It was approximately 10 p.m. There was no radio in the car to offer them news or entertainment. They talked. They yawned. Heroically, David and Eunice cuddled. The siege of the Worst-Wedding Night-in-the-History-of-Hillsboro had begun.

At approximately 6 a.m. sounds were heard from the nearby service station. The proprietor had returned from the dance in Detroit Lakes. Paul Simonson filled the tank and they were off for the hotel in Detroit Lakes to complete the second installment of this now deranged honeymoon scenario. They arrived in the neighborhood of 8 a.m., much to the bafflement of the hotel's day clerk, who had prepared the facility's bridal suite in the expectation of a more traditional arrival. He gave them the bad news. Checkout time was 10 a.m.

But preacher's kids just naturally tend to be indomitable. They thanked Paul and Bonnie and also the long-faced desk clerk. They then dashed up to their room, singing silent praises for the two hours they had.

Shortly after 10 a.m., changed and renewed, they headed to the home of the Rev. Rudolph and Gladys Simonson to join the other relatives in celebrating the couple's silver wedding anniversary at the parsonage. The plan was for Dave and Eunice to spend the night at his parents' home after the festivities for at least one relaxed evening of privacy. The problems there sprouted from the geography of the house and the bulging guest list. When the hosts finished doing the arithmetic, there was no space for the bride and groom. The solution was for Dave to spend the night with two of his brothers in one room, and Eunice to share a room with his brothers' girl friends.

Amazingly, neither party seriously considered annulment.

Salvation came the next day in a telephone call from one of Eunice's aunts in Minneapolis. She and her husband had decided to go on a vacation for a week and would be glad to turn over the house to Mr. and Mrs. David Simonson while they were gone. It's not recorded in the Simonson archives how they got to Minneapolis from Detroit Lakes. This may have been out of respect for the highway speed laws, most of which lay in shambles by the time they reached Minneapolis.

For two magnificent days the two luxuriated in peace and quiet. On the third day the house-owners returned with their family earlier than planned. They also came with more relatives, which meant that on the last night of their honeymoon, David spent the night sharing a room with a male cousin, and Eunice occupied an adjacent room with a female cousin.

The next day Eunice returned to her nurses' dorm in Minneapolis, and Dave went back to his construction work in Wisconsin. This meant the newly-weds were immediately separated for three months until the beginning of the fall term at Luther Seminary, when they moved into their own quarters near the seminary in St. Paul. It was an attic made available to Simonson by a relative who owned the house. The house was old, and the attic was unfin-ished and unheated, pending Simonson's improvement plans. Until that work was finished, the place was an oven in the summer and a deep freeze in the winter.

But after the sagas of Hillsboro and Detroit Lakes, Eunice Nordby Simonson would not have traded the attic in St. Paul for the presidential suite at the Catalina Hilton.

CHAPTER 4

The aircraft they flew into Nairobi in Kenya was a World War II bomber reincarnated by the British into low-level commercial transport. It was non-pressurized and flew only a few thousand feet above ground, which was convenient because it had to stop every four or five hours to refuel. It lumbered and bounced in the wind, orchestrating a general misery among its 30 passengers.

From London it landed in France and Malta and Aswan in Egypt, and later at a couple of wadi airstrips, and then Khartoum in the Sudan, Entebbe in Uganda and Nairobi. It took the Rev. David and Eunice Simonson and their three children nearly a week to fly from London to Nairobi, and when they got there they were struck without warning by their first exposure to the new politics of mid-century Africa.

The British, still hanging on in Kenya, were battling the Mau Mau rebellion. It was receding by the time the Simonsons reached Kenya in February of 1956 on a brief stopover en route to Tanganyika to the south. Simonson arrived with his Bible and his hunting guns. The guns got to be a source of some anxiety to the Simonson entourage (Dave, Eunice, Stephen 2-1/2, Naomi 1-1/2, and Nathan 1 month). They were to be met at the Nairobi airport by the Rev. Stan Benson, a cousin of Eunice's and himself a newcomer to Africa. When Benson failed to appear (after being told by an airport attendant that the Simonson plane was going to be 24 hours late), Simonson went in search through the dimly-lit huts that stood on stilts and constituted the Nairobi air terminal. He left his wife in charge of the kids and the guns. "You'll have to guard all of that with your life," he said. "You have to remember, there's a death sentence for anybody who loses a gun or ammunition to the Kenyans because of the Mau Mau. If we lose those guns, we're in it for good."

Despite these stern instructions, Eunice Simonson paid more attention to the squirming kids than to her husband's artillery. Guarding her husband's hunting arsenal in a gloomy airport couldn't have been worse than their arrival a few minutes before. The scene then was Eunice Simonson holding onto a barf bag to accommodate herself and the vomiting kids. The pounding in their ears in the reformed old bomber added the kids' wails of discomfort to the general tumult.

And yet she felt no grounds to complain. The interminable landings and takeoffs seemed part of the adventure. They had spent a few hours in Nice in the south of France, been assigned the bridal suite in a luxury hotel in Malta, seen camels in the Sudan and survived Stephen's rampage through sleeping Arabs in the terminal at Khartoum. About that episode, she planned to have serious conversations with the boy once they were settled. But the one important fact of life was that they were in Africa. They were in Africa, and she had spent almost all of the family money getting there. They could have flown on a conventional British airliner for $20 more. "Dave's salary from the mission board was $150 a month," she said later. "I'd seen missionary wives scraping together a couple of dollars for groceries or shoes. I wasn't going to waste it."

She did reconsider her decision a few times en route when the kids got airsick in unison, and she and Dave fumbled with the bags to prevent the mess from spilling into the aisles. None of old Richard Reusch's predictions mentioned anything about turning green on the approaches to Nairobi.

But Stan Benson was eventually located with a phone call to the African Inland Mission House. The Simonsons were transported safely to their quarters for the night, and no jail time was assessed.

A young missionary family from Minnesota could not have come to Africa at a more portentous time on the canvas of African history or of Christian mission on the African continent. The gales of African independence and revolution were sweeping the continent and hammering at the fortresses of more than a century of European colonialism. The names of Jomo Kenyata, Milton Obote and Patrice Lumumbu were daily fare in the newspapers and on TV and radio around the world. The colonialists argued that the Africans weren't ready to govern themselves and didn't have the resources to deal with the world. Those arguments made sense to most of the world but were shouted down by the voices and the warriors of African revolution. Violence shook much of Africa. The Africans warred with the garrisons of the colonialists and with each other.

The Christian mission in Africa may have hastened the revolutionary fervor both because of the education it brought and, in the earlier periods of missionary history, because of its partnership with the ruling powers. But African independence meant that the work of mission would be forever changed. It no longer had the cozy paternalism of European rule to shelter its work and bureaucracies that it could comprehend. That was history. Control of the churches now began passing into the hands of missionary-trained African prelates. While mission work continued ambitiously in the years immediately after independence, dealing with government now meant African governments, and that was uncharted terrain.

The moonbeams of idealism aside, just what were the Simonsons getting into when they arrived in East Africa? The missionaries to Africa had been at it for hundreds of years, from the time of the first explorations of Vasco da Gama. Even before that Islam was a missionary force. The first Christian missionaries were the European Roman Catholics, joined by the Protestants in the 1800s and later by Americans of all denominations. They came by the hundreds of thousands over the centuries with results that were lauded or damned by their critics and admirers. Some of the cross-bearers were saintly and some were arrogant, most endured and some caved in, many died and many were killed, some were the willing instruments of the powers that ruled whether it was the power of the European oligarchs or the power of the tribal chiefs. Most of the early ones tried to westernize the African natives as part of their passage to Christianity. The later missionaries mercifully dropped that strategy as a misguided invasion that didn't serve the purpose of either evangelism or humanitarianism.

The big majority of these people were brave, willing to risk their health and their lives. Most of them were simply inspired to carry the message of Christ to people they were certain needed to hear it. As part of this message they generally recognized that some form of social service had to be performed and could not be separated from their evangelism.

Not all intellectuals agreed with that idea. Erudite conferences were held throughout the world, from Uppsala in Sweden to the Ivy League citadels of American Protestantism, to evaluate the state of mission work in Africa. The arguments reverberated off the walls of the conference halls. What comes first, evangelism or social service? Is God sending us into Africa to build schools? Do we have a right to uproot their cultures in the name of Christ? Can't we preach Christianity *without* uprooting their cultures? If we extend the hand of cooperation to other religions, aren't we surrendering the uniqueness of Christianity?

And on.

For all of the converts and churches and schools it built and the lives the missionary movement saved and the random damage it created, the history books memorialized only a scattering or heroes or giants in mission work. In Africa, there were David Livingstone and Albert Schweitzer and a few more, but over the centuries thousands of them plodded in anonymity, returning to their native countries from time to time to plead for money or to regain their health. They eventually disappeared as pensioners or, if they weren't that lucky, as aging shepherds now gone over the hill.

A lot of these people were far from ordinary, but their lives remained obscure, their work scarcely recognized except by family and some distant archivist. Usually the most obscure part of their service was the daily struggle to keep their personal lives rightside up and their families in groceries in primitive worlds. It was a trial for which no seminary training could adequately prepare them or their children.

Which is approximately where we meet young Stephen Simonson of the family David and Eunice Simonson. Stephen was one of those kids whose energies arouse in their parents both love and terror. His exploratory impulses as a growing child in such climes as St. Paul, Minn., the deck of the Queen Elizabeth II and Khartoum offer a clue to the mixed reverence and wackiness that marked at least one family's passage to mission. The adventures of Stephen may tell as much about the life of the missionary in Africa as the baptism statistics. There was one difference in this particular family. It was not destined for obscurity. David Simonson's encounter with the lion in the Maasai bush pretty well ended that possibility early.

Their African destiny was never a matter of much doubt in Dave Simonson's mind as he worked his way through Luther Seminary in St. Paul. After his admission to the seminary in 1952, he got a job as a janitor and a room with his older brother, Luther, who was also studying at the seminary. He switched to the relative's attic in time for his marriage to Eunice, sprucing it up with a space heater and a mattress and bed frame cadged from the Salvation Army. Before Steve was born in August of 1953, Dave and Eunice had ritzed up their lives by moving into an apartment near the seminary. En route to his bachelor and master's degrees in theology at the seminary, Simonson studied anthropology and missionary history there, at the University of Minnesota and in Chicago. All of this was accented on the culture of the African Maasai, about whom Simonson finished his masters thesis in 1955. He then went before the mission board for a climactic interview that would determine the direction of his ministerial career for the rest of his life.

"By then I had a kind of fixation about going to East Africa to work with the Maasai," he said. "I'd been influenced by other missionaries and the images I created in my mind over the years. Here were these tall and fearless people, nomads herding their cattle across plains that were without boundary, with codes of living that made them irresistible to me. There seemed to be something in my blood that drew me to them. I learned quickly enough when I got to Africa that there were parts of that code of living that weren't very noble. But that didn't change this affinity and brotherhood I felt for them all my life. It wasn't only the idea of working and living with the Maasai that put me in front of the mission board that day. I knew there was no turning back for me. It went all the way back to my boyhood days at the parsonage. Every year we had a mission festival at which missionaries on leave would speak. Just as memorable to me was the evangelism week we had at the church, when we heard from some of the most eloquent and powerful evangelists who ever stood in the pulpit. One I remember best was Oscar Hanson, the father of the man who later became bishop of the St. Paul Synod of the Evangelical Lutheran Church in America, Mark Hanson. They were the highlights for the kids in the house and, of course, for my dad, absorbing all of these exotic stories from traveling teachers and evangelists, spreading the word of God. The pictures they created excited me and I said, 'Boy, if I can qualify, I'm going to do that.' Somebody not long ago asked me if I wasn't also drawn to a place like Africa by the chance to hunt and that stuff, and I said emphatically no, that wasn't part of the deal for me. It was carrying the message. I was influenced that way by all of these of missionaries and evangelists and by my father, but I wouldn't want to underestimate the effect on me of the stories Reusch brought back from Africa, and the total conviction with which he told them. I wasn't exactly a dreamer. I knew about the disillusionments that we were going to run into. But I was a pretty hardheaded young Norwegian, and I was convinced Eunice and I could make a difference. One of the questions put to me by the mission board was whether I would take an assignment to another place. I said, 'Not until you show me why I can't go to Tanganyika.'"

The dialogue was closed. The hardheaded young Norwegian was assigned to Tanganyika. He made the announcement to his wife in the form of a question he asked as he came floating into their apartment on a cloud of euphoria:

"How would you like to go to Africa?"

She answered with her own question: "How soon?"

They splurged with a dinner of potatoes and baked beans. By then Eunice had acquired a job at Fairview Hospital and received training in surgical nursing. But each time she decided she had their world figured out, Stephen would pull one of his acts. The kid was a prodigy as a wanderer and creative meddler. He was walking by ten months. His mother took all of the standard precautions. She was doing some chores in the St. Paul apartment when she heard a knock on the door.

"Here was this policeman holding Steve," she said. "By the time the policeman had finished his story, I've never felt more like a dummy in my life. I thought Steve was taking a nap. I had no idea he'd gotten up from his bed and slipped out the door. At the age of ten months! Before he went out, he grabbed one of Dave's smoking pipes and a hammer I'd been using and walked out into the street with them. When the police heard about it, Steve was standing in the middle of Como Ave. near one of the busiest intersections in the neighborhood in his droopy diapers, with the pipe in his mouth and the hammer in his hand. The policeman picked him up and yelled to some of the bystanders: 'Does anybody have any idea where this baby came from?' Somebody recognized Steve, and the policeman brought him to our apartment. The policeman didn't waste any time on courtesy. He wanted to know what kind of mother would allow an infant kid like this to run loose on the streets of St. Paul.

"I've never been so embarrassed. I didn't argue with the policeman. I said I just couldn't understand how Stephen could get out of the apartment like that without me knowing. I made the lame excuse that it was a ground level apartment and it was easier for him to do that, but that made no impression. The policeman handed Stephen to me and left shaking his head. I kissed my baby. I thanked God he was safe. And I put the hammer and pipe out of sight."

What the unhinged mother didn't know was something Stephen would reveal as the Simonson ministry progressed. He had an undeniable genius for cliffhanging behavior. It erupted again after the Simonsons were booked for London by the Lutheran mission board in late 1955 to begin their odyssey of a lifetime. By tradition and protocol, the lives of most Lutheran ministers and their spouses move to relatively orderly rhythms. For some of these people it is part of the Scandinavian legacy, augmented by a favorable push from God to get them back on the rails when necessary. From the beginning, the lives of David and Eunice Simonson were never guided by rhythms that were either orderly or predictable. Whether God intervened when their lives and mission got too chaotic (or too tranquil), extraordinary events occurred in their lives without explanation. The Simonsons absolutely believed, and still do, that God was somewhere on the edges of their strange movements of August 1955. In the week of their departure from the United States, the mission board booked them to fly directly to Africa. The newly ordained minister, 26, had been posted to Tanganyika by the National Lutheran Council. But it was discovered at the eleventh hour that in order to teach in Tanganyika, a British protectorate under United Nations trusteeship, Simonson would have to anglicize his teaching certificate. He could do that by taking a five-month course at the University of London. The agenda was revised. The Simonsons were booked for London.

But on what?

Under the pressure of last-minute arrangements, the board discovered only one option to get the penniless David and Eunice, Stephen 2, and Naomi 10 months, to England. They had to go by sea. The only vessel available was the Queen Elizabeth II, the sleek flagship of the Cunard line, the QE2.

In the original bookkeeping, the paupers from Minnesota were assigned to steerage. Nothing else was affordable. The bursars re-examined the passenger quarters when the Simonsons came on board. There wasn't enough room for them in steerage.

They were reassigned at no extra charge. Their new lodging was a private, upper deck cabin on the most elegant of all passenger ships on the high seas, and they were bound for Southampton.

For the next five days they basked and congratulated themselves; they offered prayers of thanks and took seconds at the meals. But there was no way the crossing could have been entirely free of anxiety and the maternal shakes for Eunice Simonson. "It was Stephen," she said. "Even on the ship, he got away from us, and I just don't know how he did it. Two or three times we found him in the prow of the ship, straddling the rail. The worst was when we arrived in Southampton and went ashore. Dave couldn't help with the kids because he was clearing his guns through all of the red tape. While I was holding Naomi and watching what was happening on the dock, Steve got away. The ship had settled by the prow as it was docking. And there I saw Stephen with his toes over the edge of the dock, where there was no barrier. He was staring down at the water 40 feet below. He looked mesmerized, and I could feel the panic rising in me. If I called his name he might be startled and fall into the water. I had nightmares for months afterward seeing him falling into the water. I also knew there was a risk if I tried to grab him and he squirmed away. But I had to do *something*. I held Naomi as tight as I could and ran up behind Stephen, pulled him to me and fell backwards where he was safe."

At this point she considered the possibility that God might be getting tired of her prayers of thanksgiving for Stephen's hair-raising escapes.

He had one more reprise before the entourage got to Tanganyika. But in the family history of the Simonsons, the five month interlude in England was strictly an epic of Eunice facing life in a land that often seemed more alien to the young missionary's wife than the Africa that followed. Dave Simonson quickly ensconced himself in another frigid attic apartment, this one in London for his studies there. The search then was launched for a place for Eunice, Stevie, Naomi and a third child with whom Eunice was pregnant and would materialize as Nathan in January of 1956. In this, there was no doubt that someone or something intervened. Three hours north of London in the Midlands was an old manor, practically a castle, and once called Hothorpe Hall. It was said to have been used by the British government as a settlement house for displaced families during World War II, and before that as a hunting center. Later, Field Marshal Bernard Montgomery became its proprietor for a few years. Somehow it came under the aegis of the Lutherans and of a former seminary classmate of Dave Simonson's, Lloyd Swantz. At the time they arrived it was being used to house missionary candidates and their families, from the Balkans and elsewhere. Minnesota qualified as elsewhere.

"The room we got was cold and drafty with a 20-foot ceiling," Eunice recalled. "But it was home, and I didn't complain because the baby was due in January. I thought that in this country where we were just passing through we had a place, it was then called Market Harborough, where the child could be born and cared for. There was a hospital in the English health system nearby where the delivery could be made. The first step to get into the system was to prove that you were pregnant. I notified the hospital and asked permission to be registered. The doctor assigned to me was a Dr. Daniels. He was a funny little man who drove to our place in a saucy red sports car. He came bustling into the castle and I welcomed him. I was a nurse and had worked with patients all of my life. So I lay down and properly exposed my tummy to show that I was indeed pregnant. He seemed to be shocked by this brash American woman exposing her abdomen. Very gingerly, he turned his head and ran his fingers over my stomach and said, 'Yes, yes, you are pregnant. Now tell me what date you are due.' I said, 'Well, I think about the 26th of January.' And the doctor rushed out as fast as he could. When the time came for me to go to the hospital I met a matron who must have been jilted by an American serviceman. She was totally hostile, and I don't know why. She was a real battleax. She moved around with this big brass buckle on the belt of her suit, and you could just feel her disapproval, saying to herself, 'Here comes this American nurse to have her baby.' She came to me and said, 'This baby *must* come on January 26th. You're booked that day.' As though I was going to be evicted if I loused up their bookkeeping. The rest of it was like stepping back into medieval history. Before the birth, Dave came to visit from London. This annoyed the matron terribly. She thought it was totally wrong that the husband should invade the maternity ward. She didn't think men had any right to be there as part of the birthing process. She wanted Dave to clear out. I don't know what he was supposed to do. Go down to the corner pub?

"When my time came, she grabbed a leg and said, 'Get on with it, get on with it.' I tried to tell her I'd had previous difficulties in childbirth when we lived in Minnesota. I tried to say this baby seemed to be larger than the others. She thought I was trying to interfere, and she practically yelled, 'Get on with it!' So I got on with it and I ripped and I tore and I was a mess. She said, 'Oh, deah, oh deah, I'll have to call Dr. Daniels to do a repair.' She did. There I was with all of the natural anesthesia running out of my abdomen. She couldn't bear to look there. Dr. Daniels arrived. He asked for Novocain. She said 'I have none.' He said, 'We can't do a major repair like this without Novocain.' He said 'We have to have some kind of anesthesia.' She said, 'We have none.' In my miserable state it just seemed like the battleax was getting her revenge. The doctor did the whole repair without giving me any pain relief. It was absolutely brutal."

Nathan arrived, however, in reasonably good health, a condition it took his mother a little longer to acquire. None of them had much time. In London, Dave Simonson's classes were nearing an end. His benefits weren't confined to the certification he was receiving to teach in Tanganyika. Simonson was and is one of the great networkers in the history of Concordia College at Moorhead, Minn. He'd met the man who was able to give his family entry to the castle in the Midlands. In London he met one Eliufoo Solomon, a member of the Chagga tribe in Tanganyika, a teacher at the Marangu Teachers College where Simonson was headed and a man who would occupy a cabinet post as minister of education in the new Tanzanian government. And further down the road, Eliufoo Solomon would serve as a consultant to the young missionary from Minnesota when Simonson first conceived his landmark Operation Bootstrap Africa to build classrooms for Tanzanian kids.

In London he also met another East African, Sam Ntiro, an artist who later became minister of culture in the Tanzanian government and valuable advisor to Simonson in the times when his social service enterprises needed liaison with the government. There was one more stroke of serendipity during the Simonsons five months in England that was to remove some of the future financial stresses of the missionary couple. One of their relatives, Arthur Vikse, a pilot in the U.S. Air Force, was stationed in England. With his wife, Shirley, he visited Eunice and David and Hothorpe Hall. Vikse flew in the Berlin Airlift and, after leaving the service, became an airline pilot in the states and ultimately a prosperous corporate executive in a motel chain. From there his business expanded into other properties. Vikse's mother lived in Northfield, Minn. While the Vikses were visiting her there, they renewed their connection with the Simonsons during one of the preacher's furloughs. Simonson never had trouble motivating potential donors to his causes, whether well-heeled corporate leaders or penitents in the pews. The Vikses developed a strong interest in the Simonsons' mission work in Africa and made important contributions to it. Vikse also set up retirement and investment plans that eventually secured the Simonsons financially in later life.

But when they boarded the converted bomber in London for the flight to Africa they were absorbed more with antsy kids than with their long-range future. From Nairobi in Kenya there was no flight directly into Tanganyika. None was necessary. The British ran the customs in both Kenya and Tanganyika and would for at least a while longer. With the teaching certificate in David's hands and four-weeks old Nathan in Eunice's, where he divided time with Stephen and Naomi, the enlarged Simonson retinue headed for Nairobi and then to Tanganyika. To get there, they had to make the low-budget airline's obligatory stop in Khartoum, the site of all of the ill-starred British occupation in the 19th century, the battles and the Mahdi. The crew and passengers overnighted in a Khartoum hotel. It was an event that occupies no glory today in the Simonsons' family lore, a first encounter with the Arab world that Eunice Simonson remembers today for the long gowns and long knives she saw at every turn. There was nothing especially menacing about them but nothing comforting either. Naomi, the middle child, was beyond appeasing the whole night. Her ears hurt and she threw tantrums and broke her milk bottle on the floor. Her mother spent the night nursing Naomi on one side and Nathan on the other. With his mother preoccupied, Stephen needed a vent for his energies. The family left early for the airport, ahead of the crew, and Dave and Eunice groped around the terminal looking for something that was open for breakfast. What they saw was Stephen, running ahead of them, in the throes of discovery. He'd found dozen or so Arab men sleeping on what constituted the roof of the terminal. All were covered with blankets for warmth against the overnight desert chill. In a sociable mood, Stephen began pulling the blankets off the Arabs, calling, "Good morning, good morning." Before his parents overtook him, he'd run through most of the assembly without being bopped by the shorn Arabs. The Simonsons made profuse apologies, none of which was understood or appreciated.

The kid was clearly primed for Africa, his parents possibly less so after their five days to Khartoum.

But now it was Nairobi, and the morning sun bathed the flame trees and jacarandas. Eunice was transfixed by the color. The road led south to Tanganyika, and they were under way, the day for which they'd prayed and sweated for years.

Nothing much was going to mar this day, except a wreck of mysterious cause by the side of the road. The car had been abandoned. It was one they recognized, belonging to a missionary and his wife, people they knew. What happened? An animal? Mau Mau? What?

Where were the missionaries?

No questions in Africa, they learned soon enough, are answered quickly.

CHAPTER 5

The road from Nairobi to Namanga on the Kenya-Tanzania border today is paved and relaxed. It quickly carries the traveler from Nairobi's international commerce and political tension into an East African plain and horizon that is without time or encumbrance. Acacia trees and thornbush sometimes interrupt the endless spread of high grass. But it is never dull to the traveler. A few yards off the road a giraffe will stroll behind an acacia and munch from its highest leaves, oblivious of the thorns. If you have never been to Africa, this first view of its animal life in the wild is an exhilaration. Here is a giraffe, straight from the coloring books. Two miles further down the road a young Maasai in his red garments and wooden prod coaxes a small herd of bony cattle. Not far from Nairobi to the west roll the Ngong Hills, presenting glimpses of an earth at ease yet vaguely longing, scenes that enraptured a generation of moviegoers in the adaptation of Karen Blixen's *Out of Africa*.

Her Africa was the Africa of the early 20th century, of a mood and a society where western whites were the proprietors. Not many of them were as benevolent as Karen Blixen and fewer still clung to the idyll of Africa that consumed her and nourished her poet's soul. It was an Africa in which the natives occupied roles bluntly assigned by the proprietors when their lives connected.

That Africa is largely gone. The Africa of the effortless landscapes of the East African plateau is still here. This is not the Africa of tropical jungles and rain forests, nor the Africa of the vast deserts or baked mud or its mighty equatorial rivers. This is the Africa of the roaming Maasai, with marvelous sweeps of its wild savannahs, conical huts of its villages and, on market day, noisy congregations of cattle and traders and women hauling water on their heads in perfect balance and symmetry. And beyond the horizons from the road south from Nairobi to Namanga, what?

Beyond them is the African Rift Valley, an enormous cleft nearly 50 miles wide running in its entirety for more than 4,000 miles from the Middle East, through the Red Sea that it created and south to the edge of South Africa. It is a gash in the earth so huge that it is the one physical feature of the earth recognizable by the astronauts. Within its escarpments hundreds of feet high, the Rift is an anarchy of geology attesting to an earth in agony eons years ago—dead alkaline lakes, miles of lava rock ledges and deserts of dust. But then the landscape changes and the volcanic rock gives way to thick forests of eucalyptus and semitropical growth and pools of freshwater from streams bustling down the escarpments.

And beyond the Rift lifts the vast caldera of the Ngorongoro Crater, the remains of one of the cataclysmic implosions in the history of the earth, a volcano collapsing on itself, forging what is now an amphitheater for wild animals, 15 miles across, walled in by palisades nearly 2,000 feet high. It is home to an average of 20,000 animals on a given day. Still, you can drive through it for up to a half hour and see only a handful. The scale is that huge. And then you come upon thousands of pink flamingo on their stilt legs in an alkaline lake. Nearby in one of the sweetwater pools you can hear the guttural choruses of hippos and be amused by their small, twitching ears perched above their ugly and snorting noses. But you don't ever want to underestimate the danger from those comical beasts if you ever get between them and their water.

Not far from the hippo pool you will come upon a scene of carnage, a half dozen lions slaughtering the luckless stragglers of a wildebeest herd.

Beyond the Ngorongoro spread the surviving coffee plantations of the highlands and the wildlife refuges of the Serengeti, Tarangire and Lake Manyara. Here the spectacles are almost too much for the traveler to absorb. Here are herds of skittish zebra and wildebeest, leopard dozing on the islands of rock outcrops in the savannah, hordes of elephants moving invincibly through the marshes, ostrich, waterbuck, hyena, Marabou storks, gazelles and Cape buffalo, sprinting cheetah and the languorous giraffe.

On the edge of the Serengeti is the Olduvai Gorge where the Leakeys have excavated for decades and uncovered what they are convinced is the beginning of humanity in the bones of the earliest hominids. Maybe that is why the traveler finds East Africa so magnetic. Something in the genes may be telling him or her that this is where we came from.

Yet amid all of that wonderment, what also lies beyond the horizons of the road from Nairobi to Namanga is the poverty and sickness of East Africa, less than before, but not much less. What also lies there is the struggle of a still essentially primitive people hopelessly out of the race with the technically advanced nations, groping for something better, but falling further behind.

Dave and Eunice Simonson knew this on the February day they left Nairobi to commit their lives to the land then called Tanganyika. The highway from Nairobi to Namanga wasn't paved in 1956. It was a dirt road, all six hours of it, soupy in the rainy season, a fog of dust in the dry months. But the sun was up, this was Africa and the young reverend and his wife were thrilled. The other young missionary in the homely Chevy Carryall was Stan Benson, Eunice's cousin, who'd finally made connections with them at the mission house in Nairobi and was returning to his mission work near Arusha in Tanganyika. A few hours ahead of them heading for Tanganyika was the Rev. Bill Smith, another lodge brother in the spreading Minnesota enclave of missionaries in East Africa. One of the less reverent theologians at Luther Seminary called it the Minnesota Mafia. Simonson was particularly touched by Bill Smith's story. He'd been a wrestling champion at Carleton College in Northfield, Minn., and later one of David's classmates at the seminary. Bill Smith felt the same summons to serve in Africa that moved Dave Simonson, but Bill's wife, Lynne, candidly admitted being less than ecstatic about it. When they got there the kids were chronically sick with dysentery. She confided that she'd been praying every night for a way they could get out. A way did open, a frightful one. Bill Smith, the college wrestler, came down with polio. He would have to undergo treatments at the Sister Kenny Institute in Minneapolis, then the best hope for polio victims with its sophisticated therapies. All of the Meru tribes people he'd served were there to see him off when he left Arusha. Bill Smith told them in Swahili, "I'm coming back." At Kenny, somebody suggested that he'd better face the truth that he'd never walk again. Smith went nose to nose with the deliverer of that news and said, "I'm walking out of here."

Months later, he walked out of there. Returning to Africa, the Smiths left London a few days after the Simonsons flew to Nairobi. It happened that the Simonsons and Smiths left Nairobi for Tanganyika on the same morning, the Smiths in a Peugeot driven by the Rev. Bob Johnson, another member of the burgeoning Minnesota Mafia in Tanganyika.

Eunice Simonson's first glimpse of the true, the wild Africa was a Thomson's gazelle bolting away from the road after being surprised by the Chevy. It bounded and pranced, shifting directions mercurially, it's tail twitching, its black body stripe getting smaller as it ate up ground.

"What a beautiful little animal," she said. David nodded. It was wild Africa, for sure. A mile later, a giraffe materialized, then an ostrich and then a whole enclave of termite hills. But a few miles after that, they found a busted Peugeot in the ditch. It was the Bill Smith car without doubt. They stopped and examined it. The car was deserted, its windshield smashed.

"The first thing we feared," Eunice Simonson said, "was that the Mau Mau had gotten our friends. It was a terribly depressing sight, and the picture we had of some roadside assault was even worse. We were helpless to do anything. We got back into our car and drove toward Namanga, which was the entry into Tanganyika. We'd only gone a mile or so past the Peugeot when our car stopped. Stan and Dave got out to look and found out that a rock had gone through the gas tank. Here we were still wondering what happened to the

Smiths and Bob Johnson, and we were stranded in the middle of nowhere in a country we'd never seen, out in the bush. Stan said not to worry. Not to worry! What could possess the guy to tell us that. But we didn't argue, and Stan took our petrol can and headed toward Namanga. I had no idea where that was, how far away. Minutes? Hours? Days? I asked myself a question, Are we ever going to see Stan again? What about the Smiths and Bob Johnson? All I knew was what I could see. We were stranded in Mau Mau country with our three babies. I hadn't thought about Mau Mau when the car was moving and we were looking for animals. But once we stopped, in my mind the country was full of Mau Mau. Dave did his best to comfort us. But I composed a prayer. I said, 'Dear God, I know very well you didn't bring us out here to have us killed. We'd like not to be scared, but we are. Take care of our troubles, dear God, in your order of preference.'

"That was one of those kitchen sink prayers when you ask God to sort out everything in sight and to lay out his own priorities. The first one appeared right about then. Stan Benson came back from Namanga, which wasn't far away after all. He was carrying a full can of fuel. He also gave us our first course in how-to-help-God-in-a-crisis. He said you take a bar of soap and spread some of it across the hole in the gas tank. Water will dissolve soap, but petrol won't. So we spread soap across the gas tank. It held the fuel, and we were off to Namanga."

Namanga today straddles the Kenya-Tanzania border, half in one country and half in the other. On either side, customs agents process tourists, residents and tradespeople doing business in both countries. Aesthetically, it is a dump, a collection depot for assorted garbage of today, yesterday and weeks before that. But in 1956, it was a garden spot. Since the British were still in control in both countries, there were no international suspicions and enmities at the border and no garbage dumps. Still unaware of the fate of the Smiths and Bob Johnson, the Simonsons spent the night in a sumptuous hotel, not far from a spectacular aviary and flowering, semitropical trees. "It was as close," Eunice said, "to a Garden of Eden that we were going to get in the middle of Africa." But their temporary destination was Arusha, a headquarters for international church councils working in Tanganyika and therefore a magnet for Lutheran missionaries.

In Arusha they overtook the Bill Smith family and Bob Johnson, who were unscathed.

"What on earth happened?"

All it was, Bill Smith explained, was a rock that punched through their windshield. They were still mobile but a little while later the clutch plate seized up and made the Peugeot inoperable. They couldn't leave the Peugeot in the middle of the road, and there were no discernible shoulders on the route to Namanga. So they pushed the Peugeot into a ditch and flagged down a big petrol truck heading south. It was equipped with a large cargo box, in which were stored drums of gasoline. The driver said the only way to do it was to have Bill Smith, Bob Johnson and the three Smith kids squeeze into the space between the top of the petrol drums and the roof of the box, and Lynne Smith could ride in front with the driver.

Africa.

To live and thrive in Africa, Dave Simonson told himself about then this would have to happen: You'll have to be resourceful. You'll also have to be lucky. You'll have to be smart and durable and never forget that God had something to do with putting you here, which meant there was a reason you were here. And if you could put all that together, you were going to be here for the long haul.

Years afterward, after the Simonsons' resourcefulness, luck, durability, savvy and evident channels to God had made them highly visible in the East African missionary scene, a visitor asked Simonson what was his bottom line motivation on that day he first saw Africa: "Doing the work of humanity, the work of the Lord, adventure, what?"

"In my mind, it wasn't very complicated," he said. "I was here to bring these people something. I thought I could bring them to the point where they could come into the kingdom like everybody else. I thought that too often this invitation was clothed in western culture. Things like the clothes they had to wear, that they had to be clean, that they couldn't come to worship with anybody who had ochre paint on the skin. I knew that a lot of missionaries had gone way past that point, but there was still a residue of it and I had no time for that sort of thing. It had been drummed into my head by people who'd worked best with them that these Africans, the Maasai, were people who actually came out of the tradition of the Old Testament. At core they were monotheists. They could go back to the twelve tribes of Israel, somehow, and scholars who looked into their history called them Hamitic, children of Ham. How they evolved as they did—their color, stature and language—I had no idea. But it was part of their oral history that was carried through the generations, that they had come down the valley of the Nile and headed south. The Zulu tribes had come north, and they met somewhere around what we used to call Rhodesia and now call Zimbabwe, and they had it out. War. It was settled when they roasted members of the elite on both sides; they decided they'd never meet again, and they both turned back.

"How much of that is actual history and how much mythology, nobody is going to be able to tell you. But it got to be part of the lore, and if you want to live and work with these people, you ought to be aware of it. The deeper I looked into some of those stories, the more I became aware that their own religious beliefs—apart from the Christianity we tried to bring into their lives—were somehow rooted in Old Testament theology. There's no question in my mind that they had their spiritual roots there. So this was the challenge to me: to present the type of Christianity I knew and to do it in a way that had nothing to do with my own culture and how I looked on the outside. In other words, to present Christ and his teachings and keep them totally separate from how the white people lived and what they ate and how they talked. Christ, in other words, wasn't some guy from Jerusalem who happened to walk around in sackcloth and wore a halo. Christ and what he taught had to believable to them, something they could understand in terms of the way *they* lived, not the way we did.

"Among your own peers, the missionaries and the people who supervise them, you were never going to get agreement on the best way to go about bringing Christianity into the lives of people who didn't know it. And you obviously were never going to please the critics and the evaluators of mission in their ivory towers. You would hear, and still do, that trying to convert them is a disservice to them, disrupting their culture, introducing them to alien concepts, satisfying our own values and agendas by inflicting doctrines alien to their lifestyle and not enriching their lives. I picked that up right away. In any group of theology people, or sociologists or historians, half of them would get you into a corner and tell you it's a waste of your time and theirs trying to teach Christianity to these people and that you were bothering them. The theory there was that these folks were as far along as they were going to get and why feel sorry for them. That sort of thing. We still get it from a lot of people who feel no need to bother them, that they're all happy in their ignorance. And that's baloney. That kind of criticism has never bothered me. We, Eunice and I, were definitely called. So were Bill Smith and Stan Benson and the others. We knew we were called. We understood that the needs of these people clearly went beyond the spiritual. In those times, the 1950s, there weren't many short-term missionaries. I was called for life. Bill and Stan were called for life, all of those people were. The only reason you were going to go home was for illness or some furlough that took you away from your mission temporarily but actually was part of it in fund-raising or building awareness back home.

"When we left we told our parents we might be back and we might not. I told my brothers, if there's a funeral, just notify me. I won't be coming. So we were out there for keeps. Eunie understood that. We were sent into Africa to do what we could during the time we were there. Today, though, missions are often conducted on a short term when they're conducted at all. You go out there, see if you like it, the shorter the better so you can have your exposure to global missionary work and then go back where it's a little more congenial. They don't even do that in parishes in the U.S. There are a lot of good people who go into mission work today, but the parameters on how you do it have changed. If somebody had told me that day we got to Namanga on our way to Arusha that I was still going to be in Arusha more than 40 years later, I wouldn't have been surprised. If Eunie and I held on to our health, we expected to do that, and planned to.

"Part of the reason for that was the people with whom we did most of our work, the ones we came to know to the point where we truly loved them and became part of them insofar as we could, were the Maasai. Friends often asked me if you'd have to force-feed them Christianity. They asked if we had to be super-cautious about tying Christianity to their cultures and being sure we avoided the worst mistakes of the earlier missionaries. My answer is that most of the Maasai I've worked with have been waiting for Christianity. They had this ingrained connection with the Old Testament, which surfaced in all kinds of ways if you probed deep into their tribal beliefs. In fact, some of them actually knew the spirit of the Old Testament better than they do at the seminary, ideas that had been passed on to them through the generations. They were waiting for a Messiah to come. They knew they were separated from God by some of their acts. And if you come to respect the Maasai you do it in the full knowledge of some pretty awful behavior that you observe. But where on earth don't you find bad behavior? In New York? Miami? Minneapolis?

"Where don't you experience deceit and self-indulgence, wanton acts, drunkenness and theft, all that. Sometimes we define that differently in our own cultures. I don't know that we're so much different. Anyhow, I found that most of the Maasai were looking for a way to appease their God, our God, because of this separation and they wanted to re-establish the relationship. Let me give you a little history. In 1899 there was a famine that almost wiped them out. They went to Mt. Meru near Arusha, went up the mountain. And the women milked their own breasts in appeasement of God and in prayer that the famine would end. They thought at the time that somebody had to make it right with God, and they were the people to restore the relationship. But there was also a group of people who had no interest in renewing this tribal relationship with God, and they were the medicine men who had a stake in their own status in the community. When you talk about these people to the folks in the U.S., they tend to go blank because talk of medicine men is mumbo-jumbo to most of them and hard to take seriously. But if you're a missionary in Africa, you better take it seriously because for the Maasai, certainly, the medicine men have had a strong grip on their spiritual lives. They can perform tricks of magic, read stones the way fortune tellers do and render prophesies. They also can lay curses on people in disfavor with somebody else."

The companion to whom Dave Simonson was making this recital on his early days of mission inhaled noisily at this point and stopped the reverend.

"David, you're talking about medicine men and curses, things and people you had to deal in competition for the faith of the Maasai. Are you saying they actually have these powers?"

Simonson decided on the tolerance rather than argumentation. He seemed to be saying, "Do you know the medicine men of Africa, or do I?"

What he did say was:

"There've been cases where they placed a death curse on a man, and he dropped dead. It was witnessed, and I believe it happened. I can't give you the physical reason for it. If psychiatrists or medical people witnessed it, they might call it a case of psychosomatic suicide, where the fear by the victim is so powerful he actually makes it happen. How much do we really know? Over the centuries in African cultures like these, the medicine men were people who directed the spiritual lives and the superstitions in the tribes, and they got very wealthy at it. They'd get cattle and goats for the services they performed, which were acts like healing sick people and meting out revenge, things like that. Listen. This isn't mumbo-jumbo. This is life as it is or was in some of the tribes, and it was something the missionary had to confront. Some of those medicine men I came to respect, because they had a knowledge of human nature and of the Maasai world that I had to learn. The Maasai would often go to the medicine men before going out on a hunt, and he'd give them directions and signs; they'd look for those signs and most of the times the medicine man knew what he was talking about. I don't know how or where they get their psychic powers if they have them. It doesn't matter. But the medicine man wasn't really restoring the Maasai's lost relationship with God. The challenge for guys like me was to understand all of that and still bring the New Testament into this setting. Most of the Maasai would listen because, as I've said, they were looking for a Messiah. It was going to be years before they would come into Christianity in any sizable numbers. Among all the African tribes I knew, the Maasai were the toughest to bring in, with all of their history for independence and their adherence to their traditional religion. Still, they listened. Our big concern was that they would get frustrated and leave us before we had a chance to convince them. We kept on teaching the ones who weren't ready for baptism. We kept putting into their minds and hearts that the day is coming when they would be ready to become Christians. They understood that. And some of them told us that we'd know when they were ready for that day."

Simonson wasn't a prophet. He had no way of knowing 25 to 30 years before the event that for thousands of Maasai the day would come to all of them simultaneously, and medicine men—of all people—would volunteer to do the work of Simonson, his astonished missionary cronies, and Christianity.

But in February of 1956, the Simonsons headed for Arusha and Kilimanjaro and the Pare Mountains. It was the beginning of a life, with all of its frights and revelations, that they couldn't have imagined on the Dakota prairies.

Nor could they have imagined the night Eunice fought the skinks.

CHAPTER 6

The Jesuits who popularized Christian mission hundreds of years ago could not have visualized the Pare Mountains of Tanganyika in the 1950s. Nor could Eunice Simonson:

Preachers packing guns into the wildland; one of the preachers banging nine guinea fowls with one blast; wives of the of the preachers grappling with language lessons, dirty diapers and skinks.

Skinks?

Before you could talk about beatitudes in East Africa in the 1950s and a man in sandals walking on water, you had to get acquainted with the Swahili language and the evasive movements of the hartebeest and the impala. In its spreading wisdom, the Lutheran Church in Tanganyika made the introductions to incoming missionary families as painlessly and as earnestly as it could, in the best traditions of Lutheranism. It didn't have anything particular to say about gunnery. It was assumed that most young Lutheran evangelists coming to Africa were acquainted with the basics of domestic economics and the laws of supplies and demand. If the pantries were spare (and they usually were) you could find supplementary calories and protein in the bush. If your salary was $150 a month and you had to find groceries and clothes for three kids, the Lutheran godfathers expected you to do what Lutherans were trained to do from the first days in seminary: put your trust in God and your brains in a higher gear.

So Simonson brought three guns, enough to avert the embarrassment of getting shut out on most of his hunting missions. Going into the field with the more experienced missionaries, he learned quickly that there was practically no limit to what you could bring down in the bush. He didn't learn immediately that the British overseers required a $14 annual license for these enterprises. Lutheran missionaries weren't excluded from the rule. "I found out in time that you could bring in loads of game and still stay out of jail or bankruptcy court," he said. "In the early days we hunted a lot in the country below the Pare Range in eastern Tanganyika. The church placed new missionary families with an older family in the Pares, in our case Kermit and Dorothy

Youngdale. There we spent three months being taught the Swahili language by a teacher from the primary school in Shigitani. The Swahili language, or KiSwahili, is a beautiful language, not especially hard to learn. It's an absolute must if you want to get around in most of East Africa. Eunice and I and the kids were installed in a grass-roof guest house there after we got acquainted with the surroundings and the people at the Marangu Teachers Training College at the foot of Kilimanjaro, where I was going to teach as part of my first assignment. The first time I went hunting with the other guys we shot kongoni, hartebeest and impala, and I have to say that was pretty exciting stuff. None of it was recreational. We needed the stuff for the table. When I got my license I found out that there were nearly 200 animals on a list of what you could take. Lions weren't on the list. Lions were considered vermin. There was a limit of 50 a day on guinea fowl. You could bring in two zebra. They even included rhino on the list, which is amazing when you consider the level of the rhino population in East Africa today, down to a handful. The guinea fowl were great eating, something like the game birds of the midwest in the states. Because there was a big limit, you tried to take as many as you could when you went to the British commission station, where you had to report what you were bringing back. My best day was taking out 17 with two shots. You could do that because the instinct of the guinea fowls was to run together in the middle of the road when they heard a noise. I found out soon enough how they acted. So I whistled and they all came together. I got nine with the first shot of the 16-gauge and eight with the second. All of that may sound a little crass to animal lovers, of whom I happen to be one. But there were hungry people back at the mission station and in the little thatched huts, and no wild food I've eaten in Africa in all these years is as good as the guinea fowl. When we finished we took them all in to our housing compound at the language school. The breast of those guinea hens was better than gourmet food."

Eunie could handle the guinea fowl without much stress. But she floundered when the reverend started bringing in bigger stuff and found herself nearly in tears, as we will discover later. But while her husband was learning Swahili and energetically taking the role of the Provider, Eunice Simonson was up to her eyelashes hauling water from the river to keep the kids clean, washing diapers and trying to avoid panic when the Old Missionaries Wives' Tales got around to snakes.

"I can't say all of that is a good excuse for why my Swahili classes went kaput in a hurry," she said, "but it's better than the next one. It also happens to be true. It was traditional part of the initiation rites that people in the new families coming in had to be regaled with all of the wild stories collected by the senior families who'd been attending the language schools. It was a hairy indoctrination. Most of the stories were funny but the ones I couldn't handle were the stories about snakes. I hated snakes from the time little boys put them down the dresses of little girls in the farm country. I was just horrified by them. Well, on this night they decided to tell all of their snake stories. Every-one had a story scarier in the others, like putting their babies in their cots and having a premonition that something was there, and here was a coiled cobra in the cot. It got worse. And just before I went off to our cottage somebody said that snakes really like getting into the grass roofs of huts. A couple of minutes later I had to climb up the steps of the little grass-roofed hut where my three babies slept. Dave was gone on a hunt. I remember going around that hut with a little hurricane kerosene lantern and taking everything out of the closet to be sure there weren't any snakes coiled up in the corners or under a basket. I finally got all of the kids settled for the night and was just ready to blow out the lantern when I heard this slithering about in the grass above my bed. I looked at the ledge under the roof and there was a little black head that kept darting out. I'm got more terrified by the minute. I hated Dave for running off to hunt and leaving me there to face this nest of snakes. That wasn't fair of me, but I never think very straight when I think about snakes all by myself. I have a terrible imagination, and it took over. I couldn't think of anything else to do so I got down on my knees and I said, 'God, I'll accept what comes to me, but please, if anybody has to be bitten by these snakes, let it be me and not my babies.' I was pleading. And then I want to tell you, I actually thought I heard this voice saying 'I won't. I called you and I won't let you down.' That was it. I went to bed, and I really felt peace. I was calmed. I blew out the lantern and went to sleep, and nothing more happened in the night. Later I found out what that darting head belonged to. It was a long black lizard they call a skink. They look like snakes until you see their legs, which I didn't see until the next day, and I also learned there wasn't just one. The place was filled with them, but we finally cleared them out, and the ones we didn't clear out we had to live with. But my babies were safe, and it was one more day of education for Eunice in the bush."

The introduction to Africa brought more trials to Eunice Simonson than to her husband, but it was a tribute to the benevolence she saw in each day, snake stories aside, and her resilience of character that she accepted those trials with a minimum of martyrdom. This was Africa, poor, bewildering, primitive and a ton of work for a mother of three. But she brought to it a tireless wonder of all of its nature and the music in the hearts of its struggling people, and that curiosity never abated. Africa was as compelling to her after 40 years as it was in the first days of the Pare Mountains.

Why did that matter?

It mattered because evangelism in Africa had undergone social changes that transformed the missionary movement over the decades from one in which the old solitary agents of God had been replaced by missionary couples and families and enclaves of families. Eventually, as the 21st century neared, evangelism in East Africa would change even more radically to the point where missionaries sent by western churches would dwindle almost into invisibility, replaced by African evangelists and lay preachers. But in the years of the

Simonsons' early stewardship, the western mission presence was still substantial and with a strong familial cast. Where once mission work had been the preacher facing the bush alone, trying to bridge all of the cultural gaps and undoubtedly wondering from time to time why God had forsaken *him*, now there were couples and families like the Bill Smiths and Stan Bensons, the Paul Edstroms and Dean Petersons and Dave Simonsons. The emissaries of Jesus Christ were no longer lone cowboys. The virtues in all this outweighed the hazards. Husband and wife offered mutual support and comfort. Because in one form or other both were teachers and healers, they expanded the benefits of mission. The loneliness and homesickness that afflicted many of their predecessors largely disappeared in the dual demands and rewards of evangelism and raising a family. There were some risks in it. One was the potential identity dilemmas facing the kids. Who were they? Their friends were not only kids of the other mission families but, especially as they got older, the African kids. So which culture did they embrace? The one of the white preacher's family, reinforced by occasional furloughs to America, or the society of the African kids which was at hand? And, as the kids grew to adulthood with permanent jobs in places like Arusha or the tourist lodges, were they Americans or white Africans? How about the division of work and status in the mission family? How much of the household drudgery did the preacher escape, how much did he need to escape or want to escape? Were the spouses equals or was this the old patriarchy of the prairie?

Well, all of the above.

Were there any domestic scrapes between most of these ma-and-pa emissaries of God?

Not quite every day. It is a well-documented truth, though, that the combination of low pay, overwork, small wars among the kids and the obligation to stuff emotions for the sake of appearances tend to work against uninterrupted bliss in any preacher's household, let alone the mission household.

The Simonsons had those interruptions, mostly in the early months when life may not have seemed exactly fair to the young missionary's wife. Sharing a commitment, as David and Eunice Simonson did, hardly meant that they had equal opportunities to express that commitment in the early years when the children needed round the clock attention and when the satisfactions and excitement were largely reserved for David. Before they were going to uplift any souls or heal any bodies, they had to know the language, first Swahili. It's why they were assigned to the Pare Mountains. For Simonson, with some prior exposure to Swahili in London and the states, it wasn't any huge undertaking. Structurally, Swahili isn't a hard language to learn. Eunice Simonson knew that. So if she knew that, why was she stumbling? She was stumbling because while David could devote time to it and hone it on his hunting trips, the young nurse from Portland, N.D., was washing diapers and cooking meals and sewing clothes and looking for snakes and finding a hundred other ways of being wife and mother in the African bush. While they were at Shigitani a young African teacher from the village's primary school would drop in for a few hours in the afternoon to give Dave and Eunice some individual instruction in Swahili. One afternoon the lesson dealt with word endings and word beginnings. The student had to learn which of these short syllables—"*mo*," "*ko*," and "*po*"—applied to the specific and to the general and to the even more general. Eunice started stumbling. David started to get impatient. The lesson seemed pretty basic to him, and he couldn't understand why the flower of Portland, N.D., and Fargo Oak Grove and Concordia College and Fairview couldn't sort out those simple syllables.

"What he finally got," she remembered, "was exasperated. I was terribly uncomfortable and he was tearing me apart in front of the teacher. It was humiliating for me. I just flew off the handle. I stood up and told Dave Simonson you can take your *ko* and *mo* and *po* and go. I'm leaving this place."

This outburst eventually entered the missionary annals as one of the more original exit lines in the history of the Lutheran Church of Tanganyika. It was delivered with absolute sincerity and fury. The condition was temporary. Eunice Simonson was hardly going to book a flight for Nairobi. To begin with, what do you do about the flabbergasted young African teacher from the primary school?

The mutual devotion and respect between David and Eunice, strong from the beginning, deepened with the years in Africa. But she will admit today, "That was the closest I ever came to leaving Africa, being ridiculed that way in front of the teacher, although I'm sure if Dave knew how much it hurt me he'd never have done it. We both laugh about it now, and it's become a family joke."

But it was hardly the only one and hardly the only domestic scrum. Africa in the early months was a happy ramble for Dave Simonson. The Swahili lessons were easy and he had free time to join the other missionaries hunting in the mountains. He could do this while he was attending the language school and in the early weeks of the classes he taught at the Marangu Teachers Training College near Kilimanjaro. He was able, in other words, to be Dave Simonson in all dimensions—the teacher, apprentice missionary and hunter. In the distribution of work, Eunice cooked what the Provider brought home. If it was guinea fowl, she was home free. When it got to be the bigger stuff, wildebeest and warthog, it was literally a different game. "Dave would come back with the carcasses of these bigger animals, which had been skinned and quartered. He'd lay them out on a large table behind the house and he'd say, 'Would you please butcher these so we can feed everybody at the school?'"

"What I knew about butchering warthog and wildebeest was what I learned about dissecting back in college. I'd spend the whole day cutting and carving without having a clue to what I was doing. And then Dave would come back from the school in the afternoon to inspect my work. And immediately he was appalled because I hadn't cut them into roasts and steaks. What

I'd cut up were these great clumps of muscle. Right about there he may have wondered if he married the right person. But what did I know about butchering? I did remember some of the principles of dissection from those lab classes at Concordia. I pointed out to him that there's your glutinous maximus and there's the deltoid and the trapezius. I felt extremely smug that I could remember those Latin names for the animals' body parts. He just huffed and pawed through the meat and shook his head. I need hardly say that the mission families and the students wound up with a lot of impalaburger and no steaks."

After three months of Swahili lessons in the mountains the young reverend and his family were ready for some certified mission work. Simonson was assigned to teach classes in English at the Marangu Teachers Training College, maintained by the Lutheran Church of Tanganyika. He also found places to preach in the Kilimanjaro locale and to do pastoral work among the several tribes around Kilimanjaro including the Chaggas, one of the most influential of the tribes in Eastern Tanganyika. At the age of 28, he was now a credentialed missionary, American Lutheran Church version, after all those years of his visualizations on the Dakota prairie and in the seminary. It consumed him. He couldn't get up early enough in the day. The African students seemed drawn to him, this big, black-bearded man who looked and talked so decisively and seemed to take a personal interest in them. It wasn't a calculated classroom and pastoral style. Simonson from the beginning was an assertive and inquisitive Type A who wore well in most venues. The associations he built at the Marangu college later advanced some of his most significant service and initiatives. It wasn't only the students with whom he built lifelong connections. The African head prefect of the college later became the bishop of the Kilimanjaro Lutheran Diocese. Some of the students entered government services after Tanzania became independent in the early 1960s and listened sympathetically when Simonson would propose a building project that needed government approval. Usually they did more than listen. They knew the right buttons and pushed them. Several other students became Lutheran pastors and rose quickly in what became the Evangelical Lutheran Church of Tanzania, reliable friends and associates of their old mentor at Marangu. All of those connections meant that Dave Simonson as well as his family integrated quickly with the African community. Simonson's later aggressiveness in learning the Maasai language further sped and deepened those connections. They brought some uncommon and original benefits both to the missionary's family and to the Maasai.

The move to Marangu also put the Simonsons closer to the missionary ideal that Eunice herself had imagined. The skinks were gone. So were the long treks to the river to get water. Their new quarters were in an attractive mission house with running water and indoor toilets. She could cook in a more congenial atmosphere. The reverend didn't dump as many impala carcasses on the table for butchering because (a) she was predictably going to make hash out what was supposed to be a rump roast and (b) the reverend didn't have the time to go larking into the mountains after wild animals.

Somehow the missionaries at the college discovered that David Simonson was an athlete. It probably didn't take that much investigation. Simonson more or less volunteered this information. The football captain from Concordia quickly located the running track. He couldn't find a soccer or rugby field, so he built one, and never mind that he'd never played rugby.

He would.

Technically, Simonson was the athletic coach, for which he received no extra pay. One of Simonson's early discoveries was the generosity of the competitive rules in Tanganyika amateur sport: It was all strictly open competition. In track or any other sport, the coach was just as eligible to compete as the student. In fact practically anybody could walk on in a track and field meet, the town blacksmith or the visiting bishop, and run or throw.

Simonson found that out one day when he brought the school team to the town of Moshi to compete against other schools of the territory. He noticed that few if any of the rival contestants appeared to be students. They were a mishmash of teachers, English bureaucrats, English police and commission station inspectors.

"Well, tell me," Simonson asked the meet director. "Is this open to anybody?"

"It is. Take off your pants, padre, and see what you can do."

Lutheran ministers aren't generally addressed as padre, but Simonson took the suggestion with good grace. Lutheran ministers long since having acquired the virtue of tolerance. He took the director seriously and stripped down to his shorts. First he threw the discus and then the shot.

The later legend that grew up around Simonson tells us that he broke the existing Tanganyika records in both events. This is possible. Simonson had huge biceps, vast power and irreversible faith in the durability of his shorts. From that day on, Simonson was actively recruited by the Tanganyika community athletic clubs around Marangu, Moshi and Arusha that competed with other cities in Tanganyika and later in Kenya. Eventually, Simonson and his rippling muscles were on view in some of the major all-Tanganyika athletic meets. Radio accounts of his performances were broadcast throughout northern Tanganyika and reached the ears of some of his students, who formed a fan club and cheering claque that made these Marangu students a kind of ideological forerunner of the Wisconsin Cheeseheads.

It was inevitable that somebody from the Tanganyika rugby clubs would approach the clerical superman from the American wheat fields. A rugby captain was one of the first. He asked Simonson to expand his athletic horizons to include rugby.

"I've never played rugby," Simonson said. "I don't understand the rules. Scrums and all that stuff."

"But you played American football."

"Yes. I loved the game."

"Do you miss it?"

"I haven't thought about it. Preaching and teaching in Africa and throwing the discus and keeping a family of five together is pretty much a full time way to spend your energy."

"You'd be a very strong rugby player when you learned the rules. Even if you didn't learn all of the rules right off you'd be a strong rugby player. Give it a go, padre."

"Well, not padre. I never got around to doing rosaries."

Give it a go anyhow.

The 215-pound misidentified padre reported for practice with the Moshi Rugby Club a few days later. In his early games he played as though he had just been released into the bull ring. He had no technique and no immediate grasp of the tactics. The first and last requirement for a rugby player is that you have to play rough. It helps to be swift and to be agile, but both of those attributes can be waived if you are willing to get your nose bloody and your head battered and your body racked. Simonson answered "yes" to all of these primordial demands. Eunice began coming to the games to watch his progress. One day she had the misfortune of sitting in front of three catty Englishwomen who'd heard of this wall-crashing behemoth from America. Unaware of Eunice's connection to the monster, one of them said she understood that he was coming to the games decked out in full American football padding.

"I was sitting there starting to steam," Eunice said, "and of course he wasn't wearing all that padding. They called a line-out right in front of us and everybody from the two teams formed lines parallel to us. Dave's job on that play was to throw the ball in. So his back was to us and all of his physique was visible close up. One of the Englishwomen saw that and exclaimed, 'My God, it all belongs to *him.*' And I just was dying to turn around and tell her, 'You better believe it, and it all belongs to *me.*'"

A lady declares her proprietorship in the African bush.

It was beginning to come clear that this man wasn't going to be your usual hard-working, Gospel-reciting missionary out of the seminary. This one walked heavy and took the African dirt in his hands and hammered the skulls of rugby rivals on Saturday afternoon before limping into the pulpit on Sunday morning.

Not all of Dave Simonson's peers in the ministry found that picture endearing.

But his reputation in East Africa was enlarging, and eventually Dave Simonson was going to be an institution in African mission, with the lion pelts and sleepless nights and scrapes with death that came with it.

CHAPTER 7

The average Maasai warrior will walk approximately 30 miles a day through the high grassland of East Africa. He can cover this distance whether he's walking barefoot or wearing sandals, whether he's alone or herding cattle. The Maasai stride is long and elegant. The warrior seems to float through the savannah, his feet seeming scarcely to touch ground.

This means within three days after Dave Simonson shot the lion near the school house at Naberera in South Maasai Land of Tanganyika in 1957, hundreds of people, mostly Maasai, knew about it in the small villages of the Maasai steppes and all the way to the big market city of Arusha and beyond to the African Rift village of Loliondo. It didn't happen every day in the African back country. Preachers didn't haul out their shotguns and plug a man-eating lion in the beams of a Land Rover's headlights.

He became an instant celebrity in the Maasai bomas and the shanties of Arusha. But it wasn't the first notoriety for this rumbling man of God who seemed to show no fear whether it was lions or mountains he was tackling. The Maasai began looking on him as some kind of wonderman who could do things beyond even the strength and bravery of the Maasai. David's overriding ambition was to work with the Maasai. He'd idealized that mission for years, all the way back to the missionary festivals at his father's parsonage and the peering black eyes of Richard Reusch who prophesied that he would one day live with the Maasai. Missionaries in the Maasai steppes typically worked out of stations where they had living quarters and roamed the territory in Land Rovers, tending to pastoral work, finding salt for the Maasai cattle, preaching and building churches. Simonson's problem in getting assigned to a Maasai station was the lack of openings. Once those positions were filled, the incumbents tended to hang on to them because they put the missionary in the middle of the action and the Maasai were fascinating people to deal with although hardheads to convert. But from the first day he came to Africa, Simonson was convinced that his life was marked for some special role with these people.

"When I came to Tanganyika I just had to wait my turn," he said. "There weren't any Maasai stations open. The man in the South Massai country was a missionary named Don Johnson. He had a good friend from India, a doctor, who wanted to climb Kilimanjaro. Don wasn't a mountain climber. He smoked and wasn't in shape. But his friend came to Africa, and they decided to climb the mountain which is nearly 20,000 feet high. Both of them made it to the top, but Don got disoriented from the altitude. I was teaching at the Marangu College at the time. Some runners came down the mountain and said the missionary was out of his head and had to be evacuated. I notified the hotel at Marangu, which is the staging service for the climb. The headmaster of the college, Alan Gottneid, and I went up the mountain after him. We overtook Johnson and his friend when they'd just come down from Kibo hut at 15,000 feet, the last one before the summit. He was in the next hut down at about 12,000 feet and out of his mind, hallucinating from altitude sickness. Two of the climbing porters came to me and said, 'What do you want to do?' I said we have to get him down, but he had already descended a fair amount of the way. I looked at the porters and they were worn to the bone from carrying Don Johnson on the stretcher. The fellow weighed about 200 pounds. I said let's sleep in this hut, and we can carry him down in the morning. When we got him down a doctor examined him and said he was suffering both from heart trouble and pulmonary edema and he had to leave his work in the South Maasai. All I could think of was, thank God that we got Don Johnson off the mountain before he died, and that here was the answer to my prayers. He had to take work in Dar es Salaam to convalesce, which meant that here was my opportunity to work in the South Maasai."

The reverend's performance on Kilimanjaro in rescuing his fellow missionary spread quickly through the mission community and the Maasai. It was followed not long afterward by the night of the lion, which tended to enhance Simonson's image as the resident Lutheran superman. By then he had promoted building programs at the teachers college in Marangu, using his carpentry skills and recruiting students and local tradesmen to join in the project. "Sometimes I'd change the curriculum. Instead of teaching the students religious classes and the history of Christianity in Europe, I'd take them out of the classroom and go over and build a church near the Marangu Hotel. It had fallen down three times. By the time the builders would get to the roof they had no money left, and when the rains came it all went smash. So I organized a building project, pointing out that we could hold some of our classes in the new church we were putting up. We rebuilt the whole church. Some of the fellows were common laborers who worked with other builders, and when I went to South Maasai I invited them to come with me. Many of them were young and needed to be taught building skills. So I taught building skills. I made a deal with them. I said I hoped they would work with me as long as I was in Africa, and when I retired, they could retire. They're still with me to this day, waiting for me to retire. I've made a contract with them to do brick work on a house we built and the safari lodge we later built at Tarangire, or on this church or that church, and they turned out to be the busiest bricklayers in Tanzania."

All of this eventually reached the ears of the British district officer at Ngasumet, who Simonson met at the Maasai cattle market the day after he shot the lion. By then the lion's entrails had been flung to the hyenas and the heart was gone—eaten by one of the Chagga schoolteachers so he could be strong as the lion. The British functionary had heard the news from the Maasai. His conversation with the reverend was terse.

"Understand you shot a lion last night."

"Yeah, that's right. Did I violate some law?"

"No, I've had a man tracking him for three weeks. We couldn't catch up with him. You have any wish to keep the skin?"

"Well, yes, I'd like to have it, but I can't afford to pay for a license on my $150 a month salary."

The British agent said he'd write a letter to the chief game warden and that Simonson should take the note to the warden to see what he'd say. The warden discovered big scars under the lion's skin, suggesting that the lion's black mane was torn as he made his way through the brush. The worn teeth and exposed nerve ends meant that the lion had probably been crazed with pain, and probably attacked human beings rather than his usual prey. With the permission of the game warden, Simonson took the pelt to a factory that tanned goat skins. Its workmen did a decent job of preserving the pelt. It measured 10 feet 4 inches from the top of the head to the end of the tail. But when Simonson got it back, half of the claws were gone. The Africans who worked on it wanted to use the claws for protection against other lions.

The lion skin occupied a prominent place on the Simonson floor for the next six years. After that it began to disintegrate, and they got rid of it.

He learned something more from the British district officer at Ngasumet. The little primary school there was disintegrating, and it was going to lose its accreditation if it wasn't rebuilt in time for the start of school in eight days.

Here was a mission to tap into all of Simonson's multiple energies and his obsessions to make a mark in the Maasai country. It was also a test of his growing network of bush characters on whom he would depend to meet his breakneck building schedules now and into the future. Simonson acquired a gift for scavenging. He also acquired a gift for going days without sleep. From his connections with the Brits he located a 1-3/4 ton truck. This was fortuitous because Simonson didn't have a budget to rebuild the school. What he did have was a friend in Arusha, a Romanian Jew named Karl Fainzilber. He had come to Africa through the refugee camps and settled in Tanganyika. Fainzilber knew all about bricks. He had a brick operation in Arusha and wanted the contract for a building program at the theological seminary. The reverend helped get it for him. Remembering this, Simonson now brought in his chips for the building job at the school. To rebuild the school in South Maasai he needed some corrugated iron and doors, which he scrounged from other sources in Arusha, and he needed lots of brick. His Romanian friend obliged, handing over all of the second line brick that Simonson needed. "How much will it cost me?" Simonson asked. The question was rhetorical. Any charge at all would have wiped him out. "For you, friend," Fainzilber said, "no charge," confirming Simonson's high opinion of Romanian brickmakers. For seven days Simonson drove his truck round trip from South Maasai to Arusha at night, a distance of 200 miles, hauling brick from Karl Fainzilber and then during the day supervising the construction of the school with Losioki, an unordained Maasai evangelist. Losioki rounded up some workers. The school was built in eight days. The Maasai kids were there when classes opened. It's accreditation was saved. And the British officer candidly admitted his amazement.

The day the job was finished, Simonson drove to Marangu to spend some time with Eunice and his family. He hadn't slept for three days. He dozed behind the wheel and the truck plowed down a ravine, its box scraping grass as it swerved. "The next thing I knew I'd come to a big ditch, six feet across and at least eight feet deep. I thought no way was I going to survive this. But the truck just raised up as I hit the edge of the ditch. It just got lifted up. I didn't know what was happening. I got back on the road, and looked back and I said it was humanly impossible to manage that because the place where I landed on the opposite side of the ditch was higher than from where I took off. I found myself on the road and when I looked the truck was undamaged except for grass stains on the side of the box and the front wheels were a little skewed. I took the jack and straightened them out. I then went on to Marangu and told Eunie what had happened. When she asked how I explained it that I didn't smash into the ditch head on, all I could tell her was that God was the one. It was physically impossible for that truck to do what it did. On Sunday Eunie went with me to services. The incident was a big deal at the school worship service the next day, and we all gave a thanksgiving offering. By then all of the students had heard about it, and the place was full. I had trouble convincing the missionaries. One of my friends was Harold Palm. I told him about it, and he said, 'No way, man, you're dreaming.' So we got in a car and drove down there, about twelve miles from Marangu. We looked at the skid marks and then how the truck had leaped that big ditch. It was absolutely dumbfounding."

Once more he believed he'd been saved for work he had been called to do. In this belief there was no equivocating or wishful thinking. It was a belief that was total and enduring. It sustained him and buoyed him in all of his down times. He believed that it was a truth, and he believed in it aggressively and reverently, this hardheaded, heavy-footed preacher from the prairie. That belief would last for his entire stewardship in Africa. It would prevail against the raised eyebrows of skeptics and, in a some cases, those of his peers.

The reverend's agendas now had proliferated to these: Preaching and pastoral work; building churches and schools, laying brick, floors and roofs; hunting trips when he came up to breathe in the middle of the rest of the agenda; plus rugby and discuss-throwing on weekends. In the family archives, Simonson and his Tanganyikan students are credited with holding eight Tanganyikan records in track and field. This is probable although the Tanzanian sports federation documents are silent on records posted that far back. Who's going to argue? Who wants to? The reverend was also a sight stripped down to his shorts and bare chest, with those bulging quads and that chest expansion. In fact, he'd become a national hero in his first two years in Tanganyika.

He was a national hero but all too frequently a no-show in the family house. The explanation: Like most missionaries, Simonson understood that bringing Christianity and something better into the lives of Africans couldn't be done with a Sunday morning service alone. The reasoning behind that: You had to be there on Monday morning, looking after needs, showing concern, befriending, solving problems. Because of the driving distance from South Maasai to Arusha, 90 miles, and to Marangu, more than 100 miles, the family decided in the interests of the kids that David would commute first to Marangu and later to the former German mission house into which they moved in Ilboru, a section of Arusha. Evidently he didn't commute enough. He'd come home for supplies from two or three weeks in Maasailand, on the edge of exhaustion. After a day or two of replenishment he'd drive back into the bush, leaving Eunice with the vague feeling that she was living with a stranger and the kids with practically no relationship with their father. They accepted it reasonably well, understanding from a dozen pep talks from their mother that daddy was doing important things for the Africans and for God. Eunice's thoughts, perhaps more charitable than most, were these: He's missing out on a critical time in the development of the children, but this is the way of it for the missionary family. It was what we were called to do. She believed that, and her commitment to that idea was as unalterable as her husband's. Beside this, she loved him. But one day the reverend came home while Eunice was entertaining two people they held fondly, Rev. Elmer and Lillian Danielson, who'd regaled Eunice for hours with the kind of mission tales she liked best: a lot pratfalls and a lot of laughs and no snakes. They were having tea when little Nathan came running into the living room and exclaimed, "Mommy, Mommy, Uncle Dave is here."

Uncle Dave. The reverend had lost his father's credentials in all of the commuting and had been displaced by Uncle Dave. Elmer and Lillian Danielson gasped. They went outside to welcome David, who joined the tea in a few minutes. After all of the amenities were finished, Elmer said confidentially to him, "Dave, I think we need to talk." This was the Elmer Danielson who as a missionary in Africa had gone through a living death for weeks during World War II, knowing that a passenger ship carrying his wife Lillian and their six children had been sunk in the South Atlantic by a German surface raider. It was an international story for days. The Egyptian vessel carrying 140 missionaries and members of mission families had been attacked in April of 1941, en route from the states to Mombasa. The incident occurred while the United States was still neutral. All passengers were presumed lost. For more than a month, Danielson's grief was unrelieved. He received the good news in late May: His family and the other passengers had been rescued from their lifeboats by the raider's captain, transferred to a German supply ship and taken to unoccupied France, where they were allowed their freedom and eventual reunion with their loved ones.

In the ensuing years after his talk with Elmer, Simonson never confided the details of the dialogue with his wife. Elmer was talking about Dave Simonson's prolonged absences from the house. No more evidence was necessary than having his own son convinced that his father was actually his uncle. In Eunice's mind, the kids didn't necessarily feel neglected. Eunice understood the real world of mission. She also understood the powerful drives within her husband to make a difference, to do it every day and to do it with his hair laid back and all adrenaline flowing.

But it took some symptoms of sainthood to be *that* understanding.

At least the children didn't act neglected. They were aware of the special kind of work their father was doing, that it was beyond the church's expectations, that South Maasai was far away, that he couldn't be around every day. Simonson didn't get to be a minister or pledge a life's work to uplifting Africans by being an insensitive lug. He listened to Elmer Danielson. The long absences became less frequent, and the reverend rejoined the family.

His adventures drew mixed reviews from some of the other missionary families, although by and large he was seen by most them for what he was: an uncommon man with something to give and something to say in the mission movement and yet a man who declined giving up the essentials of being Dave Simonson, whatever the whispers. The whispers were that missionaries were there to tend to missions. They were there to bring Jesus Christ, health and education to the Africans, and a dozen other services if they had the skills and available money. They weren't there to play rugby and throw the discus. Playing rugby and throwing the discus sounded frivolous to some of these folks, and it may have been. But it wasn't frivolous if you could play rugby on Saturday and get back in time to preach on Sunday. It wasn't frivolous if you spent Monday through Friday being a friend to the Africans, building a school for them and fixing up their church so it was a place where they could come on Sundays and sing their songs, and listen to the Gospel and feel part of a congregation.

Missionary critics answered that. Dave Simonson was here and there. He was in South Maasai and Marangu and Moshi and Arusha doing the work of the church, all right. He was also in places like Mombasa in Kenya playing rugby on Saturdays, when the missionary families liked to get together and socialize. In lands like Africa, mission families in those years lived in a peculiarly cohesive and tightly-woven social colony. They were bound by a commitment and a sharing of the burdens and hazards of mission. Among those were threats to health, the lengthy hours and the stress that went with them. They tended to be mutually sympathetic and self-protective. A lively sense of gossip, however, often intruded on the hallelujahs and the daily sagas.

Dave Simonson was viewed by some of these people as a renegade from the idea of social communion and the gathering of clans. "He was usually off playing something or doing something that he said couldn't wait," one of his colleagues said. "He usually sent Eunie as the family representative. Most people just loved Eunie because she was so open and thoughtful, and it was always a better gathering when she was there. But a lot of times he was the only absentee, and some of the folks simply resented it, because these were collegial times and he didn't seem to think they were important."

Did Simonson think they were unimportant?

"I didn't. It was just that I had a pretty full plate. I certainly didn't apologize for taking a few hours off to play in a game of rugby. Competition is part of who I am. I didn't think I had to forsake that, because it took absolutely no time from my ministry. I told my mission friends in Arusha that the day would never come when I missed a worship service on Sunday because I was banged up from playing rugby. And I never did."

It was a pretty fiercely observed principle with Simonson. Which doesn't mean he didn't get mauled playing rugby. There was a day later in his rugby career when he broke three ribs in a game in Mombasa and rode the hundreds of miles back to Arusha in a Land Rover, flopped in bed at 4 a.m., got up at 6 and asked Eunice to drive him to Monduli Juu, another hour away, for his service. She had to help him out of the Land Rover but he was there in the pulpit at the appointed hour. He got variously maimed in one game even further out, in Dar es Salaam in eastern Tanzania, and arrived in the pulpit practically at the sound of the bell. Once in a while he'd confide the slapstick events of the previous hours to his congregations, usually setting off a merry twittering in the audience.

Would you call that bravado?

If you had skimpy tolerances for mission preachers mingling with the jocks, you could call it that. Burning the candle on all available ends? That too.

How about another way to describe it? Getting involved to the max. Plunging into another world with the gusto he came with, exploring new environments, getting a different kind of fulfillment in a new camaraderie. Is that a rationalization? It wasn't to Simonson. All of that sweat and body-slamming might not enhance his ministry, but there was no reason it was an impediment, either. In the early organization of one of his rugby clubs, a number of white South Africans volunteered for the team. Simonson welcomed them. He also decided to recruit some native Tanzanians. They turned out not to be very good because of their inexperience. But, Simonson reasoned, they ought to be part of the ethnic mix of the club. The South Africans grumbled. The jocks were segregated in South Africa along with everybody else. "The Tanzanians are staying," Simonson told the South Africans. "We'd like you to stay, also. Integrating this club is not a problem as we see it. If it's a problem, it's yours."

The Tanzanians stayed. The South Africans stayed.

So Simonson the budding institution grew. And the institution grew a little more in 1957 when one of the celebrated tycoons of American baseball, Walter O'Malley of the Dodgers, then in the process of the team's move from Brooklyn to Los Angeles, arrived in Tanganyika with a small entourage. O'Malley wanted to hunt big animals not far from the Maasai land where Dave Simonson was working his evangelical territory. The O'Malley group had contracted with a guide and outfitting service operating out of the Lake Manyara district of the African Rift. They retained Johnny Fletcher, a respected professional hunting guide, and one of Fletcher's partners. Since O'Malley's group was dividing into hunting partnerships of two each, they needed a third guide. A guide from Kenya was added to the team, but after several days in the field, frictions developed around the Kenyan guide. Johnny Fletcher had heard of Dave Simonson, the young missionary with steady nerves on the shotgun trigger, and discovered he was in the territory. Fletcher approached Simonson and asked him if he could spare some time in the field with them as an add-on to the guiding team. He introduced the reverend to O'Malley. It didn't take the two very long to develop an affinity. Simonson had just finished handling exam papers of the pupils of the primary school for Maasai children near Naberera and was driving them to Arusha to give them to the British school authorities. He said he had some free time coming and could join the hunting safari for a few days.

The Kenya guide hadn't been dismissed, which would have been a breach of protocol. Simonson joined the O'Malley twosome at O'Malley's request, however, and he and the baseball millionaire shared a tent.

"I suppose he had reputation as a hard-charging guy in the business of baseball," Simonson said later. "I don't know about that. What I know about Walter O'Malley is what I learned on the hunt and in our talks in the tent and simply by watching how he conducted himself. It would be hard for me to respect a man more. Here was a guy who was super-rich, out in wild Africa, hunting big game. But before he would go to sleep each night, he went to his knees and said prayers, just as we had done when we were children. I learned enough about him to know that he wasn't doing that because he had a minister under his roof. You knew this man did that every night of his life. After the day's hunt, we'd talk for hours about our lives, about how we related God with our lives, about mistakes we'd made and tried to rectify. We'd also have those talks when the sun started going down and we were set up near the baits we'd prepared. During days in the Land Rover we'd play a kid's game you have to remember from your young days if you were about as old as we were. It's called "Battleship," a board game back in the states. In the middle of Africa we didn't have any board. We did have sheets of paper, though, and we made a grid like the margins of a map, and put our warships on that grid. Your opponent had to try to locate the ships by calling out the letters and numbers on the grid. We did that for hours—waiting for lion, or elephant or leopard, all of which Walter had on his license from the authorities."

So they became almost immediate friends, two strong personalities with a well-developed sense of winning and of camaraderie in the field. That kind of hunting might meet with disapproval today. This was 40 years ago. The values were different. The taking of wild animals did not encounter the social disapproval it sometimes does today. Simonson has seen those changes, of course, and does not object to the attitudes of today. But 40 years ago he found himself tracking big game in the company of a man who, to Simonson, did not seem like a man who viewed an African hunting trip as a plume to his vanity. He seemed to be a decent guy of substance. So they hunted, and the safari became a huge success, and O'Malley had a hard time believing that here was a man of God equally adept in the use of high powered hunting weapons as he was in the pulpit, as flinty when looking down the barrel of gun as he was compassionate in the presence of a suffering African child. And it may not be a coincidence, in view of O'Malley's appraisal of hunting guides, that the baseball millionaire filled out his license.

On their way back to Arusha, O'Malley asked Simonson what it was that his wife missed most from the states. The reverend went through the usual litany of relatives and friends. "But apart from that," O'Malley said. "What she probably misses most of the material things," Simonson said, "is the piano we had to leave behind with her parents. She loves music and the piano. But when you choose this life, you have to give up things and she has no regrets about that."

"Let me ask you," O'Malley said. "Is there anything like that available in Tanganyika?"

We know, of course, that God probably does not micro-manage the affairs of his folks. Still, sometimes you might want to wonder. It happened that a professor of music from Minnesota had been in Arusha recently working with local choirs. He hauled his piano with him and, when he returned to the states, left the piano in Arusha on sale at $500. David and Eunice were aware of that. But the missionary's salary was still only $150 monthly, with no immediate prospect of changing. There was no way they could handle $500 for a piano, no matter how much Eunice missed Mozart and the old hymnal.

The night of his farewell dinner with the O'Malley party, Simonson received O'Malley's parting gift—a check for $500. "Tell your wife," he said, "that it's the least I can do."

More than 40 years later, the piano is still there in the Simonson house that looks out on Mt. Meru.

"You're quite a guy," O'Malley said before David left the hotel. "Tell you what. If and when we play in another World Series, and you can get away, I'd like you and your wife to be my guests in Los Angeles or wherever it's played. It would be an honor for me. Do you think you could manage that?"

Simonson knew for dead certain that if he was in Africa, he wasn't coming to anybody's World Series. But it also happened that after nearly four years in Africa, the Simonsons were due for an extended furlough in the states. They were now six. Rebecca was born in a hospital in Arusha. Her arrival occasioned a mild uprising from the kids. To introduce the forthcoming baby, Eunice had played a game with the kids. She was then working as a nurse in clinics around Arusha, feeling eminently needed, now adjusting to African life and loving it. But she was also mother. So she said, "We have two children who we'll call our American babies because they were born there, Stephen and Naomi. We have one we'll call our English baby, Nathan, because he was born in England. And now we're going to have one we can call our African baby, because this baby is being born in Africa." Applause followed this announcement. When mother and baby arrived back at Ilboru from the Arusha hospital, the other children appeared heartbroken. They also were mad and put on a scene. They accused mother of breaking her promise. "You said we were going to have an African baby."

"That's right, I said that. This baby, beautiful Rebecca, was born in Africa."

Their rebuttal: "Well, it doesn't *look* like an African baby."

Extended explanations followed.

Which made all routes clear for the Simonsons to return to the states for a year. And it just happened that in 1959, the year of the preacher's furlough, the Los Angeles Dodgers won the National League pennant.

But those routes back to America would bring Eunice Simonson to a day three months later when only a small decision in a parish in North Dakota separated her from death in the skies over Indiana.

CHAPTER 8

To the American ear, the word "safari" first conjured pictures of troops of African porters threading through the jungle, preparing the way for great white hunters ensconced in sedan chairs. The picture later changed to the fearless, hard-drinking hunting guide risking limbs and anatomy so that his bumbling client could squeeze off one shot, usually nowhere near the contemptuous lion. Still later, "safari" came to mean squads of tourists rolling through the Africa game preserves, heads protruding from the roof hatches of their Land Rovers, scanning the landscape for lions and elephants.

Eunice Simonson struggled for a time with her Swahili, but soon discovered that "safari" in Swahili simply means you are making a trip. It can mean a hunting trip, but it is hardly confined to hunting. If you are going to the next village to visit friends or relatives, you are going on safari. If you are traveling to Arusha to shop, you are going on safari. That use of the word quickly became part of her language and, when she planned to visit another town, it was commonplace for her to tell her African friends that she would be "on safari" that day.

When they returned to the states for an extended furlough, the Simonsons were welcomed by assemblies of well-wishers, classmates and church pals dying to know about their adventures in Africa. Was it all they'd hoped for? Well, it was, and there were still something like 40 years in front of them, but they responded by making themselves available for a procession of adult forums, Rotary meetings, church socials, pot lucks and mission gatherings. For most of the time they lived at a mission house in Moorhead, Minn., the site of Concordia College. Eunice became "the program" for dozens of women's gatherings in Minnesota and North Dakota. At one of the first she was giving a description of her typical day and David's. Because David was usually on the road, hauling building supplies or doing pastoral work, she referred frequently to her husband being "on safari." He was on safari to South Maasai or Moshi or Arusha and it became clear to one of the listeners that the reverend was on safari a whole lot of time. With evident irritation, she confronted the reverend's wife after the program. "Well, my goodness," she said. "I thought missionaries were over there to preach and convert. I didn't think they spent all their time hunting."

Henceforward in her speeches, when Eunice referred to "safari" she took meticulous care to define it. While she was doing that, her husband was booked for a series of speeches that often took him out of the state. Eunice became increasingly comfortable with her own talks, learned that audiences found them appealing and found that her accounts of the family life of missionaries were absorbing to her listeners. She began introducing the sagas of the irrepressible (and often dangerous) Stephen, who was now six years old and by all odds lucky to have reached that age.

Stephen as a child was a tireless scamp with his nose in everything. He was one of those kids with a genius for finding himself in harm's way, whether he was blameless or the provocateur. There was a day at Ilboru when, while playing with his father, Stephen jumped off his shoulders and struck his head on the concrete floor. He began projectile vomiting. One eye fluttered nonstop. It was obvious he had been injured grievously. There was no hope of immediate aid at a hospital in Moshi. Facilities there were limited. They had to get to Nairobi in Kenya, more than nine hours away. A district commissioner who was planning to drive to Nairobi agreed to take them. The trip went well enough as far as Namanga on what is now the Kenya-Tanzanian border. After that the road was brutal, the same gravel road they had traveled their first days in Africa. The British had committed most of their available money in Kenya to fighting the Mau Mau, and the route from Namanga to Nairobi wasn't paved until years later. It was a grinding, bouncing ordeal that almost put Eunice, three months pregnant at the time, out of her mind in fear of her child's life. When they arrived at a Nairobi hospital, Stephen was diagnosed with subteral hematoma, bleeding under the skull. Surgeons were ready to operate to drain the blood, but after a time the boy began to recover, and no surgery was necessary.

The greater damage fell on the mother. As a result of the stress and the long trip, she had a miscarriage. She was placed in one hospital, Stephen in another. Stephen's condition cleared relatively soon. Eunice mourned the loss of an unborn child but, when calm returned to her life, she made her assessments: This was missionary life in Africa. Nobody said it would be sweet tropical fruit. It would come with hazards that were unpredictable and might seem cruel. But the conviction that they were meant to serve in Africa never left her, in that trying week or later. Nor did she lose the faith that when some intervention was needed to protect her family, it would come. It might come in the form of a commissioner driving to Nairobi or a Chagga women who invariably appeared at her side in time of crisis. There was never any complication in her mind from where the intervention would come. She was a woman of dignity beneath her unquenchable cheer, an adaptable women and a healer. But what she was at core was a woman of belief. It nourished her in the bleakest times, kept her mind working to deal with crisis not only as a trained nurse but a woman quick to recognize the heart of a problem and to find a solution. So she told her audiences about Martha. Martha came to live with the Simonsons shortly after they moved into their house at the Marangu college and then accompanied them when they acquired their new place in the Ilboru section of Arusha. It was a large red brick building that had been part of a mission station the German Lutherans had built when Germany controlled Tanganyika. Martha was part of the group of native women and girls who worked with mission families as house helpers. When needed, they served as nannies or what we'd call baby-sitters. Martha was a slim, mature and deeply spiritual woman who'd never married because of a congenital defect that made it impossible for her to have children. Partly for that reason, it seemed to Eunice, she showered all of her maternal love on the Simonson kids. She became so much an intimate part of the Simonsons' lives that David looked on her as a gift from God. During the move from Marangu to the new home in Ilboru, workmen had brought some of their belongings in packing barrels loaded a on truck that was backed up to the front steps of the house. The building was set on a steep hillside above a school. During this work in progress, Stephen, being Stephen, decided to take a hand. He jumped onto the barrels and was busily occupied playing hopscotch when the brakes on the truck gave way.

The truck rolled toward a wall above a large dropoff to the ground below. Standing on the top of the stairs, Eunice saw it and was horrified. One of the college students who was helping the Simonsons with their relocation jumped onto the truck. Just as it was about to nose-dive over the wall, he grabbed Stephen and leaped out of the truck with him, risking serious injury to himself. The young man was Marko, who later became a certified minister and then a district president of the Arusha diocese. "If it hadn't been for Marko," Eunice said, "Stephen would have been crushed between those spinning barrels when the truck went over the wall."

Intervention had come from somewhere.

"I was still badly shaken," Eunice said, "but Martha took me in her arms and looked into my eyes and said, 'Don't think of what might have happened. Think only that Stephen is safe.'"

Martha then took over completely. She sent runners to all of the workers in the mission area. She gathered them in the Simonson house and conducted a service of thanksgiving for the safety of Stephen. It was Eunice's first lesson of how much there was for the mission family to learn from the Africans about Christian community in the midst of Africa.

Part of their furlough in the states was going to be devoted to Dave Simonson's advanced education in the Maasai language. It was critical to Simonson toward his larger goals of ministering to the Maasai and, insofar as he could, integrating with their lives. The heroine in this process was a woman named Ruth Shafer, one of the western world's legitimate experts on the Maasai language. She planned to be in Florida in January and February of 1959. The Simonsons and Mrs. Shafer knew each other well from Africa and would know each other even better beginning in 1979 when Stephen

Simonson—the one and only Stephen—married Marilyn Shafer, Ruth's grand-daughter. In their early months in Tanganyika the Simonsons had heard of this strong-minded woman who'd studied at the Moody Bible College in the states and married an evangelist who worked in Kenya. In Kenya, Ruth Shafer acquired a fluency in the Maasai language and later a post as instructor in Maasai at the African Inland Mission in Nairobi. She was a brilliant, all-around linguist and violinist and, decades later, nearing the age of 100, had finished an autobiography, "Road to Kilimanjaro," shortly before her death. In the late 1950s she was much in demand as a teacher of Maasai, having organized a dictionary attempting to put the Maasai language in written form. She later was asked by the Lutheran church to translate the Lutheran hymnal into Maasai. The Simonsons and Mrs. Shafer met, and it was arranged for her to come to Arusha to teach Maasai to Dave Simonson and some of his colleagues. It was also arranged for Mrs. Shafer to live in the Simonson home, which meant that she was going to deal not only with the missionaries' ignorance of Maasai but with three kids wilder than most. Neither prospect seemed intimi-dating to her. To the Simonson house she brought not only a knowledge of the Maasai language but some unsentimental advice on how to deal with wild kids. This advice she gave freely to Eunice Simonson. "The best thing about the modern home," she'd say, "is that there's a switch in every room," to which she would add, sometimes within the kids' earshot: "The Bible says you can b-e-a-t a child with a r-o-d and he won't d-i-e." The kids weren't all that delighted with this formulation, having figured it out early. But they didn't have much to worry about from Dave and Eunice Simonson, who kept no switches in the house and depended on lung power for discipline. Occasionally, this worked. But from that time on, the lives of the Simonsons and Ruth Shafer were interlocked. Years later her physician son and his wife came to live in Tanza-nia, where he took a job as medical director in Monduli near Arusha. They arrived with five children and another on the way. One of them lived with the Simonsons for a time to ease the housing crush on the family, and another, Marilyn, married Stephen. Thus did mission families connect in Africa, often with joy and happy-ever-afters, but not always.

David went great guns with his Maasai language lessons from the stern schoolmistress and arranged to resume them when both would be in the states in 1959. The plan was for David to spend January and February taking lan-guage lessons in Florida. Being a minister didn't mean you had to ignore the climatic differences between Minnesota and Florida in January and February. Eunice, meanwhile, stayed in Moorhead those two months. Eunice Simonson knew just as much about climatic differences between Florida and Minnesota as her husband did. But there were four kids in this family. Under the agreed-to distribution of work that evolved somewhere between Luther Seminary and Fairview Hospital before they went to Africa, David would give sermons and evangelize and build churches and shoot an occasional impala. Eunice would raise the children in her creative way until they were old enough to let her get back to some serious nursing.

Which happened. Still, Eunice couldn't help but give some grudging admiration to the reverend's selection of January and February for his professional enhancement program in Florida while she waded around in snowdrifts. But there was going to be a big bonus in all of that. When his classes were finished, she was going to fly to Florida and they would enjoy a semitropical vacation in style—David and Eunice alone while her parents came from North Dakota to Moorhead to take care of the kids in Moorhead. It was planned as a second honeymoon without the threat of anybody running out of gas in the middle of a rainstorm.

But nobody ever claimed that these people lived normal lives. The start of that second honeymoon turned out worse for Eunice than the first. She booked her flight reservations at the end of a lovely gift shower by her friends. Among other things, they gave her a negligee in tone with the reunion in Florida with her husband. She shared her travel plans with her friends, and it looked like a go from Moorhead.

On the day she was to take a bus to Minneapolis to catch her plane to Florida, her parents called to say they'd be delayed for a day because of a problem that had come up in her father's parish. This meant she had to change flight plans. Although she did, she didn't advise any of her friends of the change. It didn't seem all that important.

The flight that she had originally booked, an Electra, blew up over Indiana with a terrible loss of life.

Was this one more intervention?

Her friends assumed she was on the Electra. The mission house in Moorhead was swamped with telephone calls. Eunice answered as many as she could and made the explanation. Almost all of them ended with the appropriate, "Thanks be to God." Eunice changed gears. She had to take a bus from Moorhead to Fargo, N.D., neighboring towns on the Minnesota-North Dakota border. From there she rode a train to Chicago, from where her new flight to Florida originated. In Chicago, it was agreed that she would spend the night with Dave's brother, Jim, a medical student, and his wife.

From their home in Chicago, she called Moorhead and learned that Naomi and Steve had come down with the mumps simultaneously. Somebody on the other end said not to worry. Tell that to a mother on her way to Florida, one who had just learned about the fate of the Electra she had booked three days before. Eunice worried. She also grieved for the families of the airline disaster. But she finally decided that all was in God's hands, and she flew to Florida. By then she'd been shaken by more than the Electra crash and the news from Moorhead. On the train to Chicago she encountered two men who apparently wanted to move in on her. She was traveling alone, and she was an attractive woman. They approached her several times. She discouraged them, politely at first, but they then grew annoying. She was unsettled by the incident but got off the train safely in the Chicago terminal, expecting to be welcomed by her brother-in-law. She couldn't find him. The two men from the train materialized, declaring they would take her wherever she had to go. It was getting scary. Eunice quickly returned to the telephone booth and called Jim's place. His wife answered, explaining that Jim had to work overtime at the hospital. Nervously, Eunice briefed her, trying to kill time and hoping the two menacing strangers would disappear. They did. Alone again, Eunice clutched her handbag and raced down the street outside the terminal, waving to a cab driver standing beside his car. He opened the door and she got in. Two men were already in the back seat, the same ones who had been harassing her.

"I panicked," she said. "They started to manhandle me. I cried and I prayed. I said I was going to be with my husband. I fought at them and I bit, and the cab driver just sat there. Finally, one of them said, 'It's not worth it,' and they got out. I didn't know what to do about the cab driver but I just gave him the number of my sister-in-law's home and he delivered me there. I was totally disheveled when I got out of the cab. I just was out of my senses. I didn't get the cab number so I couldn't identify the driver. I just ran into the building. By the next morning I'd pulled myself together. Jim drove me to the airport. When I got there I heard my name being paged. At that point I was very close to breaking down, being summoned that way in a huge airport where almost nobody knew where I was. I would have died if it was more bad news."

The attendant reached down under the counter and handed her a bag contained something rolled up in tissue. She opened it and found an orchid.

Pinned to it was a note which read, "I love you so much. Get here as soon as you can."

She wept in relief. Jim and his wife must have telephoned Dave and described events of the previous day. She boarded the plane jubilantly.

It was another Electra.

She subdued any lingering anxiety until they reached their destination in Orlando. A storm struck as they approached the city, severely buffeting the plane. Swaying and lurching, it fought through the wind and landed safely.

The reverend was there, wrapping her in an enormous hug that they held until she was almost breathless with relief. It was a security she hadn't felt for days. She told him, "You've never looked better to me in all the years I've known you. I've never loved you more. I've never felt so fragile."

They celebrated with dinner and laughs, prayers and all the rest. They frolicked for a couple days in Florida and then, with a friend of theirs, drove back to Minnesota. On the way, she began feeling symptoms of something alien. She was a nurse but she had trouble identifying it. Friend and relatives were waiting for them in Minneapolis, but her fever worsened and she had an examination in a hospital.

The news was that she had the mumps.

What else?

The nurse and mother of four had escaped potential assault, a flight that ended in catastrophe and a storm in Florida. She couldn't dodge the mumps. They took the train to Moorhead and learned on arrival that Becky was down with the mumps.

This made four—Stephen, Naomi, Becky and Mama. There weren't many left standing. Fewer, actually, than she'd counted. Her mother was also ill. It was a terrible, messy, doleful time. And her father had to leave the next day to return to his church, at about the time Rev. Dave Simonson had to leave on a two-week speaking tour in Minneapolis, St. Paul and western Minnesota.

The travails of Eunice stretched to the horizons.

But here was a lady simply hard to submerge. She dealt with her own mumps and the kids' mumps, trying to keep Nathan away. She also dealt with her mother's malaise. Eventually, all returned to health. For Stephen, of course, that condition was temporary. Not long afterward, with Dave on another speaking tour, Stephen broke out in a high fever. Eunice packed him in ice and took him to a hospital. There was some disagreement about the diagnosis, but he might have had brucellosis. The doctors calculated three or four days in the hospital. Right about this point Eunice was beginning to examine the wages of Original Sin, and frankly wondering whether somehow a disproportionate share had been piled on the Simonson brood. Clearly, these were ignoble thoughts for a Lutheran, and she got rid of them with a premonition that some good news was coming soon.

The day Stephen was due to leave the hospital, she received a telegram addressed to David but one that obviously was within her province to read.

"Would you and your piano-playing wife fly to Chicago as my guests for the World Series?"

It was signed Walter O'Malley, president of the Los Angeles Dodgers, champions of the National League and that very week in the midst of battle with the Chicago White Sox for the World Series championship.

No mumps, this. It was genuine, and in the midst of her giddiness, Eunice realized that she couldn't afford to wait for Dave's next phone call from his speaking safari. She had to act. Good nurses, mothers of kids with mumps and veterans of the African bush tend to be decisive. She called the airline and made reservations for a flight to Chicago. Her husband called from Detroit Lakes and offered no argument when his wife told him to drop what he was doing and to make tracks for Moorhead. He was back before the night was out. With Stephen out of the hospital, they drove across the border the next day to Fargo. Their flight to Chicago was due to arrive not long before what was to become the climactic game of the Series.

But what about tickets to Comiskey Park? And how we're they going to get to it without missing most of the game in traffic? They wired Walter O'Malley in Chicago: "We need instructions on how to get there." O'Malley replied: "Just get on the plane. We'll take care of the rest."

O'Malley's agents were at the Chicago terminal when they arrived. One of them had hunted with Dave and O'Malley in Africa. Another had contacts high in the bureaucracy of Chicago which meant that their car, with full police escort, went whizzing and screeching through the streets of Chicago, through red lights and one-way markers pointing the other way. The eyes of the Rev. Simonson, the custodian of law, reason and good order, began to roll. Another squad of O'Malley agents met them at the ballpark and escorted them to their seats behind first base, where they joined other members of the Dodger entourage. The game was in progress, but they saw most of it—Dodger vs. White Sox, for the big enchilada of baseball. The White Sox were the home town sweethearts, but the Dodgers weren't there to please. They were there to win, which they did. The Dodgers' entourage erupted and swept the Simonsons with it into an ante room of the clubhouse where O'Malley was being interviewed. In the midst of it he excused himself and said he had to greet some old friends from Africa. Nobody in the press corps understood what all this had to do with double plays and RBIs, but O'Malley was gone. He didn't return until he had a royal reunion with his old friends from Africa. When they parted, he said, "I'll see you soon." They weren't quite sure where or how, but at about this moment a limousine not much smaller than the Queen Mary drew up. "This," confided a dazed Eunice Simonson, "is too much." It might have been, but it was small onions beside events to follow. The Simonsons and others boarded the limo. O'Malley appeared on the curb. He asked the other guests if it wouldn't be too much of an inconvenience if he had some private time with the reverend and his wife. The others obliged. O'Malley got in and they drove to a church, actually a cathedral, and joined in a prayer of thanksgiving for their reunion. To this O'Malley appended a small thanks for good pitching and timely hitting. From there they drove to one of Chicago's stateliest hotels, where O'Malley and his wife were hosting a victory party in a banquet hall adjacent to their private suite. The hall was filled with the famous of California, with the hierarchs of baseball and eventually the heroes of the Dodger team—the rich, the elegant and the muscular. The value of their clothes could have wiped out most of the national deficit. And here was this young matron from the Dakota prairie, the wife of a preacher making a couple hundred bucks a month, wearing an unremarkable black suit in which she probably attended a funeral the previous week in Moorhead. She confessed her embarrassment to Kay O'Malley, a gracious woman who'd recently had her larynx removed because of cancer and needed a speaking tube. She pulled Eunice away from the crowd and took her on a tour of their suite. There she excused herself for a minute and emerged in an unremarkable black suit to replace her expensive gown. The preacher's wife nearly cried in gratitude. So they went out to meet the glitzy crowd, and in a few minutes both of them were hemmed in by curious people wanting to know all about life in Africa and impenetrable jungles. Well, no, we don't see many impenetrable jungles. Lions, yes. And suddenly the Dave Simonsons of Ilboru, Tanganyika, were celebrities who seemed more magnetic than the baseball tycoons and the theater idols. Even the ballplayers wanted to know about lions and warriors with spears.

"The celebration," Eunice said, "was awesome. In the middle of the banquet hall was a table 40 feet long covered with canapes and big ice rings and baseball figures with bats and gloves. They'd flown in orchids from Hawaii. I couldn't imagine so many glamorous people being gathered under one roof. O'Malley and his hunting friends somehow had gotten word to all of these people, including the ballplayers, that we lived these exciting lives and dealt with wild animals and performed these services, and it was overwhelming. Thank God we got around to the meal. Walter O'Malley invited the two of us to sit at the head table. The meal couldn't have finished much before midnight, when O'Malley spoke. He congratulated the players and then told about his hunting trip to Africa. He introduced Dave as one of his close friends and asked him, as a minister, to close the evening with a prayer of thanksgiving. I've never heard Dave give a more eloquent prayer. It had taste and humanity in it, and it couldn't have been more appropriate. Afterwards, the press wanted to know all about this powerful-looking guy in the black beard with one hand on the Bible and another on a 16-bore shotgun."

And the next day newspaper readers knew all about them. O'Malley called. He and his wife were flying off to an island. He invited them to join the party.

About there is where the Yellow Brick road had to come to a fork. They said thanks, but we have to go back to Moorhead.

Where?

Moorhead. It's in western Minnesota, where our kids have the mumps. We have to catch a flight. Real life.

Yes, you do, Walter O'Malley said. But I'll pay for it.

Back to fantasyland, one more time. They met several times in later years, at the Dodger training camp in Florida and in Los Angeles. But in October of 1959 they came down quickly from those dream worlds and began booking flights back to dusty roads and warriors with spears and churches that needed roofs. One thing surprised them. Those pictures of the real Africa seemed more inviting than the dream worlds. It was, after all, where they decided they belonged.

They couldn't have foreseen that in a few years the dusty roads and native churches came with personal humiliation for Dave Simonson, in part because of his brotherhood with the people called Maasai.

CHAPTER 9

The Africa of the Simonsons' return in the early 1960s was an Africa in the convulsion of historic change—the overthrow of colonial rule, once-warring tribal societies nationalizing themselves, asserting the right of self-government, reordering both the map and the seats of power in Africa. In some places it was a revolution that tore the guts out of the old colonial order, bringing death to thousands on all sides. In some, the white power structure yielded without wholesale slaughter and, in fact, opened the door to the inevitable.

Tanganyika was such a place. The British for years had been encouraging varieties of local and tribal rule. Approaching the 1960s, the British candidly wanted to leave. In this they had the warm approval and impatient prod of the United Nations. The agency of independence for the coming new state was the Tanganyika Africa National Union, a political party preaching a form of moderate socialism and headed by a former school teacher named Julius Nyerere, who had studied at the University of Edinborough. The Tanganyikans declared their independence on December 9, 1961, and in a couple of years merged with the island of Zanzibar, which had gone through intramural bloodletting after declaring its own independence. Together the impoverished new sovereignties stumbled into the future as the united nation of Tanzania. Like all emerging African countries, it was practically broke. It was harassed with tribal infighting and governmental confusion. The leadership brought in a political vision inspired by an idealism that was quickly bogged down by inexperience, by thin resources and ultimately by the curse of practically all fledgling Africa governments, runaway corruption.

Nyerere happened to be one of those political philosopher-activists whose lack of tools was partly redeemed by his good will. He got some things launched as the country's first president. A new and poor country, he reasoned, couldn't afford the additional hobbles of trying to spread all of its meager services to every splotch of land and isolated settlement. He was dealing with 20 million people, most of them undernourished, vulnerable to disease and undereducated. One way or another, he moved hundreds of thousands of them into villages. He scraped together enough money which, combined with loans and gifts through the international and religious agencies, eventually jumped the literacy level in Tanzania to 93 percent. It didn't mean all of these people had nearly enough schooling. It meant they could basically read and write. By 1970 the country had folded most of the mission schools into the government-run education system. The slogan for all of this was *ujamaa,* a Swahili word meaning "familyhood," which in turn meant "we're all in this together; whatever we're doing is for the community."

A lovely thought. It's workable with money and resourceful leadership and public commitment. Most of that was in short supply in the formative Tanzania. The idea was to socialize the country broadly. But the wheels rolled slowly and tended to break down, mostly because the country was so dreadfully poor, the fifth poorest in the world in the statistics of economics. There wasn't much to export. Sisal, used to make rope and a few other products, was one opportunity. Synthetics killed it. Tanzania had coffee, yes, but Tanzania couldn't compete with the big coffee growers. There wasn't much in minerals—a little gold and later a gem called Tanzanite, but it was piddling stuff in the international market. The country's biggest natural asset was the allure of its great wildlife. From the beginning, the government invested disproportionate amounts of its resources to preserving the wildlife—for tourism and simply because it had to be a responsible custodian of a natural treasure. But Kenya was the big magnet for the earlier tourism flocks, Kenya with its relatively modern Nairobi and its hub for international air travel. The global marketing of the big travel agencies and tour companies made hefty profits on their Kenya operations. In fact, most of the tourists who did go to Tanzania had to come by way of Nairobi and take buses, vans or Land Rovers from there.

It was in this environment that global missions came to operate in the new Tanzania. They had to make accommodations to an African government of paltry resources and the regulations of a socialist philosophy. Day to day, the charter of the Dave Simonsons and Bill Smiths and Dean Petersons was about the same—to build congregations where they could, add parishioners, preach, try to keep themselves and their families clear of hepatitis and lay brick when they had to. They also trained African evangelists increasingly to carry on the work of mission, putting a new emphasis on bringing Jesus Christ into the framework of the traditional religion of the Africa. There was one big evolving change in church administration. Political independence theoretically meant personal freedom for Tanzanians. It also meant that organized religion in Tanzania would necessarily come under the control of Tanzanian administrators—Tanzanian bishops calling the shots in the Tanzanian dioceses and synods, allocating funds that came in part from church agencies in the U.S.A. and elsewhere. Missionaries sent by mission boards in the U.S.A. and elsewhere would be reporting directly to these bishops.

Some of Simonson's colleagues grated under this arrangement. Simonson thought the principle was sound. If the Lutheran church or any Christian church was going to work in Tanzania, if it was going to build a community of Christians in Tanzanian, it had to be run by Tanzanians and there was no other way. What other way could there be? Missionaries were now working in a foreign and sovereign country whose institutions had the full power to decide on their directions. Either they accepted that or boxed their Bibles and went home.

That conviction should have put Dave Simonson on the side of the angels in the minds of all fledgling Tanzanian hierarchs. What it didn't allow for was the chance of a personality collision between the American missionary and the Tanzanian hierarch.

To the shock of no one who knew them, this meant a nasty confrontation somewhere down the line between David Simonson and the Tanzanian bishop of Moshi, Stefano Moshi. It got to be a fight which the willful head of diocese was not likely to lose to the willful missionary from America, and he didn't. That was still a couple of years into the future.

The Simonsons got back to their home in Ilboru with a hundred chores to divide. Among Eunice Simonson's chores was mothering a fifth child born in 1961, Jonathan. One thing hadn't changed about Ilboru or Africa: the likelihood of lurking calamity. This time it struck on Good Friday, of all days. It had been raining for days, a hard, unstoppable East African soaker. At about 4 a.m., Eunice awoke to a rising sound of cracking and crunching, and her husband was throwing himself on top of her at the moment of a horrific roar when part of the house came crashing down in a cascade of shattered glass.

Engulfed in darkness, they couldn't imagine what was happening to them. They knew they'd escaped injury. But what about the kids? They called out and heard some confused voices. Otherwise, it was quiet. Quickly they made their way through debris. What about the overhead electric lines? Were they exposed? They could hear falling glass. They called again and made their way to the children's bedrooms, locating a flashlight en route. They saw wide eyes and startled faces, but the kids were safe. A huge tree branch was hanging over them. It had smashed through a window in the collapse of a giant fig tree that had fallen on the house, its roots undermined by hours of rain. The porch and a small room used as an office had absorbed the full impact of the falling tree. It caved in part of the roof and shattered some of the windows, knocking out what little electricity serviced the house. Dave and Eunice gathered the family by flashlight. No one was hurt. They offered a prayer amid the wreckage. When it was finished, one of the kids remembered the dog, a golden cocker spaniel that slept on the now-maimed back porch.

"Sandy!"

There was no response.

One more time. "Sandy!"

They heard a stirring, and then the dog came leaping through the rubble and the broken window with a large wet tongue licking everyone in sight.

The dawn was coming in a few minutes. People were moving about the path near the house, fearful for the safety of the family inside. The Simonsons heard their names being called and went out to greet their African friends. Cheers erupted when the Africans saw the family safe. Not only had the family and dog been spared, but the Simonsons' small car beside the house was unscratched. If the tree had fallen into the house a few more feet in either direction, people would have died. The villagers knew that. So did the Simonsons. The villagers offered an invitation: "Let's go to the church together and give thanks." They did. When their prayers were finished the Africans came to the house with machetes and axes and chopped away the tree and branches so that the family could move about again and eventually restore the house. Nobody had to find passages in the Bible to understand what was happening in this moment when people with practically nothing to give but their hands and their friendship instinctively offered both to neighbors of another race, people from a far-off and baffling culture. But they were neighbors, and they were in need.

"I think right about then," Dave Simonson said, "Eunice and I decided we would never leave Africa if we had any choice in it. I don't know how I can express the respect and love we felt for those people who had so little. They came to us right there, right now, to surround us with their kinship and their care."

So a man who is a minister can go down both sides of the street, giving and receiving. It was a truth David Simonson already understood, but one that was sealed unforgettably for him on that Good Friday.

The house at Ilboru was a venue for an energetic ministry, for intramural brawls among opinionated kids and for a neighborhood clinic to help Africans in pain. It also became a refuge for those in despair and a crossroads for roving evangelists from all over creation. It was a theater for the enactment of the human condition, and one day it was transformed into a kind of slapstick purgatory for one of the loftiest figures in Christendom on his visit from the states.

There are tiny creatures in Africa which collectively are called "siafu," meaning a mess of ants. They are biting little creatures that come out in multitudes just before the rains and can create a swath sometimes 10 to 15 feet wide. It is a sight not to trifle with, because the siafu moves like an army and assaults whatever lies in its path. The long grass in front of the Simonson place in Ilboru seemed to be an especially popular staging area for the siafu army. In no way was this a neighborhood amusement. The ants' bites packed enough venom to sting hard. They were nasty and they were relentless. Eunice and the kids were introduced to them years before when Martha was still living with the family. Eunice awoke in pain and discovered herself crawling with siafu. She tried to fight them off but heard screaming from the kids and ran to them to start picking off the ants and brushing them off or whatever seemed to work. Nothing much did until Martha arrived on the scene with kerosene and a broom. She attacked the ants with that and then discovered that the bathtub wasn't yet infested. She threw the kids into it, and eventually cleared the house with her kerosene. Eunice located some medicine that seemed to soothe the kids' skin and her own. But she had to shake out all of their bedding to get rid of the lingering invaders. She also had learned something about pre-emptive strategy in facing the siafu.

It was a year or two later, once more with the reverend off in the bush ministering to the Maasai, that Dr. Franklin Clark Fry arrived at Ilboru on a tour of Africa. Franklin Clark Fry's credits in the Protestant world included being president of the Lutheran World Federation. This, some of his Catholic acquaintances joked, made him the Lutheran pope pro tem. Fry, his wife and other guests were invited to a banquet at the Simonson home. It didn't take Eunice Simonson long to discover that the house was inadequate to handle all of the guests, so she moved the festivities outside. All guests, friends and miscellaneous onlookers were naturally on their most proper behavior. At about the time coffee and tea were served, Eunice noticed some of the honored guests grabbing at themselves here and there and scratching. Among them was one Dr. Franklin Clark Fry. It had to be considered unusual behavior at any formal lawn party, particularly a Lutheran lawn party. It was the siafu, of course, striking again.

"Everybody was bolting in all directions trying to get some relief," Eunice remembered. "And right at the moment of highest chaos, a beautiful rain cloud moved in and drenched us all with water. Here was this mess of people in all of their finery, stripping off their clothes as fast as they could, rushing into the house. I quickly explained to Dr. Fry about siafu and offered him our bedroom so he and his wife could get their clothes off and get rid of the ants. They did. The scene is almost indescribable. People were in hysterics and screaming, under siege of this calamity of ants. All of the would-be emperors had no clothes. One way or another, the siafu eventually subsided. The Frys emerged from our bedroom, looking shaken and trying hard to smile. But nobody around held on to their aplomb. How could they? I tried to grope for some kind of parallel in the Bible, but I'm not sure there was one. I don't think even Sodom and Gomorrah deserved those siafu. We finally came together again in the living room. We were wringing wet and pretty exhausted but tried to put a brave face on all of the mess. I tried to be the morale officer. I don't think I brought it off very well. I put it down as one of my great social disasters in a career that had more than a few."

You could also put it down as Ilboru and Africa—entrancing today, a kick in the gut tomorrow. Somebody had another explanation. The siafu, he said, might have been God's invention to keep missionaries humble.

If the Rev. David Simonson needed any such education it came in 1964, after several years in which he had earned all of the hash marks needed for a veteran advocate of the Maasai cause.

And just who were these slender, noticeably haughty and often regal Africans called the Maasai? How much of the lore about them was real, and how much was fiction? There was plenty of mythology about where they came from, who they fought, how much of their dignity was deserved, how much they stole and whether they could acquire status in the tribe without killing a lion.

Nobody questioned their warriors' bravery. It was historic. By the tribal codes, it was also mandatory. For a long time in the wanderings of these cattle-herding, free-roaming people it was part of the young man's rite of passage that he should kill a lion. As Africa evolved through colonialism and independence, through the coming of game preserves and the shrinkage of free land, some of those mandates had to change. A young man can graduate into the warrior class today without killing lions. But if he gets into a confrontation— defending the herd against an assaulting lion or finding himself face to face with a lion in the wild—he will take on the lion with his spear. He will do it alone or with his warrior partners. He will go at the lion and go hard. It is heritage, and no options are considered.

Numerically today, the approximately 400,000 Maasai represent only a sliver of the African native population. They rove the grasslands of southern Kenya and northern Tanzania, changing the sites of their villages or bomas when their cattle need better forage. They settled in what are now Kenya and Tanzania after migrating from the Nile Valley and the south Sahara. There is strong evidence that they originally lived in the Lake Turkana district of what is now Ethiopia, that their forebears might have been herding cattle in that area as early as the time of the Old Testament. They migrated southward some 400 years ago, claiming land and performing military conquests as they progressed. Their ferocity routed incumbent tribes from whom they took what they needed, whether grazing land, cattle, water or women. For nearly two centuries they commanded an East African empire hundreds of miles in breadth from what is now the Maasai Mara in Kenya through the Serengeti Plain and the Rift Valley, south to the Maasai steppes in Tanzania. En route they absorbed parts of the defeated tribes. But by the middle 1800s, factionalism had broken out among their ruling chiefs. Then late in the century, little more than 100 years ago, they were struck by a catastrophic rinderpest epidemic that stripped their cattle herds by the thousands. It was accompanied by drought. Small pox killed thousands of the Maasai. To the wisemen of the tribe, it was an act of retribution by God, symbolized by the eruption of the volcano Oldonyo Lengai in the Rift Valley, the Mountain of God.

By the turn of the century the famine and disease and military defeats had ended the Maasai's glory days and disintegrated their power. Yet because they were historically nomads and because they insisted on providential rights to feed their cattle wherever the land offered them better grass, they were granted loose privileges to roam where they pleased. Those privileges began to disappear under a succession of colonial decrees by the British and Germans and finally by the Tanzanian government itself. For a time they could run their herds through the Serengeti, the revered place they call *"sirinket."* That ended. They got privileges to graze on the floor and slopes of the Ngorongoro Crater, the vast caldera in the mountains west of the Rift Valley. That ended. For a long time they crossed international borders with their herds, willy-nilly, to keep their cattle (and themselves) healthy. No customs agents lived out there in the savannah, and the herders were the Maasai. It was, the Maasai said, their right. The land was free and wild. We can use it if we need it.

Most of the land today is not that free or that wild. It is an Africa that is disappearing. The great Serengeti is still wild, although it is now legally preserved. Thank God. The stranger can intrude, but his stay there is brief and temporary, maybe a few hours from Lake Ndutu to Lobo or Seronera. From horizon to horizon the Serengeti seems endless. The word *sirinket* means "extended place." But it is not endless, and it is now fragile. Yet it is huge, and it is the soul of East Africa, the soul of the tall and proud warriors who were once its proprietors. How could it not be? The scenes of the Serengeti today are still the scenes of the Maasai's years of freedom-to-rove. The swaying seas of grass are stroked by a soft, velvet-yellow sun of the early morning before the grass dries and crackles in the heat. Dust devils spiral across the plain; gazelles bound distantly and hyenas drag their rear ends disreputably through the high grass, not worried much about their image or any other predators in sight. The heat of the mid-afternoon sends shimmers above the great mounds of rock outcrop the natives call *kopje*. The dancing sunlight momentarily shields from view a colony of big cats, lounging in utter lassitude atop the boulders. Further north the fever trees and acacias and thornbushes thicken among the streams. Crocodiles are here, zebra and wildebeest and hartebeest and lions and leopards. There is a small explosion of dust and a turmoil of antlers and limbs, and a young hartebeest goes down. The leopard is on it, feeds, and then grabs the carcass in its jaws and claws its way up a fever tree to keep its kill from the hyenas and jackals and vultures.

Land Rovers and vans can come through, but it is an Africa that has not lost its mystique. Africa. It's nature is pure Africa—glorious but tyrannical, full of sights and moods that nurture the mind and heart, but merciless. Disease can destroy its wild creatures almost overnight. For years the wild dogs roamed the Serengeti, shrewd and fierce hunters, but with familial habits that made them almost lovable to humans. Disease wiped them out in a couple of years. Disease threatens lions and other of its mighty. And today the Maasai can no longer roam untrammeled through the Serengeti of their legends and their history. Among the culprits in the shrinkage of their land are the Maasai themselves, selling or leasing land to which they actually have no individual right.

They should have more foresight, perhaps. But how are you really going to blame them? The Maasai's numbers are declining. Some of them are settling in the urban places, where they used to come into town with their spears and dramatic ochre-dyed togas or *shukas*. They can still come into town with their togas. The spears they have to leave back at the boma.

When he came to Africa, these were the Africans of Dave Simonson's deepest admiration. They remain that today. What the Simonsons know about the Maasai today can be understood only by people who were willing able to explore their history with them and to comprehend their language. Those who know the Maasai beyond the surface are those who can detect their wistfulness and know their legends, the richness of their ancient religion and some of the kinkiness of it. The listener can then understand the poetry of their story-telling and excuse (or appreciate) the showmanship of it but also hear the reverence in it. The best of the African storytellers are lyrical and hypnotic, and the Maasai elders are among the best. One cannot truly understand the Maasai or any African tribe without knowing the stories, and follow the winding threads of the stories, because those are not often written down, and the story tellers are both the poets and the historians.

Some of the Maasai have accepted Christianity sincerely. Some find it a convenience to make themselves available to services that come with Christianity. Most of the others have stuck with their traditional religion with its medicine men, spirits, curses, and its hard core belief in one God. Their historic monotheism, reaching back to its putative connection with the twelve tribes of Israel, is one that made them more receptive to approaches of white evangelists than some of the other African tribes. But the missionaries found soon enough that the best and most credible evangelism gives the Maasai space to hang on to some their own religion. In doing this the missionary could work the message of Jesus Christ into the body of Maasai history and into their own beliefs and concepts, such as sacrifice and demonology and pleasing God.

Polygamy was something else. No missionary was going to stamp that out overnight in this millennium or maybe in the next. Nor was any missionary going to win a popularity poll in the smoky Maasai bomas by belittling one of the Maasai's handier beliefs passed down through the centuries, that all of the world's cattle belong to Maasai by decree of God. This gave the Maasai a kind of divinely-ordained injunction to steal another tribe's cattle. The Maasai didn't consider this stealing, but rather reclaiming what was theirs by commandment. The other tribes, naturally, disagreed with this interpretation of theology. Battles and small wars resulted. Those cattle raids became the primary mission of the Maasai's warrior class over a period of time. That time is now in eclipse. There are fewer cattle raids. The Maasai don't provoke much dread any more, and theft in today's concepts of government is generally considered illegal. The Maasai today can't very well afford to live beyond the law. Along with the other tribes, most of them now understand the virtues of education as the best vehicle for self-preservation and betterment. They remain the romantic figures that attracted the zeal of young Dave Simonson back at Concordia. A lot of their tribal codes have not changed. They still maintain the principle of "age-set," in which young people of comparable age are joined in a peerage sealed by circumcision. Together they move into the warrior and junior elder and then elder classes of tribal rule. The young women also are required to undergo circumcision and are married off by their parents in prearranged matches in which cattle are exchanged as part of the bargain. In the husband's boma, the bride either begins the harem or joins it and essentially is committed to arduous, dawn-past-dusk labor to serve the needs of the man. That is one of the not so romantic parts of the Maasai legacy, and one that Simonson's schooling concepts may eventually modify. Those bomas now attract the tourists who ride through the African countryside, Westerners infatuated with the Maasai images and their carriage. The travelers will visit inside one of the huts. In two minutes, they will leave almost at a gallop. Those huts are thick with smoke and with flies assaulting the children. They are almost impenetrably dark, and it is all too much and too dreadful for the once wide-eyed tourist.

But it is Africa.

Cattle are still the mark of the Maasai elder's wealth. The Maasai don't hunt and most of them don't farm. They still live on what their cattle give them—milk and blood and (for some) meat and (for most of them) urine to mix with the rest. They will supplement this diet with grain obtained for cash or barter. They are still proud. They still look regal in those red *shukas* knotted at the shoulder. The young women can look lissome and beautiful and totally charming in their red, white and blue beaded collars and their earrings. Dave Simonson knows that the Maasai are still tough and enduring and often fun. For Simonson, they are one thing more.

They are now kin. In the 1960s, the Maasai made the Rev. Dave Simonson an elder in their tribe. The Maasai aren't as romantic as the tourists who come to Africa. When they wanted to honor him, they didn't give him a gold star and a certificate attesting to his visits to their bomas. The Maasai called Dave Simonson a Maasai. It meant he knew them and spoke their language. When he preached to them on Sundays, he spoke in Maasai. He came back on Monday and Tuesday and Wednesday and nailed lumber to rebuild their church. He drove to Arusha and got them a door. When he came into their huts he sat and drank what they poured out of their calabashes, whether it was milk and blood and urine or combinations thereof. This, it might be argued, will either make a native of Scobey, Mont., an elder in a hurry or it will kill him. But the Maasai knew Simonson well. They knew about the lion he killed not far from the thornbush fences of their vulnerable boma. They also knew the story of the African young mother in Arusha. Unmarried, she was having a baby in the hospital near Mt. Meru not far from Arusha. A post-partem hemorrhage developed. The hospital was relatively primitive. She was going to need blood quickly or she was going to die. The doctor told her brother to run out and bring back all of the relatives he could find. Coming out of the hospital the brother ran into Dave Simonson, who'd coached him on a track team. Simonson asked where he was going. The young man asked him if he could use the Simonson Land Rover to find relatives because his sister was bleeding and would die if she didn't get blood in a hurry.

"Maybe I can help," the missionary said.

He walked into the hospital and met the doctor who was trying to save the mother's life. "I've got type O blood (universal donor)," Simonson said. "Can you use me?'

"You'd give blood?" the doctor asked.

"Sure. I live with these people."

The woman survived. Within days, the word had reached villages dozens of miles away and around the environs of Mt. Meru. The word was that here's a white European (their language) who gives his life's blood to one of our women.

Years after they made Simonson an elder in their tribe, they offered him an even more expansive gift—Maasai land on which the Simonsons could build a home. It was a gift that had practically no precedent in the centuries of relationships between Africans and missionaries.

Simonson had come to Africa with the primary goal of ministering to the Maasai. There were other tribes with whom he worked, but the Maasai were the people with whom he was going to live and work. He would be their padre if they wanted, their friend if they wanted, and their advocate if they needed. He became all three, to a virtual ovation from the Maasai.

But being their advocate produced the shock of his life in 1964: an order of eviction from his missionary work by the bishop of the Lutheran Church of Northern Tanzania and an invitation—rather a demand—to "go back where you came from."

By then Simonson was splitting his evangelical time between the needs of parishioners in South Maasai and others in the far more populous Arusha district, with a total population of more than 100,000. Africans of several tribes were included. There were other missionaries working the Arusha district, of course, many of them part of the ever-present and zealous Minnesota Mafia. But there were never quite enough. There were congregations to build and tend, churches and schools to build, sickness to heal and ecumenical outreach to perform because there was a whole colony of Christian churches in Arusha: Catholics, Methodists, Baptists, Anglicans and others.

There was also money to scrounge where it could be scrounged.

This was a goad that put the missionary from Concordia on a collision course with the bishop of Moshi. At the church's request, much of Simonson's work in the Arusha-Moshi area (the cities are 50 miles apart in northern Tanzania) dealt with the Wa-arush, a tribe of agriculturalists living mostly on the slopes of the extinct volcano, Mt. Meru. The Wa-arush were part of the Maasai society, although most of them were not purely Maasai genetically. They got to be Maasai partly because in earlier days the Maasai needed or wanted more women and the Wa-arush provided a source. In any case, the Wa-arush became Maasai. Working their farms and living beneath Mt. Meru put them in close proximity with other tribes, including the Chaggas. The Chaggas represented the most powerful tribal group in the Moshi area and in the Lutheran church there. With Tanzanian independence came a shift in ecclesiastical authority to Tanzanian church leaders and away from the foreign mission leadership. Dave Simonson and most of his colleagues saw this as right and proper and that the foreign missionaries should now occupy the roles of co-workers, serving as pastors, for example, under Tanzanian leadership. So it wasn't the chain of command in the Lutheran Church of Tanzania that Simonson objected to as his stewardship with the Wa-arush churches expanded. What bothered him, and them, was the distribution of money budgeted by the bishop's office. Disproportionate amounts of the money for churches and maintenance, the Wa-arush argued, were going to Chagga churches, a suspicion heightened by the fact that Bishop Stefano Moshi of the church's headquarters in Moshi was a member of the Chagga tribe.

"Most of the funds available to the bishop's office," Simonson said later, "came from Lutheran sources in the United States and Germany. The Wa-arush felt they had to go on their hands and knees to beg for what they needed. There should have been some sensible pro-rata system for distributing the money."

Simonson saw no such sensible system. Bishop Moshi adamantly disagreed. He resented what he saw as an unwarranted attack on the fairness of his budget process. The Wa-arush's discontent flared up into anger and threats to break away from Moshi's control. It got to be a showdown in the bishop's office between Simonson, the Maasai advocate and white missionary pastor from thousands of miles away, and the African bishop with roots in the land of his own ministry. Oddsmakers wouldn't hesitate to predict that particular outcome. But while it was mostly a tribal fight in its early stages, it graduated into a personality battle eventually. Simonson acknowledges that. "He thought I was instigating, that I was trying to arouse the Wa-arush to usurp the power of the Chagga bishop."

This charge may not have been totally inaccurate. Simonson *was* instigating, although he didn't want to usurp power. What he was doing, he said, was demanding a fair deal. He was counsel to the Maasai trying to make a case in the other side's court. He might have done it more discreetly, but discretion is not a commodity in general supply in Africa, or in Simonson. The reverend harbored undoubted political skills. If he hadn't, he could not achieve in

Tanzania what he eventually did, largely through his charismatic power to extract money from willing sources in America. But while he was a politician, he was never very much of a diplomat. The two callings are not necessarily the same. And the bishop was a man with a crust as least as thick as Simonson's. The Wa-arush position was basically this, as defined by Simonson: If we can't get our fair share of the money, we'll go out on our own and raise it ourselves.

By no coincidence that also was Simonson's position, and Simonson was the guy who would be digging up the money. Going out on their own meant the Wa-arush were threatening to split from the Moshi bishop's control. Simonson and the bishop talked. The bishop didn't have much trouble defining Dave Simonson's role: He was undermining the office of the bishop and rebelling against it. The way Simonson read it, the problem was the bishop' refusal to be reasonable and to credit the Wa-arush with a justifiable complaint. His friend Bill Smith was one of the missionaries supporting Simonson. Elmer Danielson, the missionary who had once carried the Tanzanian cause to the United Nations, joined a later meeting to offer his own support and was invited to leave the meeting.

Simonson said later: "The Wa-arush told me that if they (the administrators) didn't want to listen to them, the Wa-arush would build their own churches and schools and they'd even build their own bridges. I brought that up, and the bishop had enough of it. He told me I was through with the Lutheran Church of Tanzania. He didn't want me around. He was kicking me out and telling me to go home."

Did he have the power to say and do that?

He did. This was his diocese. The foreign missionaries were there as resources volunteered and salaried by their mission boards back home. Simonson spent a couple of days in a fog of disbelief. When the shock had subsided, he and his Maasai pals began to reorganize. His superiors back home were the heads of the Evangelical Lutheran Church, which later merged with a Ohio body to become the American Lutheran Church, which ultimately merged with the Lutheran Church in America to become the Evangelical Lutheran Church in America. Lutherans customarily advance and divide alphabetically. At the time of Bishop Moshi's eviction notice, Simonson's ultimate supervisor in the states, Dr. Frederick Schiotz, protested the action and was ready to go to the mat for him. But in Tanzania, Simonson's Maasai admirers were closer to the scene. They organized a strategy revolving around old Petro Sirikaa, a highly prestigious Maasai leader from the plains, once a chief but now retired as a kind of Massai elder emeritus. They demanded another hearing. Simonson returned to the bishop's office accompanied by Elmer Danielson, Petro and a few others. The bishop reviewed. He said missionaries had come and gone but had pretty much stayed with the flow. Here were Simonson and the rebellious Wa-arush trying overthrow the system. At which point old Petro stood. He said, "Bishop, we don't know anything about what you've been doing. All these things you're telling us don't mean much. All we know about this is that we know Simonson and people like Bill Smith. They've been with us and working for us, and we want them. If they have to go, this church divides. We're leaving you."

Old Petro was a generation older than the bishop and a respected elder. Sometimes tribal differences fall away when one generation confronts a younger one with its moral force. Old Petro remained standing. He pointed his finger at the bishop. He said, "Bishop, do you hear me?"

The bishop looked into Petro's eyes and nodded, "I hear you."

The bishop's decree was revised.

Simonson, he said, stays in Tanzania if he wants to. But he doesn't stay here (in Moshi and Arusha). He was reassigned to another mission station about as far from Arusha as the bishop could make it, on the fringe of the Kenya border in Loliondo, 200 miles from Arusha across the Serengeti Plain, north of some of the loneliest steppes in Africa. It was a distance that one could theoretically walk in seven or eight days if he went through the African Rift Valley with its dust, volcanic canyon floors and its 2,000 foot high cliffs. As a matter of fact, it's a walk Dave Simonson eventually made a half dozen times.

It was also Maasai country. To hold his diocese together, the bishop regarded the compromise as worth it—Simonson's exile in exchange for peace and quiet. Later, Stefano Moshi is said to have explained to a friend his strategy in dealing with Simonson. It had the wry tones of a tribal proverb: "You never meet a charging elephant head-on," he said. "You step aside and let him bull past and after he goes through the grass, there's plenty left even for the smallest animals."

The resident bull elephant, Simonson, decided quickly that his transfer to Loliondo was no exile at all. He was here, in Maasailand, where Eunice could do some honest-to-God nursing, where Dave Simonson could preach Jesus Christ to the Maasai, build churches, eat goat meat with the Maasai and rebuild Land Rovers without a starchy bishop looking down his throat.

It also meant that he would now know, now that he was a weather-roughened veteran of nearly ten years of missionary work, what the Maasai really were thinking when he preached Jesus Christ.

CHAPTER 10

The Maasai should have been amused by the coast-to-coast fervor with which millions of Americans in the mid-20th century embraced a concept called "wellness."

It surged across the United States from the self-improvement industry, but it wasn't exactly a revelation. It dated back a few thousand years, a fact well understood by the scholars who dig into the philosophies of ancient civilizations. Holism—the philosophy that sound health cannot be achieved unless human beings recognize the interdependence of the physical, spiritual and emotional-mental parts of their lives—has been around approximately that long. But it was peddled rhapsodically in the United States as something new in the quest for Nirvana. The Maasai would have been amused because a form of "wellness" or holism has been at the heart of personal and communal health in the Maasai society for centuries.

It is such a pervasive part of Maasai life that health is indistinguishable from religious belief. Missionaries working with the Maasai made those discoveries relatively early. One of those was the realization that Western society might learn as much about health from the Maasai as it could teach them. Simonson reached that conclusion after his first encounters with the Maasai medicine men, the tribal healers and psychics who were sometimes Christianity's rivals and sometimes its partners in the struggles to mend or alter the spiritual lives of the Maasai.

"They'd be brought to somebody in the boma who was sick or scared or unruly," Simonson said. "They knew things about herbal medicine and natural cures and sacrifices, but they didn't usually ask, 'Where does it hurt?' They'd ask, 'Who have you quarreled with?' Which meant, 'If you're sick, something may be out of whack in your life. What is it? Who is it?'"

In other words, if you're not healthy, you have to look at your relationships. One of them is broken. This belief in the cause of sickness is part of traditional religion throughout Africa, no less than the belief that the universe is filled with spiritual power that flows into the body and unites with it.

"There are three relationships that are at the center of life for practically every Maasai," Simonson said. "The first is his relationship with God. Whether it's the God they learned about as part of tribal tradition or the God we preach, it doesn't matter. You have to believe they're the same God. When you talk to the Maasai, you're impressed by their reach into history. Their talk is full of allusions to events in the Old Testament. I wouldn't doubt their claim that they're descended from the twelve tribes of Israel. When you hear their oral historians describe the Maasai's meeting with God, it sounds like a fairy tale, I admit, or maybe a tall tale would be better. But I suppose you can say the same about things that come out of the Bible we use. In their tradition, the Maasai had this direct link with God. In their tradition, God made a contract with another tribe to give them all of the world's cattle, and he passed down a long leather thong from heaven to signify the arrangement. But the other tribe wasn't there. The Maasai were. They took the thong from God and the right to all of the cows. And that made them God's chosen people, and before we laugh at that we ought to consider: The idea of God singling out a people as the chosen ones isn't exactly unknown in the Bible. Anyhow, that is their traditional connection with the deity, and being right with God is obviously part of their value system.

"It follows that another one is their relationship with humanity, first with other Maasai and then with people who aren't Maasai. The Maasai haven't lost all of their old arrogance. They still consider themselves superior, which means that people like the neighboring tribes and white Westerners are just going to have to adapt to that idea. That business never bothered me very much. That's tribal pride. I just shrug it off. All ethnics have their quirks and vanities. Norwegians figure they can handle lousy weather better than anybody else, and they probably can, considering all the practice they get."

The third relationship that matters to most Maasai is their relationship with the earth, the environment. If their environment goes bad and if they lose their watering places, if drought strikes, their cattle die and their lives are in disorder. So while they may not be watchdogs of the good earth, they have a stake in it and where and how they can protect it.

If one of those relationships goes sour—Maasai to God, Maasai to family, Maasai to the land—the medicine man is going to tell his client to make sure he knows which one, and to get it restored. But the Maasai's distress may come from a more sinister force growing out of a broken relationship. Dean Peterson, a longtime contemporary of Simonson's in East African mission work, explains it in his book, *Christian Theology in an African Context*:

> The quarrel (that caused the sickness) might be among two living people or may involve an ancestral spirit and a living person. So the question a sick person asks (after deciding which one he has quarreled with) is: Who might be wishing me ill by placing a curse on me or calling on a member of the living dead to settle the score with me?

Is the western missionary, trained in the Judaic-Christian tradition, going to scoff at stories of revenge-by-curse from ancestral spirits in a Maasai boma?

He'd better not. The missionary's credibility depends on a respectful understanding of the old religion in the land where he or she presumes to evangelize. A question: When somebody is trying to figure out where the pain is coming from, do demonology and curses seem like farfetched villains?

Why should they? Those phenomena occur in the standard Western Bible. Jesus Christ himself is said to have done some impressive dispatching of demons.

So how much do we really know?

We can probably know more by listening to Dean Peterson. The notion that some ancestral spirit may be invoked to do harm to a living person and to extract vengeance, Peterson reminds us, simply embraces the religious view of life after death: "Without elaborate argument, it simply posits that physical death is not the end of a person. One can also see how this view arises out of a very close relationship between matter and spirit, between the physical and psychological. The boundary between the living and the living dead is blurred or obliterated as well as the boundary separating the physical and the spiritual. The unity of life holds these distinct themes together."

Which means that one of the traditional Maasai beliefs is that a member of the tribe, convinced that he's been wronged, can call down retaliation from the spirit world, or have it done by a sorcerer.

Does Dave Simonson believe this is possible? "I don't know anything about the spirit world," he said. "I've said before, I know of a man in a tribe cursed by an enemy. He fell dead. I don't know what was the cause of his death. What I do know is that the man dropped dead."

When he was banished to Loliondo, Simonson ultimately found himself liberated. At core he was a mission free-lancer, preferring to work his own tempos and to shoot for miracles where slower but steady progress might be preferred by his superiors. He was no instinctive rebel, but his single-mindedness in crossing the line or scaling the mountain, once he decided on a goal, tended to collide with authorities who had to guard protocol and had an occupational wariness of miracle workers. Even in his first months in Loliondo Simonson had worked out a scheme for building schools in Tanzania with money raised in America but allocated by the Tanzanian government. The schools were still several years off. But when he finally got the apparatus rolling— pure Simonson in its boldness and its reach—the results were breathtaking.

If his first months in Loliondo were supposed to be a time of contrition, Simonson found optional uses for the time. Within a few weeks he had orches-trated a strolling ministry in the highland along the furthest reaches of the Serengeti Plain. It meant getting thicker with the Maasai, preaching and listening to them and in general functioning as the one-man mission that suited his independence and resourcefulness. The bishop at Moshi had decided it was going to be a frugal exile. Simonson got neither a vehicle nor a budget. For a home he and Eunice set up in a Toonerville little cottage recently vacated by Stan and Marie Benson. It was a roof, but barely. "The guy who built it," Simonson said, "took a house plan from Better Homes and Gardens. He actually did. The trouble was, his builder mixed up the inside and outside measurements. So the ceiling boards came up short and the walls leaned in or out, and it was a mess. But we overhauled it and after awhile figured we were in great shape out there, sort of Robinson Crusoe, except that Robinson Crusoe didn't have to worry about a leopard. The Bensons told us that when you went from the house to use the outhouse, you had to keep an eye open for a leopard who liked to hang around there. He did, but he didn't bother us much and we figured it was part of the environment."

Not having a vehicle would have bothered Simonson more than the leopard did. If sin and idleness were his worst enemies, immobility was not far away. Loliondo lay beyond the Gol Mountains, on the far side of the African Rift Valley. Nonetheless, Simonson decided he would not be doomed to immobility in these remote highlands. Shortly after the bishop forced him out of Arusha, the family had returned to the states for several months furlough. For Simonson, it was also time for reassessment and recommitment. They were housed this time in Northfield, Minn., the site of St. Olaf and Carleton Colleges and one of the havens for Lutheranism in the Midwest. To her surprise, Eunice was swarmed by well-wishers from her college and nursing days in Minnesota. David quickly resumed his speaking tours and guest preaching, and the kids basked in the gifts of genuine, store-bought clothes from the relatives. When the Simonsons returned from the states, they arranged to transport the kids to a Lutheran boarding school at Kiomboi in central Tanzania, one with an excellent faculty and comfortable lodgings. For Eunice, it offered peace of mind in the knowledge that their children were safe, were being schooled well, and could come to Loliondo to visit on vacations. For the first time, it also offered her enough freedom of movement to do some serious nursing, for which there was a pressing need at a Catholic-run hospital in the village.

But first, to settle Simonson's mobility problems, they needed the reverend's growing skills at creativity-in-the-wilds. Somebody told him there was a dysfunctional Land Rover in one of automotive graveyards in Moshi. It had been assigned to the church office, built for Diesel power. But whoever had been driving it didn't know much about Diesel engines. It had been run on low revolutions and burned out within 2,000 miles. So Simonson found his way to Moshi and made an offer of a few hundred bucks. The reluctant owner said, "It's a deal." Simonson hauled the machine to Arusha seeking aid and comfort from his old Jewish pal, Karl Fainzilber, the brick and construction man. Fainzilber was one of those African characters and soldiers of fortune who had his antennae all over Tanzania and Kenya. One of his sideline businesses was buying cars and trucks at auction. He knew all about Land Rovers and Diesels and gave the reverend this advice: "If you buy anything for the road around here, be sure you first buy one that's smashed up. If it's smashed up, you know you might be able to salvage the engine or the gear box. So if it's spare parts you're looking for, get a car that's been creamed."

This was the automotive world according to Karl Fainzilber. His gospel about scavenging spare parts in the African steppes made up Simonson's mind. In Kenya he'd buy another Land Rover, this one driven by petrol instead of Diesel fuel. It cost him another few hundred bucks. Wait a minute. Is the reverend a spendthrift? Two Land Rover wrecks, not one?

"Bear with me," the reverend said. "Nobody wanted that wreck in Kenya because you couldn't straighten out the body. I took it down to Tanzania and took out the petrol-driven engine. I put that engine in the first Land Rover that had been a Diesel. I sold the gear box in the rear end to one of the hospitals for twice the amount I paid for the whole thing, so I ended up with a vehicle ready to go and I made money on it."

Concordia College's department of logic had struck again. They don't teach vehicle repair in the seminary. But if you grew up on the prairie, you remembered this: the towns were a half day apart and there was barely one car for one family and for all the relatives, and that one had to be kept running for the preacher and the groceries and Saturday night dates. All that being true on the prairie, you *better* know something about gear boxes and fan belts.

And yet Simonson hadn't manipulated all those rusty parts and fixed the plugs on the Land Rover to turn it into a prayer-mobile. The Land Rover was mainly for long-hauling, driving from Loliondo to Arusha or to Nairobi or for village and church emergency. What he came to value most about his new ministry up there in the highlands—some 7,000 feet above sea level—was the sociability of it. Simonson would walk the roads and trails to the village from that kooky Better Homes and Garden cottage. On those days he could meet the Maasai or the Sonjos on the way and talk God with them if and when they wanted. But mostly they would talk salt licks and cows and schools. He settled into the most relaxed and probably the most pleasurable ministry of his entire career in Africa. Most of these folks were Maasai, the people he'd come to Africa to live with and to serve. He was no stranger to them. There are no secrets in the Maasai's bush networks. They knew about Simonson the lion-hunter and blood-donor, the discus thrower and the school and bridge builder. But beyond that, they knew of Simonson the Maasai elder.

He'd become that in a ceremony in the foothills near the slopes of Mt. Meru in recognition of the work he and his wife had done among the Maasai. It was an irrevocable seal of kinship that had grown up between the missionary family and the Maasai. Ceremonially, Dave and Eunice received new names under codes of the Maasai, who defined a person not by heritage but by his relationship with his children. Therefore, in the Maasai honorifics, the name of the man of the family was transformed from David Simonson to "the father of Stephen," the eldest son, and that of Eunice Simonson to "the mother Naomi," the eldest daughter. There was still one other title bestowed on David Simonson, one which left him choked with emotion. The Maasai gave him the name of *kipwesi*. It is the name of a mountain near the village where the ceremony took place. In the legends and teachings of the Maasai of Arusha, Kipwesi the mountain is the place where God comes to meet his people and to bring them his blessings. When the Maasai there wish to receive God's benediction, it is to that mountain that they walk. An elder explained the significance of that title: "It means you are one of our leaders. You are a person through whom God gives his blessing to us. You are a person we ask when we want God's blessings for us. *Kipwesi.*"

Said Simonson, "It was an honor past all understanding for us. I never took the Maasai's legends and the traditional beliefs and stories lightly. I didn't in my first year in Africa and I still don't. They are part of the lives and history and the spirit of these people. And without compromising any of my Christianity, I was now one of them. We were part of them and their history in a real way. Some of them were Christians. Most weren't. It didn't matter. We now felt a responsibility to represent our people, the Maasai, wherever we went in this world, to do it not only by preaching but by building and healing where we could. I think we have done that without overlooking the needs of other Africans, as I think the body of our work there will show."

Dave Simonson got something else: The Maasai version of the old boys' macho code. They told him to insist on it. "They were probably hamming it up to tease Eunie," he said. "But they said I better make sure that when I come home at night my wife should greet me with a gourd full of sour milk and have that easy chair waiting for me with the beaded backrest."

No such reception has ever been recorded in the Simonson histories in Africa. A short beer, perhaps, or a plateful of fresh greens. Eunice's hospitality at home has always had a practical side. It stopped short of gourds of sour milk and beaded chairs. Being a Maasai elder—a working title and not a token—carried one final mark of status.

One of the titles they gave him was that of *olmoruo kitok*, meaning a person of important role among the elders. It made him an advisor to the ruling membership of the Maasai group. To signify the honor, the Maasai gave Simonson a carved walking stick made from the wood of the wild olive, and an ebony baton that to the Maasai is an emblem of leadership. David explained it: Maasai don't conduct their business as an autocracy any more. There's really a democratic base to it. When they hold their meetings as the high council, the one with the ebony baton has to watch the dynamics of the meeting closely. If he sees some potential unrest over his leadership, he'll put the baton down. It means, do you want me to stay or don't you? If they want him to stay in that role, they have to buy that baton back, which means they have to pay him in cows, sheep, goats or beer. If they don't want him, they stay silent, and he's finished as the ranking elder. It's the most democratic, low-cost election system in the world. Before the meeting finishes, they pick somebody to replace him. You don't see any big campaigns or political rallies among the Maasai. If you want the job and you start pitching yourself to the rank and file, you're ostracized. The title *olmoruo kitok* means that I'd have the last word at any of our meetings as long as I'm entitled to carry the ebony baton."

But the reverend pretty much contented himself with being an elder in name, and he respected the kinship that it conferred. Temperamentally, he wasn't suited for Roberts Rules of Orders, whether the Maasai version or the Western one.

But when the Maasai who knew about him met him on the streets of Arusha or in the boma, they sometimes called him "Rev. Simonson" or "bwana" but very often they called him "*olmoruo kitok*," in their language "the great one."

That designation may have been partly poetic at the time it was bestowed. It could hardly have been applauded by the bishop back at Moshi. But once the schools began going up all over Tanzania, the handiwork of *olmoruo kitok*, it was deserved and it may have been no exaggeration.

CHAPTER 11

A small group of parents living in a settlement in a remote corner of Tanzania near the shore of Lake Nyasa called on the district authorities. It took them hours to get there. They were routinely poor and they were frightened. They appealed to the authorities to build a school for their children, and explained why. The school nearest their settlement, Gonalamafuta, was six miles away. Their kids walked it every morning and again in the late afternoon when they came home. They walked on rude paths and in bush country where there were no paths.

The parents were scared because other life moved through that stretch of six miles, wild animals that could kill or maim their children.

The administrator met them in his spare little office in the government station. He said he was sympathetic but powerless. There were only six families in the settlement, not enough to qualify it as a village. Unless they lived in a place that met the numerical requirements for a village, the government couldn't build a school for them. It was the law. They'd heard that before. He explained it again. He heard a helpless shuffling of feet on the wooden floor and read the resentment in their eyes. But this was life in Africa. What was he supposed to do about the law?

He did what he couldn't have done a few years earlier. He told the parents the school authorities couldn't help them, but there was an agency called the Community Development Trust Fund. He said this agency could approve a school on its own authority if money had been given by a donor. The parents went to see the regional director of the Community Development Trust Fund, which was a semiprivate liaison agency that acted as a clearing house for village building requests. They needed a school, they told the director, for the sake of their children's safety.

They got notification several weeks later. There was money in their fund from a donor. The parents in this tiny settlement may never have known the name of the donor, but their school was built, and not long afterward a house for the teacher stood nearby, built with money from the same source. And their kids no longer walk twelve miles a day through wildlife country.

The money, some $3,000, probably came from churches in Minnesota. It came indirectly from the zeal and the blast-the-torpedoes commitment of the Rev. J. David Simonson. Without Simonson, in fact, it would not have come at all.

Today the school near the shore of Lake Nyasa can be multiplied by more than 2,300, the number of classrooms built with money raised by an organization called Operation Bootstrap Africa, the creation of Dave Simonson and some of his friends in the mid-1960s. The number of Africans whose lives were bettered or enriched by it reaches into the hundreds of thousands. Among them are the thousands of pupils to whom the door to a school was now open, the members of their families and the people in their communities. The numbers are stunning. As much as any missionary work in East Africa in the second half of the 20th century, Simonson's Bootstrap represented global mission at its most constructive and humane and resourceful.

Not all of it represented saints in action. Quarrels and personality splits developed from time to time on the Minnesota-based board that supervised the budget. Simonson's dominating style as the field director and project architect, as its broker and its fund-raising spellbinder did not charm all of the directors all of the time. The Tanzanian government itself had to insist that more of the money should go to distant reaches of the country instead of being concentrated in the Arusha environs, as it was early in its history.

But sometimes there are no more compelling ways to measure value than by what shows on the bottom line. And the bottom line for Bootstrap is not measurable only by the hundreds of thousands who have benefited from it directly and indirectly. The bottom line for Bootstrap also joins men, women and children in hundreds of churches in America and Europe with the lives of impoverished kids and their families in Africa. It is measured in the recognition of those thousands in America, in their churches and homes, that the bedrock affirmation of human service is contained in three small words: "We can help."

There is one other dimension to the bottom line of this extraordinary school-building commitment spread over three decades, embracing close to $7 million in donations from the main streets of Minnesota and America to the dusty villages of Africa. This one has to be seen to be understood. It appeared on the face of a girl of ten or eleven years of age on a late summer day in northern Tanzania. The day marked the opening of the school year but, more important, the opening of a classroom that was now the pupils' own. The nearly 40 pupils were seated at their work tables, tidy in their blue and white uniforms, awaiting the arrival of a group of Americans to whom they were to be introduced. In it were twelve Minnesotans, members of a club for which I produced adventure travel, in this case a photo safari in Tanzania. As an acquaintance of the Simonsons, I asked for a few minutes with the pupils of one of the schools built with Bootstrap funds. One of the kids acted as a lookout and alerted his classmates to the Americans' approach on a path through a nearby banana grove. They began singing as we came into the schoolyard. They sang in one of those wonderful syncopated chants whose meaning was lost on us but whose rhythm was magnetic. We entered the large single room with the respectful smiles and demeanor of strangers coming into somebody's house. When the kids finished their song, we were welcomed by the schoolmistress.

English lessons were printed on the blackboard, new. Underfoot was a concrete floor, new. In front of each student was a blue work notebook, and on one of the walls was a multicolored sign in large letters proclaiming, "Welcome!"

We thanked the teacher and the students for their songs and congratulated them on their new school. Based on what we saw on the blackboard we also congratulated them for their advances in the English language, silly language that it was. The teacher translated, and the kids twittered. And then the teacher introduced the girl, ten or eleven, who had memorized a little speech, which she gave in her own language to be translated by the teacher. She was a tall and attractive girl in braids and ribbons, her brown eyes slightly scared. She began by giving thanks to the visitors from America for helping to make this new school possible. Then she looked around at her classmates, sitting primly at their tables, and then to her teacher and then to the blackboard with its imprinted words in fresh chalk. Her voice broke. She struggled to continue but couldn't. Her face was damp. But there was a muted pride in it, expressing what her voice could not.

Her face was saying: We have a school. We don't have to do lessons any more under the trees and in the rain and under the hot sun. We don't have to do our lessons anymore in rockpiles and in the dirt and in all the flies. This is our school. We are like children everywhere in the world now, in America and England and Japan. We have a school where we can study and laugh and play games and grow up.

We applauded, and when she turned her eyes to us, they sparkled with her tears. She looked at the visitors, and saw that hers were not the only moist cheeks in the schoolhouse.

The first commandment of the dedicated missionary is uncomplicated: When you see a need, respond to it. There are responses and responses—they depend on the resources of the missionary or the mission station, they depend on the wisdom and resolve and sometimes the ingenuity with which those needs are met. Meeting spiritual needs with the skills and fervor this requires is sometimes tricky. Do these people really want or need Christianity. When and how?

Physical needs announce themselves more emphatically. They are called hunger, sickness and dirty lots where schools ought to be.

Simonson made it the watershed of his ministry to face those needs. His disposition was to define the most important need that could be sensibly met, and to go after it with passion, with creativity and without much sleep when it came to that. If he'd been a military commander he would have added: And go after it in force.

Simonson was no military commander, but he went after it in force. Which is what happened when Bootstrap was conceived. The Tanzanians achieved their independence in 1961. One of the first priorities of the new socialist government was to improve education, especially in the primary grades. The country was almost bankrupt from the very beginning, but it scraped together enough money to increase literacy in the country by making more schooling available to the kids. Mission schools were being phased out in these onetime colonial countries. But none of newly-independent countries in Africa had the money to build enough schools.

Simonson, of course, saw this. He had been building schools around Arusha and in Maasailand as part of his early ministry. He had also been approached by the Tanzanian minister of education, Eliafoo Solomon, whose friendship with Simonson stretched back to their studies at the University of London in the mid-1950s, and was renewed at the teachers' college in Marangu. At the time of Tanzanian independence, only 30 percent of the country's children had received a primary school education. "We need hundreds of more schools, thousands," Solomon told him. "We need help, an organization of help from the outside."

No such school-building structure financed by donations from abroad existed at the time. The money came piecemeal, from church agencies or occasionally from foundations and citizen groups. With luck, it was eventually converted into a classroom. Nothing was systematized. Tanzanian independence was part of the problem. These were public schools Solomon was talking about, schools that would be operated by the country's public school system. The donated funds would not go directly from donor to the village. They would have to be forwarded to a governmental agency for allocation. The formula for the government was this: Help us build our schools. It will be mostly our responsibility to decide which villages get the money and the school. We want it to be done on the basis of need.

The problem for Tanzania was that everybody needed.

In the parenthesis of this formula was a loose understanding that the people creating the donation (which became Simonson's Operation Bootstrap Africa) might themselves nominate a village based on the informed judgment of their people on the scene—which more or less meant Dave Simonson.

The formula (and the parenthesis) made sense to Simonson, who needed no further blueprint from Eliafoo. He knew the villages could build the schools themselves if they had the money for the material. He'd seen that in his recruitment of his bricklaying pals around Marangu and Arusha. They didn't need professional guidance. If they were willing to expend the sweat, they had the skills. And why wouldn't they want to volunteer their labor? The school was for their kids. Simonson knew that what Eliafoo was talking about was some kind of apparatus that would fill the space between mission and government. He also figured that in the market values of the time, they could build a school for 40 or 45 kids for something like $1,600 to $1,750. The figure leveled off a few years later at approximately $3,000 for each school—one room, about 20 feet by 30 feet, with a concrete floor, roof, blackboard and, in most cases, windows. In parts of Tanzania and elsewhere in Africa where Bootstrap operated, it was too hot for windows so they left the window frames open. The cost for those one-room schoolhouses stood at $3,000 through the late 1980s and rose to its present $4,500 in the mid-90s. But the schools are still being built.

In Arusha shortly before the American furlough that preceded his exile to Loliondo, Simonson fine-tuned the prospective campaign. If you raise the money in America, it will be used for building the school and not for the actual teaching. The government pays for the teachers. The volunteer village workmen handle the labor. What then? Well, you need roofing timbers and corrugated iron sheets for the frame, Portland cement for mortar, windows, door frames and nails and a half dozen miscellaneous materials. You need mud bricks for the basic structure, but the village workmen will make those with their own mud and their own sun. You'd like tables or desks. But those will have to come later. In the earlier years, the kids will have to sit on the floor. Not the best, but this isn't a prep school. This is Africa. What the kids need most is a shelter in which to learn and a blackboard on which the teacher can do the lessons. The Africans can honestly call this a school. It's called the same thing in America. The Africans can honestly say they built the school, which they did. But it becomes more than a school in what it does symbolically. For those who provide the money for the material, those who give their sweat to build it, those who study in it, the school bridges the continents in one of the most precious of all causes, improving the minds and health of impoverished kids.

What's missing, Simonson asked?

He asked the question wistfully because he knew from the beginning what was the missing piece: What is wellspring for this dream of Eliafoo's and now Simonson's? Where do you find that spring and how do you channel it? Who gives the money and how do you reach the givers and organize this . . . what would you call it?

Generals would have called it "the offensive." Simonson's mind wasn't that military. No, not a campaign, not a crusade. Call it Operation Bootstrap, let the African villages lift themselves with their own work and the dreams of their own. All we would say here is, "We can help."

A couple of days after he and the family settled in Minnesota for a few months prior to the move to the mission station in Loliondo, David's brother Luther and his sister-in-law, Audrey, called. They invited the Simonsons and

Richard and Evelyn Kvamme to spend a few days with them in a cabin on Alice Lake near the northern Minnesota town of Bigfork. Kvamme was a highly successful construction man from Moorhead, Minn. David remembers their second morning at the cabin.

"It was difficult for me to sleep so I got up and I was leaving the cabin to go for a walk. Dick Kvamme was up as well and we walked together. I remember we stopped under a huge tree to talk about Africa. Dick was interested in what Eunie and I and the rest of the missionaries were doing in Tanzania. We talked about that, and what we thought lay ahead and what were the biggest problems. The talk got around to schooling. Then Dick asked how he could help us."

Simonson gave the businessman a long and thoughtful look. He said, "There's a way."

He told Dick Kvamme about his conversation with Eliafoo Solomon. It's not just a vision, Simonson said. It can be done. What we need now is some form for the fund-raising, some structure and getting it before the public.

A few days later they were in Kvamme's construction company office in Moorhead. Dick Hefte, a Fergus Falls lawyer and friend of Simonson's, was there with them. Kvamme's secretary took the minutes. It was a beginning. Eventually they incorporated as a nonprofit with a board and skeleton staff. Hefte drew the papers. But that came a year later. First they needed some public exposure. Kvamme volunteered first his car and then his plane. They hit their business cronies, fund-raising boards and adult forums at church. Simonson hit the pulpits.

Almost nobody sells the needs of Africans the way Simonson sells them. His listeners needed a picture: An African village with its dirt and shanties and grass huts. Smoke in those huts. Kids trying to study. A teacher holding a class on some old floorboard from an abandoned shanty, the equatorial sun bearing down.

It wouldn't take much to give those kids a school, the preacher tells the congregation. They weren't asking for a school like the ones with beautiful red brick and roomy corridors and lockers on the wall like the schools in America. All they wanted or needed were walls, a roof, a floor and a blackboard.

The bearded preacher in the pulpit wasn't selling snake oil. He was selling truth. His voice rolled through the audience, and not many in it moved. The faces of the Africa he was describing were almost physically present in the church. The preacher was believable because his life and those of his loved ones were invested in those scenes in the African villages, committed to giving hope to the people who filled those pictures.

The first big donation came from a freedom-from-hunger-walk in Madison, Wis. The money was forwarded to the Tanzanian community development agency. "Eight schools," Simonson said. "I think we can raise enough to build eight schools." The fledgling organization formed its first board of directors. Kvamme and Hefte were on it, along with E.F. Johnson of Waseca, Minn., Dickran Sarkisian of New York, Paul Kovacs of New York, Ann Wright of Washington, D.C., G.T. Scheldahl of Northfield, Minn., and Earl Madson of Mankato, Minn., who was succeeded by his wife, Lenore, after his death.

It has to be noted that not all of these folks were from the Minnesota and Dakota prairies. Simonson's reach by then—through his speaking tours and his clans of admirers, through his business friends who had their own business friends—ran from coast to coast. Bootstrap never was a local or regional organization. It worked to attract friends with large pockets and big hearts. The corporate community service offices never gave Bootstrap much comfort or cash. If they're going to give away some of the company's cash, most corporate executives like to be able to show the stockholders and directors the results of their generosity. Not many of those stockholders were going to take field trips to Engaruka in the middle of the African Rift to see a one-room school built with mud brick and bare concrete floor.

While it had a national venue, Bootstrap by and large was underwritten over the years by hundreds of church congregations, clubs, by church agencies for a long period and by fund-raising organizations concentrated in Minnesota and the Midwest. It did function as most non-profits are supposed to function, with budget and a board, with a field director (one more hat for the reverend) and with an administrative director and a national office in Minneapolis. But not a whole lot happened in Bootstrap's operation that didn't bear the personal prints and warm-breath-from-Maasailand of J. David Simonson. The book-keeping wasn't always tidy. Simonson sometimes functioned like the oldtime newspaper columnist who carried tomorrow's column in his hip pocket on the back of an envelope. Simonson's major was theology, not accounting. But those original eight schools began to multiply. So did Bootstrap's mission, which spread from raising money for schools to a multiplicity of other African needs. The architecture of some of the buildings it was funding—apart from the schools—had to meet the peculiarities of East Africa climate and soil. Building designers don't usually have to worry about protecting the foundation from termites. They do in Tanzania. Those and other fascinating elements in building construction in East Africa were presented to Bootstrap by a Dane named Poul Bertelsen. He was a young architect who answered an ad placed by the Danish Missionary Society, which needed an architect. In time Bertelsen became a missionary-architect, and in time he and David Simonson made connections, and Bootstrap contracted with Bertelsen's MSAADA (a Swahili word meaning "assistance").

Bertelsen was a resourceful free-lancer with a missionary urge that fit in with the cast of mission individualists who'd by then dappled the landscape in Tanzania. He specialized in designing handsome but relatively inexpensive churches, hospital and mission schools. He explained some of the guideposts of building in East Africa: "In Africa, you can't depend on air conditioning. So you design the buildings to take advantage of the prevailing winds. That gives you natural air conditioning." In time, Bertelsen's business, although closely tied with Lutheran enterprise in Africa, went ecumenical. "There was a Roman Catholic hospital in Tanzania that needed a new building but couldn't afford to go the conventional route," he said. "They had no solutions so they just started praying. Then I showed up. I never looked on myself as the answer to a prayer, but I gather they did." Eventually Bertelsen moved MSAADA's headquarters from Africa to Wayzata in suburban Minneapolis, a place not famous for savannahs and herds of wildebeest. But it made sense to the practical Dane. "I knew there were many Lutheran missionaries in Tanzania with Minnesota connections. It seemed like a logical place to locate."

As a result, a comfy synergy developed between MSAADA and the Lutheran mission movement, which means most of the recent Lutheran church construction in Tanzania is probably going to be free of termites and suffocating breezes. It's further likely that Martin Luther would have approved of practical Danes.

Bootstrap's early administrative director in Minneapolis, Art Dale, created much of the early foundation for the organization, especially in its appeals to the public. One of the most dramatic schemes was to organize a service with cooperating churches, in which members of the congregation—on their hands and knees at the front of the sanctuary—would make mud bricks using sand and gravel mixed with water, the same materials the African workmen use to build the village schools. It was an exercise in *ujamaa,* or "familyhood," in which neighbors unite to build the community. Art Dale's successor, Ernie Holman, made additional contributions to the expansion of Bootstrap, together with a board that changed and expanded over the years. But it wasn't until the early 1980s, with the installation of Deana Miller as the executive director, that the administration of Bootstrap stabilized in Minneapolis. Deana Miller revealed herself as one of those office fireballs with inexhaustible energy and traits rare in most office fireballs—a strong sense of direction, a sort of benign competence and an ability to adapt (and sometimes to humor) the strong wills of her board members and especially the restless field director. She was a former church secretary who did volunteer clerical work for Bootstrap and its architectural partner, MSAADA, for several years. When Holman left, the directors decided that Deana would probably be a good fit to run the show day to day in the Minneapolis office. Another thing they liked was her salary, $16,000 a year, compared with the combined $60,000 they'd been paying their directors in salary and car allowances and other amenities of the position. They thought a good interim title for Deana would be associate director, meaning they wouldn't have to give her director's pay. Because she found the job stimulating and because she immediately grabbed onto it and ran with it, practically always under control, she accepted. The bulk of the job was supervising and initiating fund raising, for which her best resource was always Simonson's resonant pitches in the pulpit or on a potential rich angel's putting green. The beauty of Simonson's appeals was that the potential donors, whether congregations or millionaires, didn't hear or see them as slick recitals from an experienced hustler. He **was** an experienced hustler. But what they heard from him they saw confirmed in his eyes and the ardor of his voice. This guy believed. There was no showmanship about that. The people whose needs he was advocating were people whose lives mattered to him. His listeners gave for the best of all reasons. They understood the need, and they were willing to serve.

To a gathering of Bootstrap donors one year, he explained the bonding that takes place at this moment, when this act of pure service is performed, linking the lives of the giver and the receivers. He explained it in terms the Maasai might best understand. He talked of the closeness with the earth he and his friends felt in one of their walks in the African Rift to raise money for the schoolrooms. The cause of those days of trudging, he said, had brought them closer to the Africans, closer to the earth of Africa itself, its history, suffering and its beauty.

"For many of us," he said, "for the first time this was the moment when *oneness* takes on a beauty of its own. You traverse a country covered with every variety of plant life imaginable, not only involved with its own survival but at the same time seeming to offer itself for the well being of other life, including ours. The thorn tree and its ability to protect itself and other plants, birds, animals and humans; the aloe with its juice that can be used to heal; the cyclod, offering us a traceable continuity to the past; and the desert rose blooming profusely where no other vegetation can be seen. The desert rose gives us hope. By giving of ourselves and by giving some of what we have, we give hope to those who desperately need it. We are together, and the sight of that desert rose where nothing else grows seems to anoint that whole idea."

With this appealing metaphor, Dave Simonson seemed to have defined not only his ministry but that of his colleagues, most of whom pursued their mission with less visibility than he did. With some of those he quarreled about the direction of mission. His buildup of Bootstrap, with the relentless fund-raising it demanded and its departure from the conventional channels of mission fund-raising, produced private complaints among some of his associates, and in some cases direct complaints to the church authorities. Were missionaries supposed to be missionaries or building contractors and empire builders? Simonson responded to those complaints without a huge amount of gentility.

"There were those who thought I had quit my mission work and gone to building schools," he said. "Well, while they were golfing and playing horseshoes in their time away from pastoral work, I was building schools. So what's the difference? It got so bad that a mission director back in the states sent one of his officials to talk to the leadership of the Lutheran Church in Tanzania about whether I was doing my job as a missionary. They talked with Bishop Laiser (Thomas Laiser, the bishop of the Arusha diocese and a onetime student of Simonson's). Laiser acknowledged his connection with Simonson. He said, "Well, we know he's doing church work equal to or better than other missionaries who are not doing the extras that Simonson is. So what he's doing with his time outside of church work is pretty much his own business, and from what we see, we appreciate it."

Among the Lutheran mission overseers, was there any serious objection with Simonson's distribution of time and energy in Tanzania?

The Rev. Bo Sorenson of Minnesota was the director for the Division for World Mission and Interchurch Cooperation of the American Lutheran Church (ALC) during part of Simonson's ministry. He'd received reports about what Simonson's critics saw as his cavalier attitude toward accountability for his time and work, whether on the athletic field or arm-twisting for school money or cajoling a merchant in Arusha to donate brick. To them it seemed that Simonson fundamentally answered to God and to himself, a rather limited form of accountability. It may have been a fairly accurate assessment. When required, though, he also answered to the church overseers and his answers were generally satisfactory. "In the end," Bo Sorenson said, "it got to be pretty obvious that although David was unorthodox in how he pursued his mission, he was a powerful worker in behalf of the people he served."

In evaluating Simonson's ministry, Sorenson was saying, it finally came down to what he and his friends and all those contributors achieved, and that was pretty monumental. But they did grapple, Sorenson and Simonson.

"He and some of the others in Africa were bothered by guidelines we thought we had to set to protect the overall mission program and to keep ourselves focused. I suppose you have to know Lutheran church people to know we fought over one particular phrase in those guidelines, and this was that the mission work should be "essentially evangelistic."

The question the dissenters raised was, "What does 'essentially' mean?" All right, they said, doing mission work in Africa meant trying to bring people to Christ, among other things, conversion, the prime and historic role of mission. But how about today? What is mission today? Isn't social ministry—improving lives, feeding, educating, building where and how you can—as important as conversion? Don't you do the work of God by doing the work of humanity?

There was no way that the Bo Sorensons, veterans of years of mission work themselves, were going to argue against that proposition. What they were trying to do with the guidelines was to assert the *continuing* importance of evangelism. Eventually the "essential" part of the guidelines was modified to the apparent satisfaction of most of the contending parties, and Lutheranism forged ahead with its usual wary handshakes among the combatants.

"The squabbling over whether that word ought to be narrowly or broadly defined," Jim Knutson said, "got down to the historic description of a Lutheran discussion: Ask two Lutherans a question and you get three opinions."

Just three?

Knutson, like Sorenson is retired from ministry now and a veteran of mission supervision. In retrospect, he said, he could see why Simonson's concept of missionary work made sense to the Maasai. Knutson drew a circle. In the center he put the name of Jesus. From that center he drew lines radiating to the rim of the circle. "In Western thought," Knutson said, "we're prone to create priorities. What is the most important, what leads all the rest? Decide what that is and pile most of your energy and money into it. But the thinking of most tribal people is circular. Each radius from that center is equal. For and from Jesus comes worship, schools, health, making the village better, making the individual better. You can't separate them. All are part of the work radiating from Jesus."

Simonson could have carried that circle around in his pocket, because it perfectly characterized his personal mission.

And Bootstrap broadened. In Minneapolis, Deana's interim three years ended, and she acquired the title of director with the deserved salary increase. During those three years the gap widened dramatically between the organization's expenses (considerably lower) and organizational income (higher). At the height of the school building the budget had been raised to nearly $350,000. The expanded goal, 100 new schools a year at a price of approximately $3,000 in donations for each, was never quite reached, partly because there were competing needs.

"We tried to install a school-funding program in Madagascar," Deana Miller said. "It didn't work. Art Dale found that out after a lot of hard work to get it started. The village elders there knew what we'd been doing in Tanzania and they wanted us to do the same thing in Madagascar. But we just didn't find much interest among the local people to build the schools as they had in Tanzania and Gambia. There were power struggles over how to use the money and who controlled it. In one place the mayor left office and wouldn't give the key to the supply shed to his successor. But there were teachers there who were getting no money at all from the government, so we set aside part of the donations we received to pay the school teachers.

"In Zimbabwe rural villages had been destroyed in the long civil war. They wanted to rebuild the school system and asked us in as a partner. The best we could do, through a contract arranged by Ernie Holman, was to provide financial assistance to young adults trying to complete their educations. Later, our board decided we should have a stronger emphasis on educating young women and mothers, so we made progress that way."

School building continues today as part of the Bootstrap charter. But, moving with Simonson's shifting initiatives ("when you see a need, respond to it") increasing amounts of the money it raises now go to the Selian medical clinic near Arusha and for scholarships at the secondary school for Maasai young women in Monduli. The fund-raising itself had to diversify. From development walks and random contributions from individuals and churches, it has graduated to a full-court press on church congregations and service clubs. Money once available to Simonson from the big national church agencies has shrunk, amidst Simonson's audible grumblings. Service clubs like Rotary have bylaws that prevent direct financial contributions to church-related enterprises, but there is no prohibition against the donation of equipment, up to and including steam rollers, piping, hardware, machines and a hundred other needed materials.

And the flow of that equipment comes from all over America.

Why and how? "We do a lot of promotional work out of our office, of course," Deana Miller said, "and God bless those thousands who have given and are giving. For many of those churchgoers, missionaries seemed like gods coming back to church to report on the mission work because it just seemed so worthy. And today here comes David Simonson, and anytime Dave Simonson comes into a room, people are going to turn around and notice him. There just aren't many people as striking in mission work. He has that presence. His beard is white now, which may add to the picture. When he speaks, he instantly arouses attention for what he's talking about. And what he's talking about is lifting the people in Africa. I got a call once from a newspaper woman in Denver. She said she had to meet Simonson at the airport and she wanted to know how to find him. I told her to stand in the concourse and look for the broadest, tallest guy in a white beard who sort of swaggers a little but looks more like he's heading for the nearest wall to walk through it. I told her to go up to that man because if he looks like a combination of Ernest Hemingway and John Wayne wearing a Crocodile Dundee hat, it has to be David Simonson.

"The reporter called the next day. She said she recognized Dave Simonson instantly in the concourse, and they had a sensational conversation."

Simonson had undergone an enduring exercise in humility in his banishment to Loliondo. By that time, though, Africans from the Serengeti to Kilimanjaro were convinced that this guy was endowed with powers not available to other preachers they had known. A body of mythology had grown up around him. One of the stories dealt with that leopard that stalked the road to Loliondo. A friend of Simonson told of hearing a Maasai boy telling a leopard story after being asked by his teacher if he knew Simonson. He told the class about how Simonson had been walking in the woods and met the leopard. "He grabbed the leopard," the boy said, "and he first took off his ears. Then he broke the leopard's legs and took him by the tail and spun him around his head and threw the leopard into the woods and he told everybody that it was just a cat, and what he did was nothing."

Maybe all Concordia fullbacks could do that. But that was the size of Simonson's image among some of the Africans by the 1980s, and those stories, of course, eventually reached the reverend. They were met with smiles of due modesty, a modesty Simonson admitted had to be reinforced one day at the dedication of one of the Bootstrap schools in the Usambara Mountains of Tanzania. Simonson was invited to take part in the ceremonies. The formula for the school building had been the same. Bootstrap money paid for the material. The hard labor of the kids' parents built the school. In that way, everyone's dignity was preserved. "We had this celebration of the school opening," Simonson said. "Nobody celebrates like Tanzanians. Afterwards, I was standing against the wall of the building with other elders, and a lad came up. I assumed that 'here comes this boy to thank us.' But he didn't. He ignored me, walked right past me and went to his father and said, 'Thanks, Dad.'"

Simonson thought about that scene on his way to the talk in Denver. "It taught me something pretty basic," he said. "All along, we wanted to be seen as sort of silent partners in these villages. And here it was. The boy thanking his father, not us, for his new school. We'd been a success. We'd preserved the dignity of these people."

And the contributions to Bootstrap from his talk later in the day netted more than $10,000.

It all reached back to Simonson's schemes when he was exiled beyond the Serengeti. One of those schemes had ultimately delivered $7 million to deepen the lives of thousands of men, women and children in East Africa. And from that furlough in America, the Simonsons now headed back to Loliondo, where Eunice was to find herself in a hospital setting that would have rattled her brain back at Fairview in Minneapolis.

CHAPTER 12

She stood beside a makeshift operating table in a back country hospital in northern Tanzania, the nurse and apprentice anesthesiologist, Eunice Simonson. In one hand she held the tubes of the anesthesia apparatus, in the other a textbook. She'd never performed the procedure in her medical career. She was terrified but under serviceable control. The patient, near death and about to lose consciousness, couldn't have been aware that anesthesiologists rarely bring textbooks to the operating table.

There was one other uncommon sight in the room. The operating surgeon was holding his own textbook.

The patient survived, as did the anesthesiologist and the doctor.

Back in the states and in Europe, there were very few volumes in the medical libraries to prepare the bush physician and nurse for that kind of crisis. If they were going to save lives in a place like northern Tanzania, they had to make an early discovery: The volumes that exist may not be as important as their ability to hold their jangled nerves together when the hour of panic comes.

And yet Eunice Simonson today would never surrender one hour of the years in Loliondo. They were supposed to be a punishment for her husband's alleged sins as an ecclesiastical rebel. She imagined weeks of uninterrupted isolation and loneliness. It was an anxiety she'd developed from missionary wives' tales in Arusha, something they'd heard.

But to both David and Eunice, four years in Loliondo became the maturing of their mission, sometimes their joint mission and their sometimes separate missions. He was a bringer of the gospel to native Africa, a builder and teacher. She was a healer and, in her fashion, missionary to the lonely, to the frightened mothers and to their children. Loliondo revealed an Africa that was daily adventure and daily suspense and yet, remarkably, a sociable Africa in a part of the continent condemned by the map as "nowhere." It was an Africa that tightened their family despite the hundreds of miles that separated the Simonson parents from their children—Steve, Naomi, Nathan and Becky— who were at school in central Tanzania for months at a time. Jonathan, 3 at the time his parents moved to Loliondo, lived with David and Eunice and assorted baby-sitters. The separation enriched the days the family was able to spend together. This was an Africa of the Serengeti Plain at its most maddening and hilarious in the winter rains, when they found themselves marooned and lost in mud in their vehicles, while the kids laughed and the preacher and the nurse tried to explain that it wasn't amusing, until they had to break out in giggles themselves.

How could Eunice have foreseen the Flying Doctors, the hospital at Wasso and the Catholic Sisters of The Precious Blood from Austria?

"That little house that we moved into," Eunice remembers, "it was a little out of kilter because Bill Jacobson, the young missionary who lived first there with his wife, gave those Better Home and Garden plans to an African builder who didn't read them very accurately. So the inside dimensions became the outside dimensions and vice versa, and it was amazing that the house was still standing with its rock walls when we got there. And yet we got to love the place. Stan and Marie Benson followed the Jacobsons in the house and fixed it up a little more, and we did the same. You had to watch your step because the house was built on a steep hill and getting out of the place in the Land Rover was an engineering feat. We used kerosene for light and nothing special for heat and for water we depended on a cistern to hold the rainwater. If all that sounds pretty ugly, it wasn't. We found out early that Loliondo was a place where missionary families from Arusha and Moshi would come up for a few days to vacation, of all things. It wasn't exactly your classic Norwegian place-up-north, but it was a change, and it was adventure. So we'd often have the house full of people and we'd have picnics together and mingle with the African folks. When the rainy season came, we'd exchange Serengeti Mud stories. Washouts and ravines and uncharted miles of muck. All of that. It would actually graduate into gamesmanship. Our days in the mud had to be the worst, we said. No, they weren't, somebody insists, and now we'd get a 20-minute monologue describing the deepest ocean of mud in creation, mud that could devour machines, mud so bad and so wide that it had to be a sequel to the Flood of Noah."

When missionaries get together, where else but in the Bible are they going to find horror stories to end all horror stories?

Eunice had met the Catholic sisters early when she volunteered to work in the Catholic-operated hospital in the village of Wasso not far from Loliondo. It was managed by a physician priest from Austria named Dr. Waschinger, with whom Eunice Simonson would work hundreds of hours in the months to come. She found the hospital sisters sweet but instinctively distant in their first meetings. Eunice had to deal with a mild awkwardness of her own. How does a Lutheran nurse from Minnesota achieve a comfort level socially with these nice but reserved nuns from Austria. "In today's world," she said, "I don't think there would be much hesitance at all. People of different faiths approach each other a lot easier today. But they were a little restricted in what they could say, I think, especially with unsaved folks like Lutherans. They were very polite. And then one day we suddenly became closer, and it was a personal grief in my life that made it possible. Mail always got to us months late. And then it came in bunches. Telegrams also came in piles and I was always wary about opening those telegrams, because the news we got in them was often bad. One of the first I read after we'd been there for two weeks came from my family. It said: "Mother has had a stroke and is very seriously ill. Can you come home?"

With mounting fear she read the next telegram. Her mother had a second stroke. Could she come? And the third. No word from you. Mother died last night. We don't know what to do about the funeral. Will you be coming?

She had never experienced the helplessness and grief she felt at that moment, reading telegrams in the middle of Africa that tersely carried her in one awful stage after another toward the news of her mother's death thousands of miles away. And the final telegram: Still no word from Africa. We had the funeral.

To her grief she now added guilt. Unreasonable guilt, yes. There was no way for her to have known of her mother's stroke earlier than this. If she had known, she could not have left Africa. No money was available for the flight. The accumulating weight of the news, the rising dread she'd felt with each succeeding telegram, the hard and almost judgmental question at the end of each—will you be coming?—and finally the realization that her mother was gone put her in depression.

Her belief pulled her out of it. She truly believed that she and her husband were in Africa as the will of God. Events would happen in their lives that would leave them isolated from the lives of those they loved in their old world. She and Dave had talked about it. Mission had become the most important fact of their lives and inevitably it would widen the distance between those two worlds. Being thousands of miles from her mother at the time of her mother's death could not lessen the closeness she felt with her at this moment, the gratitude for the years they'd lived together and for her mother's counsel and love.

"In God's wisdom," she told Dave, "he knew I could not be at mother's side, so although her death was so hard to accept, I was spared all the work and anxiety it would have taken trying to get home, which was impossible."

A few days later she received a visit from three of the Catholic sisters, Amadea, Anna and Guida. "They said they came to express their sympathy," Eunice said, "and that they had offered masses for my mother. I was touched in a profound way, because we didn't know each other well, and they were extending their arms in this way. But I also had to chuckle to myself realizing how mother would have gotten a kick out of that, a sturdy Lutheran like her being the recipient of masses dedicated by these Catholic sisters in the middle of Africa. We talked of my mother. I told how painful her death was for me, but that I'd remember her as a saintly woman and I rejoiced that she was with the Lord and I would see her some day. And to this Sister Amadea's face brightened and she said, "Oh, then she was a Catholic."

Not quite, Eunice said, but she was a Christian and a believer, a condition that seemed to resolve all questions, and the visit ended warmly. They became friends, the Lutheran nurse and the Catholic sisters, and their paths connected constantly in the four years in which Eunice worked as a nurse at the Catholic hospital. When the Simonsons left Loliondo four years later, Sister Amadea embraced Eunice and said quietly, "I'm going to ask our Father to put you next to me in heaven."

Her healing, though, was hardly confined to the hospital. She made home visits. She saw sick people in their huts. And some days she went miles and made discoveries about tribal medicine that amazed her. One of them came in the middle of a day when visitors had come to their quirky little house and were pummeling them with questions about life on the edge of the Serengeti. In the midst of this, a young Maasai warrior came to the door frantic for help. With one of her guests, Eunice headed across the plains in the Land Rover, getting directions from the warrior. He couldn't explain what the emergency was but there was no doubt about his distress. There was also no doubt about the terrain they were riding through. It had no roads and no hint of any roads to come. It had dips and holes and unpredictable ridges, and the Land Rover nearly overturned several times before they reached an older man bending over a herdsboy. They learned later that the boy had driven his spear into the ground at a place where he and his companion were going to rest. The point of the spear struck a rock. The spear spun and shot straight up, striking the boy in the head with its tip, cutting an artery.

Eunice examined the first aid the older man had performed. Using grass, he'd made a compress the size of a quarter and then pulled a safety pin out of his ear and caught the two ends of the artery and pulled them together. He then applied the compress where he'd tried to join the arteries. After this he tore a strip of clothing from his *shuka* robe and bandaged the wound.

There are no Red Cross manuals in the Maasai bomas for this kind of life-preserving treatment. It comes from the survival savvy of generations of people for whom there were no hospitals and whose lives were never far from hazard. When Eunice arrived the bleeding had subsided although the boy was nearly unconscious. They drove back to the hospital at Wasso, where Eunice grabbed all of the instruments that would be needed to suture the artery. They did the requisite patching at the hospital and, incredibly to Eunice, the boy lived and appeared to suffer no brain damage.

In time she became a scrub nurse at the hospital, often working with the teams of Flying Doctors. They were surgeons and physicians available for emergency calls from the back country. They also made periodic visits to hospitals like the one at Loliondo to handle patients who needed specialized surgery or treatment. Often they would bring their own specialized nurse with them. The hospital management asked Eunice if she were willing to broaden her skills to include anesthesiology, which would allow the hospital to treat cases that otherwise would have to go on hold to await the Flying Doctors.

Of all the facets of medical work, Eunice looked on administering anesthesia as the scariest. She would do anything but that, she told some of her friends. But if you're working at a hospital in Wasso on the far side of the Gol Mountains, and the hospital asks you to learn about anesthesiology, you learn about anesthesiology.

"I went to Nairobi," she said. "I spent two weeks with an anesthesiologist at a Nairobi hospital learning the use of an ether oxygen machine. He gave me some training with their more complex machines, but he also made sure I knew about the simpler ether machines that I probably would be using. I'll have to admit that the more I learned the more frightened I became. It's such an awesome responsibility to have a person's life basically in your hands. The hardest part for me was doing the first step where you'd have to manipulate the breathing tube in the patient's mouth and throat. After two weeks in Nairobi I told my instructor I thought I was ready to do the work. He took me to a hospital unit where a lot of orthopedic surgery was being done. There'd been a major polio epidemic in that part of Africa in the late 1950s, leaving many people with shriveled and useless legs. They had a process in the hospital for replacing useless legs with artificial limbs. My first patient was a young man with two withered legs that were to be removed so that he could be fitted later for the prosthesis. He was a pleasant fellow but anxious, of course. I explained to him what I would be doing and what the effects would be. All went well and I got him into the proper sleep, but I don't mind tell you I was frightened by the whole thing. It was still going well when the doctors began to work with their big saws, and that was all overwhelming. I kept my face close to the young man's to be sure he was getting the right amount of ether. And now I was inhaling ether as well as the smell of the bones being amputated, and there was all of the exposed flesh from that, and while I was a relatively experienced nurse by then, I nearly passed out, the closest I've ever come to do that in a hospital. I think the big reason was that suddenly there was all this responsibility, and I was a novice doing it, and the whole scene came together into something that turned me inside out. But I got through it, and I must have done the job well because I received high recommendations when I returned to Loliondo and Wasso. But it was still hardly second nature, doing the anesthesiology. Dr. Waschinger, the hospital's priest-physician, came to my door not long after I got back from Kenya and said, 'Eunice, we've got to do surgery. I've got this young warrior with an acute appendix and he won't live if we don't get it out. Please come and do the anesthesia.'

"We had a generator that produced enough electricity to give us light in the operating room. I noticed that Dr. Waschinger had all of his medical books laid out. He said he'd never done surgery alone except in medical school. And this was my first attempt at anesthesia on my own without any backup whatsoever. So the doctor and I had no professional secrets. We knew both of us were walking into new terrain, and the knowledge that we were in it together might have strengthened us. The warrior was in severe pain and we had to begin right now. I got out some of my books and did a quick review, and then we went to work. I'd just gotten the patient asleep, and we both went to poring over our books and it developed that we had a special case on our hands. Dr. Waschinger got the abdomen open and located the appendix, about six inches long, highly inflamed and twisted up. It developed into a long and tedious piece of surgery. We didn't have much help, only one sister in the room with us. They put a sterilized glove on me and I tried to assist the doctor with that hand, holding the oxygen and the ether mask in the other. It took us four hours. It may have been one of the longest appendectomies in history. With the amount of ether I gave that young man, he didn't wake up for three days. But he emerged from it relatively fresh. I don't think the same could be said about the nurse and the doctor."

Almost nothing that happened in that hospital was routine and it was probably inevitable that the resident preacher at Loliondo would find himself as one of the players in the continuing drama of medicine in Maasailand. Waschinger operated one day on an elderly Maasai who'd developed a huge cyst in the region of the liver. With Eunice at his side he removed the cyst, but the patient began hemorrhaging and was getting weaker by the minute, his blood pressure plummeting. He was going to die unless—unless what? Unless something unforeseen intervened. The arrival of J. David Simonson was, of course, totally unforeseen. Between chores he got inquisitive about what was going on in the hospital and walked in at just about the time old Maasai was going under.

"Grab him," Eunice Simonson told the doctor as the preacher came in view. "He's Type O."

With the briefest explanation they instructed Simonson to lay down beside the Maasai. In minutes they were pumping his blood directly into the fading patient. They weren't quite sure how much blood they drained from the surprised but willing donor. It was enough to put him in la-la land for a few minutes. But the patient survived and for days after leaving the hospital he would walk up to his Maasai pals, hold up his arms triumphantly and say, "I have the blood of the pastor in me."

Those were landmark days for the back country nurse, wife and mother in a time full of landmarks. One of those landmarks was a decaying old shed in the middle of the Serengeti Plain. By then, the family had spread out. Jonathan, the youngest, and Becky were attending the boarding school for youngsters at

Kiomboi. Stephen, Naomi and Nathan were off to high school in Kenya, where the chances for a versatile secondary education were better than in Tanzania. The big events for the Simonsons were the holidays when the whole troop could assemble in Loliondo. And the most exalted of these holidays, of course, was Christmas.

It was a time of the year that coincided with the rains of East Africa.

The plan was for David to drive the high schoolers to Loliondo a few days in advance of Jonathan and Becky's arrival in Arusha from Kiomboi, school having let out in Kenya earlier than in Kiomboi. To pick up the younger children, Eunice drove to Arusha with Andy Clark, an American veterinarian living in Loliondo, where he worked with the native Africans to protect their animals. Andy was droll and likable. He was also a little different, a man popping with ideas and innovation. One of his projects was to rebuild a Land Rover he'd acquired. Putting windows in the Rover must have been a later priority, because there were none on their drive to and from Arusha. It's rusted roof hatches had been removed, giving it the appearance of a junk yard convertible. In this battered carriage Eunice and Andy rode across the plains the more than 200 miles to Arusha, met Jonathan and Becky, and piled Christmas presents and foodstuffs in all remaining crannies of the Land Rover. The journey went well for a couple hours until they reached the loneliest spread of the Serengeti, where the torrents struck from above. Within an hour the Serengeti had reverted to its most ancient heritage, when it was the ocean floor. Water stretched for miles in all directions. It splashed through the open windows and hatches of the seagoing Land Rover. The kids were delighted with this unexpected adventure, but the Christmas parcels and food were getting soaked. Darkness settled while they were still hours from Loliondo. The crude road on which they were riding got to be invisible. The road was still presumably there, but the headlights weren't confirming it.

Andy decided on some seat-of-the-pants directional finding. He might have been wearing the wrong pants. They made a wrong turn. The Rover dived into a large hole and got stuck. The adults got out to make an estimate of the situation with their flashlights. Not far from the hole they could see bushes and small trees and scattered rocks, which they gathered to put under the Rover's tires to prevent any further slippage. By now it had stopped raining. The decision was to try to push the Rover back out of the hole, an operation that required them to unload all of the cargo. They unloaded and pushed. The Rover was stubborn. They pushed some more and then became conscious of other creatures on the scene. The clues to this were bright eyes shining among the bushes and in the high grass, moving and circling.

The presents might have been safe, but the food wasn't and if the food wasn't safe, the Rover's occupants were probably in no better shape. They quickly reloaded the Rover and packed themselves in for the night, not exactly sheltered from the lions and hyenas that clearly were out there. The kids seemed unfrightened. They kept up a steady chatter during the night and found the interlude, which was spiced by Andy's stories, more entertaining than threatening. The adults picked up the cue. Andy told more stories and sang songs. The others joined. The night passed. In the morning light they saw the remnants of an old shed that had served as a bus station. In it they found some wire mesh and chunks of concrete, useful for traction in extricating a mired Land Rover. They got the process started by backing the Rover out of the hole. But there was a half mile more to engineer, muck so deep it needed shuttles of concrete chucks and mesh to keep the Rover inching toward drier ground. Eventually they located terrain firm enough for the Rover to get out of they swamp, but there was more bad stuff ahead and they were elated to come across another Land Rover with more automotive juice. They roped up and rolled into Loliondo, leaving a trail of spilled carrots halfway across the Serengeti.

It gave Eunice the championship of the mud-I-have-known horror stories in the next parlor session of gamesmanship in Loliondo. That lasted for two days, when somebody came up with saga more hideous.

Dave Simonson, in the meantime, was finding his deportation to Maasailand increasing stimulating and fruitful. He built congregations and chapels. He made conversions, found feed and water and salt for the Maasai cattle and became a familiar figure in his walking ministry that took him up and down the highland trails. He was free to work independently. Independence did have a down side. It meant no budget from the Tanzanian church, among other things. Running a bankrupt, private little ministry didn't intimidate Simonson for long. There was no rule in the Lutheran guidelines, nothing nailed on a door in Germany, to prevent a Lutheran minister from raising cash from Indian Sikhs.

Simonson's roster of friends and advisors from his Arusha days crossed all ethnic lines. On the streets of Arusha, he was a social free-lancer. There was the Romanian Fainzilber who operated brick factories and dealt automobiles; a Polish butcher who shared with the American preacher the street smarts he needed to work the tricky alleys of the Arusha market place. He also, incidentally, made delicious sausage, the identity of the meat usually being in doubt. There were also the Sikhs. So when he encountered a small colony of Sikhs in Loliondo, it was a kind of reunion. "They were friends of mine," Simonson said. "They were merchants. What else are they going to be doing in Loliondo? I don't know all the businesses they were in, but it didn't matter. I do know they trucked in maize and other produce and they also sold salt to the Maasai for their cattle and they sold some goods from Loliondo in the markets at Arusha. They ran a couple of shops in Loliondo, way out there on the Massai plains, and they made money doing it, which the economists will probably tell you can't be done. But every Sikh I've met is a born economist with his own rules about what the market will bear, and I've never seen one of the Sikh merchants in the welfare line. We got to like each other and trust each other. One other thing, we looked like each other with those black beards. The only difference, I told them, was I left my turban back in the states."

The Sikhs found Simonson an agreeable character whose friendship—as an American Christian minister popular with the local Maasai—might have been an enhancement for the Sikhs' enterprises. But the relationship wasn't that calculated. They just hit it off comfortably, and the added bonus for David was that the Sikhs usually had available cash. With none of his own from the church to build his ministry, Simonson borrowed from the Sikhs. There weren't any contracts. Simonson said he'd pay them back after Christmas, when he'd receive contributions from American congregations who took Christmas offerings for mission work. He (and the American congregations) always repaid the loans.

An unconventional ministry? Sure. But the ministry grew. Simonson taught and, when the Maasai said they were ready, he baptized. He went into the bomas to join the Maasai in drinking their sour milk and whatever came with it. One day young Nathan and Stephen came with him. They sat in the smoky hut in which a Maasai elder produced a gourd and passed it around to the other Maasai and their guests. Simonson wasn't sure about the ingredients in the gourd. Sour milk and what else? Maybe cow's urine. Maybe cow's blood. Maybe both. Simonson sipped from the gourd and passed it to his wide-eyed sons. Most of the contents were gone. The reverend leaned over to his sons and said privately, "I don't care how you do it, but when you pass that gourd back to the Maasai, it better be empty."

The gourd was returned to the Maasai, drained. Nathan and Stephen have always kept their own counsel about how they did it, but they still gulp when they remember the episode.

The esteem in which the preacher was held by the Maasai obviously flowed from deeper wells than his designation as a Maasai elder. They were captivated by the sight of the preacher walking down a trail carrying a shotgun in his arm and a Bible in his jacket. Simonson didn't slight the value of either one in his solitary hikes between the family cottage and the nearby settlements. There was that leopard story, the one that actually happened. Simonson had encountered the leopard not long after he got to Loliondo. He was walking the path south from Loliondo to a church in the Sonjo country, a track that begins at more than 7,000 feet above sea level and winds down through the forest to 4,000 feet. "On that trail you often meet leopard and buffalo," he remembered. "As I was walking down I saw the leopard coming up. I snapped the gun to get a shell in the chamber. He heard that and went off into the woods. If it had been a lion, he would have kept coming. Leopards will run off the track and then get back on once you're gone. The rest of the way to the village church, I walked backwards all the way. You'd be surprised sometimes what good time you can make walking backwards."

He may have been the first reverend to get to church on time, rear end first, hauling a shotgun.

There were days and weeks in Loliondo when the separate callings of husband and wife—David's in mission and Eunice's in nursing—came together in work and service that gave their mutual commitment, in fact their marriage, a special kind of testament. The village of Sonjo was the largest settlement of the Sonjo people living in the Rift south of Loliondo. The medical facilities there were nil. Infants were dying from disease for which they had no immunization. They were dying from diarrhea and lung disease. The villagers asked for help. Simonson enlisted the support of the church, and the hospital at Wasso joined. The Flying Doctors—the American, European and other physicians who piloted light planes—were asked to bring their resources into the project.

A small clinic and an airstrip were built, Simonson supervising some of the work when he could. The year before the clinic and airstrip opened, all but five of 35 children born in Sonjo died. "We flew in whenever one of the doctors came to Loliondo," Eunice said. "The doctor would diagnose and do whatever treatment was available, and I'd administer the medicines and the immunization. The airstrip wasn't exactly built for jets. It was carved out of the Rift floor. The big line of cliffs that walled in the Rift wasn't very far away. When we'd take off we had to head straight for the escarpment. The doctor got the nose of the plane up in a hurry and we were right on the edge of stalling out a couple of times. Other times we'd get into one of those thermal currents rising out of the Rift floor and just float above the cliffs."

It was medicine in the middle of Africa. But Sonjo was a landmark for Eunice and her husband in the lifesaving service that could be given to once-neglected people by uniting ingenuity with the concept of a motivated team. The year after the clinic and airstrip were built, approximately 30 children were born in Sonjo. All but five survived.

The Maasai had heard some of the Simonson stories, of course. It was his willingness to go the extra miles for them, reflected in dozens of spontaneous acts, that left the most powerful impression on the Maasai. He came to preach one day in the village of Kitumbeine in the African Rift near the big alkaline lake, Natron, which the Maasai used as a source of salt. In that particular year the lake had shrunk. The Maasai cattle around Kitumbeine were dying for lack of salt. Simonson talked about Jesus Christ for a while and then got into his Land Rover to drive to Arusha. He returned the next day with great blocks of salt. The accounting for that transaction appears in no existing ledgers.

"I knew people in Arusha who were in a position to give us salt," he said. "We made an agreement. I got the salt."

How? The little congregation in southwestern Minnesota may not have considered the salt market in Arusha a very dramatic destination for the Christmas offering. But it's probably what happened.

Not quite as clear to Eunice Simonson was what happened to her in the Maasai hut near Loliondo the day of one of the Maasai's big feasts.

Throughout her stewardship in Africa, Eunice Simonson believed as intensely as her husband that inexplicable events in their lives represented the will of God. It was a belief that might not have impressed people of less tepid faith. But that unflinching conviction identifies a person of faith, and with this person there is no arguing or serious demanding of evidence. But Eunice had seen enough of life to avoid the traps of guilelessness. People of any culture, she knew, are capable of skullduggery or abuse of trust. She remembers being invited to attend the circumcision ceremony of a daughter of one of the Maasai elders near Loliondo, an old chief named Olromi, who spent most of his time at his boma and was very wealthy with a horde of wives and children. The old chief had become a great friend of Simonson and had given him a bracelet that would normally have been handed down to his favorite son. So it was not surprising that Eunice should be invited to the circumcision ceremony, which had graduated into a full-scale celebration because of the chief's status in the tribe. Most of the big Maasai circumcision parties were fueled by alcohol. The missionaries walked careful steps in trying to deal with that phenomenon. Nobody who preaches the principles of Jesus Christ is going to feel comfortable in the midst of a drunken blowout. But the moment they were tempted to get judgmental about it, they were going to remember those lovely church weddings in the states, the ones that ended up in a drunken blowout. Eunice was not permitted to witness the circumcision ceremony, a blessing considering the pain that accompanied it.

"But one of the older women came up to me and asked if I'd like to see the circumcision hut. I wasn't very enthusiastic about it but I thought it was the courteous thing to go with her. It was a pretty large house that had been built especially for the occasion. It was very dark inside and I was quickly disoriented. I felt people reaching out and leading me further and further into the smoke in the hut. The people in it had been drinking and were sounding festive and greeting me and I was trying to respond as politely as I could, but I couldn't see anybody and soon it turned strange. There were hands all over me, on my arms, going up under my blouse, under my skirt. The hands were feeling, feeling. I started to panic, realizing I was in a circumcision hut and all kinds of things were going through my mind. For the first time in my years in Africa, I was afraid of these people, afraid of the ones in the hut. I felt ashamed for that, but I was terribly afraid. I wanted to get out of there, but I didn't know how to find my way out. And suddenly I heard this wonderfully gentle voice of a man asking in perfect English, 'Are you afraid?'

"I said, 'Yes, I am. Would you lead me out of here?' He said, 'Yes, please, give me your hand.' He had a warm and wonderful big hand that led me out of the hut, through all those reaching hands and drunken voices. As we neared the doorway, I tried to adjust my eyes to the brightness and I turned to thank him. But I was alone. He wasn't there.

"I can't explain this. I'll never know whether this was an actual person, or an angel taking me to safety."

When you believe, and when you believe you have been called to do the work of God, either explanation makes sense.

But that was an isolated interlude for Eunice Simonson in her life with the Africans, and she realized it was lubricated by alcohol, and it did not alter the affection she held for the people she had come to live with and to serve. Nor did those sieges of mud in the Serengeti dim for the Simonson family the hours of familial intimacy they later treasured in recounting Loliondo and the other drives from Arusha through the Serengeti. The kids had been in school, the preacher in Maasailand and the denmother and nurse in the hospital. But when they came together on those rides through this mysterious and powerful land, so full of a history that was beyond their grasp, it was as though their family was graced by an ancient and guarded beauty that seemed to erase the cruelty and poverty of the land's history. It was a land lonely but lovely, and it embraced them with a special kind of kinship. On some of those days for the Simonsons, it was a place and time that seemed to bring nature and God and the human spirit together, and it all assembled in family. When that happened, there seemed something of divinity at work.

They always started from Loliondo at 4 a.m. It was an hour that wouldn't have survived a democratic vote if you asked the kids when they wanted to get going. But it was judged by the family patriarch to be the best for all hands. The first 10 or 15 miles were the roughest, and since the kids never really woke up at 4 a.m. they spent the first hour or so being tossed around the Land Rover in their pajamas, still asleep. At about the time night was ending they had come down from the Loliondo highlands and reached the edge of the Serengeti and the site of a tree that had always attracted Dave and Eunice with its character and the sense of welcome it conveyed. There they'd stop and unpack the food. Near the tree was a large flat rock that became their picnic table. Assembled around their breakfast table, the family watched the sun rise over the Serengeti. There is almost no sun like the East African morning sun. It is huge and benevolent, so close that it spreads its geniality to the horizons and to a family celebrating its hours back together around a stone breakfast table, where wildebeest and zebra graze nearby. It is a sun that seems to unite the most benign power of heaven and earth, to dispel all mysteries and bless the face and soul.

"We'd linger around that round stone table, feeling that nature had made it for us," Eunice said. "We enjoyed the sunrise and the sounds of the wild animals, and we'd enjoy each other. We were alone in the Serengeti, our family. There was a marvelous innocence to those mornings. I don't know a more graceful place or time in all the years we lived in Africa."

Little Jonathan might not have been old enough to understand the quality of those moments, but a few years later there was another place for Jonathan. A couple hours down the road stood a dormant volcano, where the family would stop. The first time that happened, David crept up on Jonathan and, laughing, grabbed him by the foot and said, "Little boy, deep in the heart of Africa." Then he squeezed Jonathan's knee while the boy squealed happily. The scene got to be a family ritual, something between Dad and little Jon. And each time they'd stop there, Jon looked a little tense, worried that his father would forget to play their game.

He never did.

CHAPTER 13

When Naomi Simonson was five years and children of her age were playing with skip ropes in America, Naomi was playing a game called Mau Mau with other missionary kids in Africa. The object of the game, if you were a pretend Mau Mau, was to catch a missionary kid and to squish a geranium on the kid's cheek and spread the bogus blood around while the bogus Mau Mau howled "gotcha."

It may sound gruesome. It wasn't. They were kids playing a game without malice but conscious of the world in which they lived, the revolutionary Africa of the mid-century. When they acquired African friends, which was quickly, they dropped the game. What it meant was that Naomi Simonson was the daughter of white missionaries living in a world profoundly different from the one from which her parents came. About that world, the little girl knew almost nothing. Which might explain why, when she visited that strange land for the first time with her parents over Christmas, the face of Santa Claus suddenly appeared in her window, and shook her down to her toes. She'd never seen or heard of Santa Claus. Santa Claus wasn't part of the family holiday in the middle of East Africa in December.

Psychologists have had a field day looking into the minds and lives of the children of expatriates who grew up in ethnic and racial environments radically different from the land of their parents, especially in primitive countries. What are their true identities? How do they *perceive* their identities? When they visit the land of their parents or live in it for any extended time, what are the cultural conflicts that confront them? What are the competing pulls (if there are any) on the emotions and mentalities? How enticing are the material gifts of a country filled with high technology and razzmataz, with casual wealth, comfort and luxury? How dazzling are those gifts that can instantly thrust the Third World countries from which the visitor came into the Dark Ages by comparison?

Who are you today at the age of 42, or who were you, Naomi Simonson?

"I suppose the shortest answer is that I'm an American citizen who probably prefers living in Africa," Naomi Simonson said.

And why?

"This is the country I know best. It's the place where my son seems comfortable with himself and with his friends. It's where he seems comfortable with the world around him and a place he seems to understand. My family roots go back to the states. I'm an American. I lived there part of my life and so has Seth (her son, now 15). For Seth it was a pretty traumatic experience after his childhood in Africa.

"He came to the United States when he was six, and I took work in the travel business in Minneapolis. I'd lived most of my life in Africa although I was born in Minnesota and I'd gone to college in Minnesota and visited there fairly often with my friends. Seth grew up in Tanzania. When he came to Minnesota from Africa he had nothing in common with the kids in America. He didn't know how to make friends. He didn't know the TV shows, and he didn't know the games or how it was done in school. He was an outsider. He didn't know how to be an American kid. He lived with me for seven years in Minnesota, and he never really adapted. He thought Lake Street in Minneapolis was a battle zone. (Lake Street is a business street of car dealerships and fast food shops surrounded by residential neighborhood with a mixture of white, African-American, Hispanic, Indian and Oriental residents). He'd crouch down in the car afraid of being shot. If he saw more than two African-American kids together, he'd get frightened because he'd heard about guns. He never had that feeling in Africa. The African kids were his friends. He couldn't understand why he'd have these feelings so different from Africa but he didn't know anything about cultural differences. In Africa he rode his bike anywhere he wanted to around Arusha, in the streets and around the *shamba* gardens or the paths in the woods or in the banana groves, and he felt completely safe. In Minneapolis, he was afraid to ride around the school."

Not surprisingly, school itself was no source of joy to the youngster, and certainly not a venue where he achieved.

When he returned to Africa with his mother at the age of 14, he felt liberated.

And for his mother, was the collision of cultures for her that jarring when she was a child?

"I don't think so," she said. "This was partly because I was exposed to the United States off and on from my earliest childhood and I was born there. And there was the fact that Seth grew up in a single parent household (Naomi and the boy's father did not marry), while I grew up with a houseful of other pretty independent and squabbling missionary kids. After that you could deal with just about anything."

The five Simonson children were born within a span of eight years, Stephen and Naomi in Minneapolis, Nathan in England, Rebecca and Jonathan in Africa. All of them attended the Lutheran mission primary school in

Kiomboi in central Tanzania and then the Rift Valley Academy high school west of Nairobi in Kenya, another boarding school operated by a conservative mission group. No home school was available to them during their adolescent years, years in which Dave was running about Tanzania and Eunice was nursing. They *were* together as a family during the early years in Arusha, when the innocent inquirer might assume the missionary kids spent their free time acting the part of apprentice angels.

"You can't be serious," Naomi said. "We had hell-raisers like any other family. And I was probably the ringleader."

It might be remembered that this was the family whose early centerpiece in the playroom was Stephen, the incurable spirit who stopped traffic in his diapers in St. Paul and ran roughshod among sleeping Arabs in Khartoum, and later was almost smashed to pieces among petrol drums of a runaway truck. He was into trouble big time again in the early years in Arusha. His father had been painting a cistern tank at the family house before leaving on a mission. Everything looked relatively safe. Stephen was in view on top of the tank. Nathan was toddling around under the tank. A can of green paint left by his father seemed safe from Stephen's venturesome urges.

The green paint wasn't safe. The kid located the can on top of the tank and poured it over the edge. Unerringly, the falling paint located Nathan and spilled over his head. Other missionary kids who were visiting gleefully pointed out the sloppy sight to his mother, who told the assembled audience that she would wash the paint out of Nathan's hair before dealing with his brother. On the verandah they kept a large petrol drum for the Land Rover and house lamps, and near it some big metal pans for carrying cement and plaster. Eunice put paint solvent into one of the pans to clean Nathan's head and, afterwards, took him into the bathroom to soak him down with water to remove the petrol and final splotches of paint. While they were there, the neighbor kids came running in to announce that Stephen had set the house on fire.

The irrepressible kid had found some matches, lit one and thrown it into the remaining fuel in the tin of petrol on the verandah. Flames shot up from the pan, within feet of the 44-gallon petrol drum. Martha, the Wa-arush nanny and guardian angel, ran to the scene, grabbed the flaming pan and got the flames out in some nearby grass. In the meantime, Eunice Simonson was steadily going out of her mind. When all dangers had passed, she herded the kids into the house and took Stephen into a room, where she took down his pants and spanked him so hard that she actually sprained her wrist.

She then locked him in his room, taped her wrist and prepared for a siege of Stephen's bellowing. It came early and stayed long. Predictably, the mother developed deep guilt. It got worse as an hour passed, and then another. In the throes of regret, she opened the door to his room. "There he was, crying, his face red as radishes. His little hands were quivering in anger. And he said, 'Jesus forgave me a half hour ago. Why can't you?'"

What she did was to fall apart. They cried together. They cried and cried, and then—"We just swam out of that room on a tide of mutual forgiveness."

So whatever the level of casual anarchy in this missionary house, it usually wound up being theologically correct. Naomi, however, remembers more protracted battles and today, in the full bloom of perspective, confesses that she instigated most of them. She was, she admits, "just an obstinate and willful kid."

Any particular member of the family from whom those traits might have been acquired?

"I always kept saying I was my father's daughter but as a kid I probably took that headstrong stuff to another level. He was gone a lot, Dad, but I can't say I ever resented that. The others might have. I think for a while my sister Becky did. Maybe he spent more time with me because we seemed to have this affinity. Maybe we understood each other better. I think he showed plenty of affection to us when he was there. I know I felt it. He'd hug and play games. I remember once in Loliondo we were playing hide-and-seek outside and Dad was supposed to find us. It was pitch dark. All I saw was eyeballs. There was that story about the leopard hanging around, and we never forgot about it, and all of sudden Dad jumped out and scooped us all up, and we just about wet our pants."

The fact that Jesus Christ seemed a constant if invisible lodger in the house—the prayers at each meal, the casual little invocations that Eunice would make as part of their religious training—didn't quite deter the mission-ary kids from the traditional mayhem in a house full of young ones. At one of her mother's tea parties on the porch, Naomi remembers bending over to pick up some toy and getting belted over the head with a baseball bat by Nathan, who had a better swing and follow through than Naomi although he was a year younger. The little girl considered three options. One was to go crying to mother. The second was to go crying into the neighborhood. She chose the third. When Nathan came around the corner, she hammered his head with a brick.

Blood ran down his face. It was messy but not critical. Naomi said, "For-give me." Nathan probably did, after all of the blood was wiped away. The forgiveness piece of Christian theology was something the kids discovered early and summoned often. It was an escape hatch, duly blessed, from the wages of rowdyism. The parents marveled at the kids' precocity in it. Hit your brother with a brick and announce: "I have sinned." Some form of mercy always followed, although with the kids it might have been postponed a few weeks.

If Naomi's heart belonged to daddy in her earliest years, her life with Eunice—Eunice of the open arms and giving spirit and the open door to all souls in need—was an almost daily war.

"It always makes me feel a little guilty looking back on it now that I have this beautiful relationship with Mom and fully understand what she's done in all her years in Africa," Naomi said. "I was just an unruly kid. I don't know how else to say it. I was totally disrespectful to my mother. I couldn't believe anybody could be so **good!**" I'd call her St. Eunie, and I'd do it really sarcastically. Maybe it was because I felt so far from the kind of goodness that her life reflected, serving so many people, trying so hard to be a good mother and wife. I'd taunt her. And she'd seem so mystified that this stuff was coming out of one of her children. People I talked to later in life would tell me that Mom just glowed in the comfort of her faith and service she did. To other people that sounds syrupy and unreal, as though there's some kind of act there. There wasn't. She did glow. She still does, and now I have so much respect for her because I understand how she bears herself and the courtesy she shows to others."

Four of the Simonson children eventually were to spend the bulk of their lives in Africa. It was a choice common to the children of the expatriate missionaries, doctors and educators who formed the American colony in which the Simonsons moved. Becky, their fourth child, married a young rancher and settled in western North Dakota. Eunice Simonson reflected on the reasons for Africa's appeal to those who chose to stay.

"Most of those young people who grew up with their parents in Africa later were exposed to life in America, and in most of the cases it was a good part of that American life they saw. They saw the material benefits available to them there. All of our children attended some form of higher education in the states, most of them at Concordia. So there were opportunities there. But here was our oldest son, Stephen, the bratty kid when he was young. He was a pretty serious-minded young man when he grew up, and he had strong leanings toward teaching or the ministry for a while. When he went to Concordia he majored in biology. By then he was in the middle of a dilemma about what direction his life should take but beneath that was a drive to return to Africa, and biology probably was a compromise on the best academic route to take."

For Steve as the oldest son, and to a lesser degree the others, there was always the picture of J. David Simonson as a model for their lives and as the planter of footsteps that had to be observed if not filled. Steve had played rugby back in Tanzania but in America the game to play was American football, which Steve roundly disliked. But Dave Simonson had captained the Concordia team, and Steve Simonson reported for the squad, probably to please his father. He enjoyed middling success in his senior year, and he didn't regret the choice although he was never going to appear on the professional scouting charts. But he had a quick and photographic mind and found his way back to Africa working for Lutheran World Relief in a reforestation project in—by no fluke of coincidence—Tanzania. From there he went into conservation work in northern Kenya where, again by no twist of coincidence, he met Marilyn Shafer, the grandchild of the woman-legend who taught Dave Simonson the Maasai language. Marilyn was also the daughter of a doctor working in Kenya. It was a familiar pattern in the expatriate colony: Young people choose to stay in Africa, children or grandchildren of mission and medical families particularly. They meet other young people whose lives have been shaped by the same experience. There is an America 10 or 15 hours away, an America with its glitz and suburban lawns, supermarkets, call-waiting, freeways and shopping malls. America with its speed and strength and turmoil and dynamism.

But here is the Africa of their childhood. An Africa of struggling tribal life, destitute new countries light years behind the developed world in technology and wealth. It was an Africa of meager financial reward for young married couples from the expatriate enclaves. It was an Africa of dirty roads and illness and poverty in the villages. But it was also an Africa whose needs could be understood by a missionary's kid who grew up there and who understood the gifts of service he or she could bring to that Africa as an adult, even as a workaday office manager or engineer and not necessarily as mission or medical worker. It was an Africa whose yearning these same people understood: its silences on the Serengeti, the great herds of zebra and wildebeest streaming out of eyesight. This was an Africa that offered a freedom they might experience nowhere else. Get into the Land Rover and ride to Lake Ndutu on the edge of the Serengeti. The flocks of flamingo have flown. The gazelles and giraffe are nowhere to be seen at dawn, and the lion's roar subsided an hour ago in a gruff arpeggio of descending aarghs and oofs. And here on the white soda shores of Ndutu the sun rises in all of its immensity to an audience of only two.

And the witnesses thank God for being allowed the privilege.

Steve and Marilyn were part of the community that comprehended this Africa. It was no special community of the elite. The Africa of their childhood, with its vulnerability and lyrical tongues and dignified black faces, had reached into their insides and become inseparable from their own longings and their spirituality. Steve and Marilyn married and raised a family and with that acquired a passion for horses that quickly extended to the kids. Eventually Steve found his way into the Simonson family's business enterprises that came later. Jonathan, the youngest, and Naomi did the same from different directions. It happened because J. David Simonson and Eunice were in Africa for the duration. A lifetime. Their children knew Africa. Each had skills and particular drives in how they were going to occupy their lives, but J. David did not become J. David by leaving events in his life (and theirs) to chance. With some contributions from his sons, but primarily in partnership with the prominent Norwegian-born entrepreneur, Kjell Bergh of Minneapolis, he acquired in the 1980s the safari lodge at Tarangire and created a booking and touring agency in Arusha, Serengeti Select Safaris. The transactions represented the adoption of one more hat in Dave Simonson's haberdashery of creativity in Africa, the hat for J. David the industrialist. It was a role with which his church had no ethical problem. If he fulfilled his mission for the church, which he seemed to be doing in four or five dimensions, he was free to pursue personal initiatives as well.

A few of his critics in the missions saw it a little differently. Here was one more outlet for Dave Simonson the free-lancer, exploiting his position in mission work. But to that the neutrals and certainly Simonson then asked: Is building churches and schools and clinics and feeding starving Maasai cattle an exploitation? Of whom?

But operating a commercial enterprise is something else, the detractors said. And it might have been, except that the reverend's clear intention was to make use of some of his free capital to build enterprises his children would manage and in which they would eventually become primary owners. It ultimately happened that way, although the bookkeeping has always been slightly fuzzy to the corporate traditionalist, Kjell Bergh, who retained 40 percent interest in the safari lodge through the transitions and a sizable equity in the touring agency in Arusha. The lodge's managership by Jonathan Simonson has been strong. It was a niche his father hoped Jonathan would fulfill once he had outgrown the hostile gropings of his adolescence and early adulthood. He did and became a first-rate manager. Steve eventually took over the management of the touring agency, where Naomi also worked. And Nathan, good straight Nate as his mother called him, eventually joined in his father's crowning commitment (at least the one that gave him the deepest personal satisfaction), a secondary school for young Maasai women at Monduli near Arusha.

And yet all of the Simonson children pursued independent lives and independent work at different times in their lives. It couldn't have been easy given the hardheaded benevolence of Dave Simonson in wanting to bring stability into those lives with his own devices. Do you call that an urge to control? You could. You could also call it being a father and being available to his children in a part of the world where it was hard to put down roots of security.

In what way? Here was Jonathan Simonson, who became a kind of terror in the schools he attended in Tanzania. His father gave a capsule evaluation of Jon the student, one that was not challenged by Jon himself: "He was unteachable. He was disruptive. He got thrown out of the academy in Kenya. He wasn't going to get involved with the academic groves for love or money but one thing he cared about and knew something about beside Africa, which he loved, was car motors and Land Rovers. There was a school in Madagascar. I said, 'Jon, this is it. You've got to decide where you want to go and how you want to get there. If you don't work this out by yourself, there isn't much more we can do for you.' I knew the headmaster and talked to him about Jon, so he knew about him when Jon got to Madagascar. The headmaster said, 'Jon, you haven't done well in your other schools. I'll make a deal with you. You have a gift in auto mechanics. You study and get through your classes, and I'll open a class in auto mechanics. You'll run it. You, Jon Simonson.'"

J. David remembers the outcome. "The schoolmaster bought some broken-down Volkswagon from a Frenchman on the island and sent me the bill. Jonathan and the other kids overhauled it. They tore it apart and rebuilt it. Then they took it out on the sand dunes and had a great time. He finished the high school there to fulfill his part of the deal, but he was never going to be cut out for a traditional college education. One of my friends back in Moorhead in Minnesota was in charge of vocational school that was highly funded by the federal government. The farm kids spent their winters there and got paid for it. All the openings in the school were filled. But somebody in the federal government pulled the subsidies. The farm kids went home, and there was room for Jon."

Well, reverend, *that* wasn't the will of God.

"I don't know what you call it. But Jon went to vocational school for two years, lived with my brother in Glyndon, Minn., and came back to Africa with a two-year degree that he had every right to be proud of. And I said, 'All right, Jon, what are you going to do? You can't sit under the trees.' He said the only thing he knew how to do beside overhaul cars was to run safaris. I told him I'd get him a Land Rover. Margaret Gibbs who ran the Gibbs Farm for tourists on the way to the Ngorongoro Crater said she'd hire him to take her clients on photo safaris. But it didn't work out."

Jonathan Simonson had Africa in his guts but very few words on his tongue. Running a safari with a small group means you have to socialize with the travelers, to answer the good questions with some enthusiasm and the dumb questions with some generosity. At that stage in his life, young Jonathan had no skills with customers or with most people he met. "Tell you, Jon," Margaret Gibbs said, "what you really need to do is to start your own tour company and hire people to do what you don't want to do." Not long afterward J. David put Serengeti Select Safaris together with Jonathan and others, and not long after that he negotiated the Tarangire Safari Lodge deal. Jonathan was installed as the manager and supervised the improvements, and the operation has been making money since. Remarkably, Jonathan Simonson discovered some limited gifts of sociability and how to relax with the tourists. He learned how to share his enormous knowledge of the East Africa's wildlife and its moods, and how to share his ardor to preserve the animals and the land.

It might not have worked out as well without Annette Lillelid, a missionary's daughter he met in Madagascar. Once more, the mission kids found each other, knew about each other's troubles and their visions, married and formed a partnership. Annette ran the lodge when Jonathan was gone, which was often. He was in the field with tourists or off to Pangani on the Indian Ocean, where he has been building another lodge. But he was now mature and knew about what work ought to be managed by the manager and what could be delegated. The math teachers at the Rift Valley academy in Kenya wouldn't have recognized the surly, disruptive kid who was unteachable.

Straight Nathan created a roaming life as a water engineer but also a life of service that put him closer to the careers of his parents. He made the mandatory beginning by attending Concordia for two years and then transferring to North Dakota State for his final two years and a degree in civil engineering. For the Lutheran World Federation he worked in a refugee resettlement program in western Tanzania after starting as a water engineer. More refugee resettlement in Mozambique, then to South Africa. But from there he returned to Tanzania and an international romance, deep in the heart of Africa. It was on one of his refugee projects where he met a remarkable young woman named Susan Down, a nurse who rambled around the world from Botswana. She was born there to a Scottish mother and English father, a mining consultant. The family moved to Ireland, where she received her early education. The next stop was Canada, where she took her nurse's training and then Hawaii for a degree in public health, from there to Mozambique in public nursing and then to Tanzania where she met and married Straight Nate Simonson. He was still working on engineering projects in the 1990s when his father's medical problems took Nate, Susan and their three kids to Monduli, where his technical skills helped to expand the new secondary school for Maasai women.

One way or another, the Simonsons' energies and needs kept most of the family in the same orbit in Africa. The flower child, Rebecca, the girl Eunice called "the gentle one," moved in her own sphere. She loved the more subtle nature of Africa as her mother did, its blossoms and vivid skies. She responded to Africa's mystique in relaxed and curious ways that seemed to make her encounters with them a private devotional. She was a child of impulses and, while she was attending Concordia, one of her impulses was to take a job in western North Dakota, where in 1980 she met Jim Weinreis, one of seven brothers of a ranching family near Beach, N.D. They decided to be married in Fergus Falls, where Dave's preaching family had connections with Bethlehem Lutheran Church. What could be a more appealing place? Right?

But Becky was part of the family, and she got the deciding vote. First Lutheran in Fergus Falls was beautiful but too grand. They wanted an unpretentious wedding, or at least Becky wanted an unpretentious wedding. How about Bethlehem Lutheran, somebody asked? A little less grand, Becky thought, but still a little too grand. She then discovered a little home mission church called Zion, which was mostly wood and definitely unpretentious, so this was the place. Still, it wasn't easy to be unpretentious about a wedding in which a flock of guests showed from western North Dakota driving large cars and wearing cowboy boots and Stetson hats. But little Zion made Becky's world safe from pretension, and the wedding was beautiful, tasteful—and full of cowboy boots. They settled beyond the painted Badlands of North Dakota to raise a family. Years later, Becky was to survive a terrible seizure and brain tumor that put her and her unborn child, three months into her pregnancy, on the edge of death. They survived, Becky's mother would say, only because of an intervention that nobody could explain, except the members of the Simonson family who had experienced those mysteries all their lives and simply said: Prayer saved her.

Still, such a family could hardly escape heartbreak, considering the abnormal environment of their lives and the risks in them. Naomi may have been more vulnerable than the others. As her respect for her mother deepened and she approached adulthood, she was attracted to her own kind of service. She wanted to get into some form of child psychology. The needs of victims of schizophrenia made that venue of psychology appealing to her. She grappled with some personal dilemmas. She wanted to stay in Africa. It's where she had confidence in who she was and what she could give. Growing up in the missionary household, she watched the gradual evolution of her attitudes toward her parents. She always admired her father for tackling goals that seemed impossible to achieve. She was also drawn by his absolute faith and the care and love he showed for her. Still, she realized after a while that he was a head-knocker as a manager of events and sometimes a tyrant around the house in the turf struggles with her mother. "Dad was a chauvinist for most of his life," she says. "He doesn't really deny it now. It was supposed to be part of the culture of the time. That was the rationalization for guys. It didn't bother me. One of my attitudes growing up in Africa was that I could do what the men could do. If they could fix a car, so could I. And I did. I could do that without losing my femininity, if that's what you want to call it. Anyhow, I kept coaching Mom when the two of them would argue. Much as I admired both of them, I was a real agitator. I said, 'Stand up to him.' And sometimes she did. Once she got real mad and decided to tell him off. She just got disgusted and said, 'Go fart in a barrel.'"

Fiercer expletives have been spoken, occasionally in Lutheran households. But Eunice retired from the scene horrified, believing she was on the brink of banishment from the kingdom.

Africa was too much fun for Naomi to want to leave permanently. She studied at Concordia and came back after a year, and then returned for her degree. Back in Arusha she got into a relationship with a young man who was part of the expatriate enclave and became pregnant. The young man revealed no interest in marriage. Naomi had been given a scholarship at the University of Minnesota to pursue child psychology and then got an opportunity to study under a renowned psychiatrist in India, who had developed a new approach in the treatment of schizophrenia. While she was there she developed stress from some laboratory incidents and nearly lost the baby. She telephoned her mother, who now learned for the first time about her daughter's pregnancy. After hospitalization in India, she flew to Minnesota at Eunice's suggestion and lived with friends of the family while she studied at the university. But she developed a toxicity in her third trimester and nearly lost the baby again. Eunice flew to Minneapolis and was there for Seth's birth.

"She went through hell," Eunice said. "She tried to find work after the baby was born and couldn't find day care for him, and we said: 'Come back to Africa. It makes sense. You know this place. You'll be with people you love.'"

She got a job teaching primary grades at a Greek school in Arusha and lived pleasantly in a small apartment with Seth. She later spent two stimulating years helping Margaret Gibbs manage the Gibbs Farm tourist resort. When Jonathan moved from Serengeti Select Safaris to manage the lodge at Tarangire, she moved into the Serengeti Select office to manage, but eventually returned to the states with Seth to work in travel offices. The environment was all wrong for Seth, and they came back to Arusha. By then her father had bought majority interest in the Bishop Travel agency of Minneapolis, where Naomi worked as an agent. Since much of its business was African travel, Naomi moved her portfolio from Minneapolis to Arusha.

Her son's life settled. His father, who met another woman and is now married, sees him more often, something important both to the boy and to Naomi. He's back with friends and not worried anymore about getting shot on Lake Street or the constant flow of blood he saw on television.

"I found myself understanding Mom when she talks about what it is that draws people back to Africa," Naomi said. "For all the things that are great about the states, you find yourself getting sucked into the speed and the running around. If you've lived in the states all your life, I suppose that's OK. But if you've gotten used to a different pace, like the one in Africa, you find yourself spinning trying to keep up with everybody else. You have to do this and do that, be here and go there. Mom brings up the African word for European: *wazungu*—one who runs around in circles. Isn't that a great word? In Africa, things usually can wait if they have to. You don't have to have your foot on the pedal all the time. Relationships seem a little closer. What living in Africa means to me is more freedom and more honesty. It means more wildness of the earth. I love driving out to Tarangire. It has the deepest effect on me. I can't wait to get up in the morning and see the animals again, driving through the acacia forest at sunrise. You feel this is a place that God created, a special place that God created. I feel it there more than anywhere I know. I love identifying the animals for people in my Land Rover, the little dik-dik, the Thomson's gazelle, the guinea fowl, the birds, the waterbuck. I see something new each time I do it. There are days when it's absolutely heaven, the quiet, the animals in the distance, the African sky."

She is a woman who *can* go home again, each day at sunrise in the acacia forest.

CHAPTER 14

Before they began walking south from Loliondo to Arusha, a distance of 200 miles, David Simonson tried to explain the phenomenon of the Great Rift Valley to Stephen, 13, and Nathan, 10. No geology texts were at hand and he didn't want to scare the kids, because this was going to be the journey of their young lives. He did tell them about the Mountain of God, Oldonyo Lengai, and the steaming basin in which Lake Natron lay. Finally he settled for the generic "awesome," which more or less delighted the kids.

It's a description impossible to deny. Nowhere on the earth's surface are its subterranean upheavals and wrenchings over the ages revealed on the sheer scale of the Great Rift Valley. Millions of years ago the tectonic plates supporting the land masses of East Africa and the Middle East crunched and ripped. For a length of more than 4,000 miles running from the edge of what is now Syria to Mozambique, the earth violently rearranged itself in cycles of volcanic explosions. The earth buckled and caved in on itself. It created mountains on the rims of its convulsions. The Red Sea emerged. A vast ravine, more than 50 miles wide in some places, formed in East Africa. Today it is called the Great Rift Valley, but the term sounds paradoxical in places like Ethiopia, where the Rift takes the form of great dead plains of sun-dried mud plaster, creased by the broiling heat into patterns of hexagons and octagons. Near Loliondo the Rift rises to heights of nearly 8,000 feet and the terrain to the Simonsons on their arrival there whimsically resembled northern Minnesota's rolling forests.

But temperatures in northern Minnesota don't often rise to 140 degrees Fahrenheit, which is said to actually have been recorded on the soda shores of Lake Natron. There, in the sinks of volcanic depression, the Rift radically changes character and becomes a boiling prehistoric vat of heat waves, alkaline water and lava cliffs. Mixed with these, amazingly, is a freshwater stream coming down from the mountains of the Ngorongoro Crater miles away.

This is the Rift. People live near Natron. Settlements exist there. A crude route exists in the northern Tanzania Rift, from Loliondo to Arusha. "Boys," Simonson said, in what was supposed to represent a democratic discussion of whether they should undertake it, "this is a trip for you and me. I don't know how many people have walked this before, but it doesn't matter. Do you like the idea?"

They did. Their nods reflected more than filial loyalty. They were inquisitive and capable kids. The 200 miles of the Rift seemed huge, but they were primed for adventure and they trusted the big man in the lead, carrying his shotgun. Their father, being a father, pushed them toward shortcuts in their passage to adolescence, but he wasn't a fanatic about it. As a kind of bonding rite to tighten the fraternity of David, Stephen and Nathan, he'd considered a climb on Kilimanjaro but turned that down. He wasn't sure that at ten, Nathan could handle Kilimanjaro's 19,340 feet. It was even less sure about the old man. But the Rift was ground level, and it had enigma and power, and it was a world that a father and his two sons could enter with shared excitement. It was also a symbolic salute to the four fruitful years he and Eunice had spent in Loliondo. In a few months they were going back to Arusha for a more conventional and expanded ministry for Dave and a nursing life Eunice hadn't foreseen.

The shotgun? To add to the oven heat and tortured terrain of the Rift's 200 hundred miles, they were also going to encounter wild animals. Part of their route would take them through lion country. The rest of the wildlife ensemble—giraffes, zebra, eland, waterbuck, giraffes—they wouldn't have to worry about. Elephants they would give a wide right-of-way.

Today there is a rough if suspenseful road running through the Rift from Loliondo to Arusha. It is negotiable only by powerful 4-wheel drive vehicles and drivers with cast iron kneecaps and durable duffs. When David, Stephen and Nathan walked it in the late 1960s, there was no road. There was, however, one presence that may or may not be available to the Rift travelers of today, a presence that David Simonson never doubted but which could not be seen. Agnostics never get far with Simonson when he talks about God's protection in the parade of potentially lethal events that confronted the Simonson family in its African stewardship. "We were called to do a work," he says unarguably. He says it again and again. "The call was from God. We were going to be allowed to carry that work to a finish."

The agnostics would incline to other options in explaining those escapes and survivals. But they might run out of options to explain what happened on the walk through the Rift.

"We (read "I") didn't tell Eunie too much about what lay ahead," the reverend said. "That wasn't only to spare her the anxiety. We didn't really know ourselves." They did know of the Sonjo settlement down the ravine from Loliondo. Simonson had preached there and done some baptisms. The Sonjos were sociable when they encountered Simonson, which was a comfort to the kids because some of the Sonjo still fought and hunted with poison arrows.

"A Peace Corps director in the district joined us on the hike," Simonson said. "We'd arranged for porters to meet us in the Sonjo settlement, from where the trek started in earnest. Some of the Sonjo we met on the way asked what we were doing and where we were going. I told them, and they couldn't believe it. 'Those young boys!' they said. I said the boys would make it. The first couple of days weren't too tough. The kids were really high about it and couldn't wait to get into a campsite at night so we could start a fire to cook. It was interesting for a father to watching the dynamics between Stephen and Nathan. Nathan was tall for his age but he was three years younger, and Stephen was a hero to him. Steve was a good deal more aggressive, and Nathan stood in the shadows when it came for them to do stuff around the camp. It took time, but Nathan gradually asserted himself more and more as a partner on the trip. He had trouble keeping up with Steve. As a matter of fact, so did I. Steve's stamina at the age of 13 was hard to believe. He carried something like 30 pounds in his pack and when the Peace Corps director got tired, he volunteered to carry that pack as well. We had great times at night. We'd put up a thorn fence to keep the animals out, just like the Maasai, and lay a fire in the middle of our little compound and spread our sleeping bags or blankets around it. On one of the earlier days one of our porters began to sing. I asked the head porter about him. The head porter had been one of my students in Marangu. He said the singer was one of two balladeers who lived in a Sonjo village, and what the balladeers would do was get people together as an audience, and they would sing the stories of the tribe's history. They were like minstrels. I loved that idea. Anyhow, this singing carried on the rest of the way because the balladeer was rehearsing his stuff and we were a trial audience.

"When we got past Lake Natron, where the Rift floor was practically on fire with the heat, the trek brought us to a sand river that ran down the slopes near Oldonyo Lengai. It was a stream that everybody knew pretty well and one that we were counting on to give us good drinking water, which we were beginning to need badly. When we tasted it, the water was brackish and undrinkable. What we hadn't counted on were the effects of a major eruption of the Lengai volcano a year before. It radically changed the drainage and contaminated the fresh water channels. We explored for water for hours but came up empty. The porters were going dry. So was the Peace Corps director. The kids and I weren't in very good shape, either. The porters lay down in the shade of trees along the polluted river. They weren't going to be any help finding water. I started walking upstream trying to find drinkable water. To me, it was getting pretty desperate. We had no water supply left. Here we might as well be in a desert. Nobody lived here. We couldn't use anything in the river, and the channel had dried up. The rest of the valley was parched. I kept walking up the dry river bed and worrying about the kids. As I walked I noticed some mud on the sides of the channel. It got more watery as I moved upstream. There wasn't enough to siphon, but I tasted it and it seemed fresh. I kept going up, and the mud kept getting more fluid and then I reached a ridge, and I was stunned by the sight.

"I'd come to a lake. There was no lake on the maps. How could there be? There was no basin in there. There wasn't even supposed to be a ridge. Except there *was* basin, and this *was* a lake. It wasn't any mirage. The lake in this new basin was deep enough to have waves. You could wade in it, right out there in the desert flats beneath Oldonyo Lengai, and it was sweet water. Drinkable. We learned later that the volcano's eruption had created the ridge, this natural dam, and over a period of time rainwater collected in it."

The native's translation of Oldonyo Lengai?

"The Mountain of God."

"I ran down to the others and got the kids and went to the porters, who were laid out in the shade and pretty lifeless and didn't seem to want to move. They didn't believe the lake, either, because they'd been through here many times and there was no lake. I told them you can stay and leave yourselves for the hyenas or you can come with us. They said, 'We're coming,' and in a few minutes everybody was gulping water and filling every container we had and finally we actually did some swimming in this lake that wasn't supposed to exist."

The lake may not have been the will of God. The reverend's decision to follow a dry river bed uphill toward volcanic rock in search of freshwater might have been a closer explanation. Who could really know?

"I do," the reverend said. "I was directed there, to the only place where there was water."

Case closed.

They camped on the far side of the nameless lake, splashing around on the shore, and headed back into the deep Rift the next morning. A few months later the ridge and the lake were gone. The ridge eroded and the rainwater drained into the sour wastes of Lake Natron, to turn into soda.

Three quarters of the way to Arusha, days out of Loliondo, they came to the Maasai village of Kitumbeine, near where they'd camped. Simonson thought the kids needed milk. He went to the village and part way there met a Maasai woman. He asked if they could have some milk. She said no. And then she looked at Nathan and asked who the boy was. Simonson said he was his son. The woman asked where they'd come from, and Simonson said, "Olgosorok," the native name for Loliondo, meaning "black throat" because of the black-barked trees. She looked again at the boy and began to cry, "All the way from there? This little boy?" He nodded. The woman's matronly urges took over, and they weren't polite. She lit into Simonson for taking the kid on that long and exhausting walk. He started to defend himself and then caught himself. There were times when you talk to the Maasai. There were times when you kept your mouth shut. The reverend shut his mouth, and the woman walked back to her village. She returned a few minutes later with a full gourd of milk.

"None of it is for you," she snarled at the reverend in Maasai. "It's all for the boy."

Simonson was not about to quarrel with her. They left with thanks and returned to camp. It was a big gourd and there was no way Nathan could down the whole thing, which meant that all hands drank milk before they went to bed, and little Nathan became the toast of the expedition. David found himself deeply respectful of Nathan's handling of his stress, all of which brought the three even closer than they'd been. When they got to the village the next day, the reverend popped for Cokes at a Somali shop. Toughened now and gaining confidence, the party headed into the final stages of the trek to Arusha, through terrain filled with knee-high dust as fine as talcum, up great palisades and then to a plain where they found a herd of elephants on the move.

Simonson: "When we found a gap in the herd we crept across this plain until we felt we were safe. I counted noses and Nathan's wasn't among them. I almost died. I looked into the elephant herd thinking he might have got tangled up with them, but I didn't see him. When the elephants passed I went back to where we'd come from, and there he was, watching the big elephant parade. He thought it was fabulous, which of course, it was. It took me a half hour to get my color back."

By about then they had descended a slope and were about to camp for the night when then noticed the tail lights of a vehicle receding in the distance. To the elephants and the rest of the day's excitement was now added an element of mystery. Why tail lights out here in the Rift? They also noticed vultures circling ahead of them. Simonson handed his shotgun to the head porter and asked him to investigate. The porters found a freshly killed eland and cut all the meat they could bring to camp. But before they organized a roast, Simonson asked about the water supplies. "If we're going to eat meat," he said, "we've got to have water." Nobody had much. The porters, somewhat more fatalistic than the reverend, roasted the meat and went ahead with a night feast. Simonson, the kids and the Peace Corps director abstained. By the mid-morning, on the trek again, the porters wilted. One of them remembered a stream coming through a range of low mountains several miles away. Simonson told them they could investigate if they wanted, but he, the kids and the director were going on. The porters caught up with them several hours later with a glum report. They'd found no water.

Simonson said, "They were on the edge of collapse from thirst, no doubt about it. We couldn't leave them out there. Our own thirst wasn't that severe, but it was bad enough. We kept going. The country we were in had been devastated by volcanic action. It had a thick crust of ashes on top of the soil. And then all of a sudden we came on some green grass which was holding standing water. It was unbelievable. It reminded me of the late spring in Minnesota and the Dakotas when the snow melted and left water. None of the porters could remember water ever being there before. They drank and drank, and we filled our bottles. Then in the distance we got the explanation for those tail lights. You could see the road to Arusha. We were just about out of the Rift. We told the porters they could walk in their own good time, but we were heading toward that road as fast as we could. We'd walked for a couple of hours, and one of the kids was about to take a sip of water when he turned to me and said, "Why don't you just hit that rock with your stick and we'll have water."

Light sarcasm from your own flesh and blood. OK, oh, great rainmaker. Do it again.

"The little buggers."

They reached the asphalt highway after dark, close to 8 p.m. Nathan was dragging. All those days in the heat, 200 miles. They came to a local shop where Simonson bought some pastries and sodas. When he came out Nathan was draped out on the porch, sleeping. Some Maasai warriors who had stopped to rest on their walk into Arusha removed the blankets from their shoulders and covered the boy. He slept for awhile and then awoke. They kept walking, Stephen at his brother's side. By midnight they'd reached the house of a family on the outskirts of Arusha and were welcomed with tea. From there the welcome deteriorated somewhat. "My friend's wife was completed frosted with me for putting Nathan through that. My ears were ringing when we left."

Which made two chewings on the reverend's vulnerable kiester in three days. But Nathan made an announcement a little while later: "If I have to sleep," he said, "let's sleep in the ditch. I don't want to be picked up after we came this far."

His father decided that at this moment, Nathan had become a man. Considering Nathan's ten years, it would have been a pretty precocious adult-hood. What his father *meant* might have been more agreeable to the psychologist. The boy had discovered something important about the fabric of Nathan. It had strength and could carry him through strain and fatigue. He had earned the respect of his father, which mattered, but might not have mattered quite as much as the respect he had earned from his brother.

But that couldn't have been the first reason for subjecting a kid 10 and a kid 13 to the trial of a 200-mile walk through the cauldron of the Rift?

No, Simonson says in retrospect, it wasn't. "It was an experience that I thought a father could share with two of his sons in a part of the world that had become intimate to our family and was full of wonderful scenes and sounds. It was going to be tiring and unpredictable and have some risk, yes, but I thought it was a risk that we could manage. We did. We had the kind of shared moments that became an indelible part of our lives. When you think it through, what is life about, anyhow? For some people, it's about finding out; exploring your world and yourselves. It's exploring how you can serve and what you are capable of doing and what you aren't. If you can do that together, with your family, it makes the exploration so much richer."

If the kids were overextended, you would never hear that from them. They had been on an odyssey unlike any most kids on earth had experienced. They had found water where it was never supposed to exist, elephants in their midst, heat waves radiating from lakes that looked like mirages. They'd built thornbush fences and listened to the songs of African minstrels.

In later years they would tell that story with increasing laughter and yet with quieter moments of puzzlement. How *did* the water get there? They'd tell the story together, brothers linked by blood and by something else, the memory of a walk past the Mountain of God and over palisades. Like their brotherhood, it would last a lifetime.

CHAPTER 15

When Christianity first confronted polygamy in its attempts to convert black Africa, the evangelists usually retreated in a mess.

The tribal stakes in the institution of multiple wives were too high to abandon it suddenly to the preachments from Christian scriptures or legal arguments about changing the law. Polygamy has receded somewhat by now. Many who came into the Christian faith accepted the idea of one spouse, along with the rest of the package. Some of the converts decided to accept it eventually. A problem for the evangelists was that polygamy was a critical part of the family structure in many of the tribes. More than one wife was the male's safeguard against a marriage without children. Wives meant large numbers of children as a measure of familial strength and status. Wives meant more male sons for working (whatever work that wasn't done by the women) and fighting and also for performing the sacrificial rituals critical to the spiritual afterlife of the father. Some of the wives themselves felt threatened by monogamy—a loss of their own status, such as it was, and their security.

The institution still hangs on in much of Africa. As some of the Africans mirthfully point out, it had the same stubborn longevity when Solomon and other erotically active monarchs in the Bible practiced it thousands of years ago. In fact, it had a fairly vigorous run for a while in the United States in the Church of the Latter Day Saints.

The missionaries of today in Africa have fundamentally made their peace with it. The shrewder ones decided some time ago not to get bogged down in making the case for Jesus Christ by trying to overturn a tribal power system that has been entrenched for centuries. Compromises were available, the shrewder missionaries decided. They made their deals with the prospective converts, and then were not especially inquisitive about whether the agreements were being strictly observed. A lot of times, they weren't. It's life, some of the missionaries shrugged. Jesus Christ was also pretty explicit about disapproving divorce. But not many Christian pastors in American pulpits today overexert themselves complaining about divorce, especially where half of the members may have been divorced.

Polygamy was one issue on which the Christian message and traditional African lifestyle met uncomfortably. There were and are plenty of others. But there is another side to the encounter between Christianity and native culture that should open the door between the two, at least wider than it's been. Simonson as well as other perceptive missionaries understand today that traditional African spiritual beliefs offer the Christian church opportunities to enrich its own experience and to broaden the channels for its invitation to the Africans.

Several years ago Simonson startled some American listeners by relating the story of a Maasai medicine man whose community had resisted Christian conversion. In the 1990s, his people agreed to baptism largely under the persuasion of the medicine man, who claimed to have been walking one day when he heard a voice from the sky. The voice, he said, told him it was time. It was time for his people to enter the kingdom of God. He believed absolutely that the voice was that of God, and his summons into the kingdom could not be refused.

Simonson was asked if he believed the story, that this man actually had heard a voice from the heavens.

"I do," Simonson said. "I don't have any doubt about it. It happened."

The discussion moved to another theme. Simonson wasn't going to argue about the story. He'd been down this road before. Our own culture is full of stories about dreams being fulfilled, about uncanny coincidences, about miracle cures, about people inexplicably being moved to make a telephone call that eventually saved a life. Why, he asked, do we reduce it to superstitious mumbo-jumbo when the same thing happens in another culture? Why should miracles and visions be respected in the New Testament but draw rolling eyes if they're reported on the road to Loliondo?

Dean Peterson talks about it in a section of his book probing epistemology, or how we acquire our knowledge. In that field, he says,

> the richness of the African tradition serves to accentuate the poverty of the West. When humanity is seen as no more than one aspect of the material world, knowledge becomes limited to that which can be scientifically-proven or rationally explained. Acknowledging only one part of human experience, our ways of "knowing" are delineated by a poverty-stricken world view. This is why "revelation" is such a strange word (to us) and this is why the Western church is uncomfortable with visions or dreams or intuition as a way of "knowing" truth. The Book of Acts thus purged becomes unreadable. Or, when dealing with the "transfiguration" of our Lord, the Western preacher often skips over the experience of Jesus with Elijah and Moses (appearing to him in dazzling light). Things like that just don't happen. So the last part of the text about healing through prayer gets

all the attention. Not so with African preachers. [From them] I have heard a lucid, forthright message on Moses and Elijah as the personification of the law and the prophesies which Jesus came to fulfill. What would be more fitting than that the Lord Christ have a conference with them as a witness to his lordship?

Within the give and take of class discussion it is not unusual for African students to share an insight or message received in a dream or vision. In a similar class in the U.S.A. I have known students who hesitated to tell any such experience even to the teacher in the privacy of his office, lest they be branded as balmy. African traditional religion/culture does not intend to negate reason and its blessings; neither does it intend to encapsulate the human experience within a closed spacetime box.

Simonson's ministry accepted that idea almost from the beginning. It's one reason it wore well with Africans who weren't crazy about turning Christian when he or his colleagues first approached. Prominent in that category, of course, were the Maasai who—despite the ministries of Richard Reusch and a few others—had no thick history for converting to Christianity. They had their God, *engai,* their ancestral spirits, their medicine men and curses and sacrifices, and they had no special imperative to accept the God or Christ of a Western society that didn't much interest them. They roamed the land, herding their cattle and living in the oval huts of dung and mud. They were independent; they were the chosen people of *engai,* and it might logically be argued, what more status did they want or need. Whose God was going to be any better?

"But the more I learned about the Maasai in all that time I spent with them," Dave Simonson said, "the more I was impressed that they were missing something. They conceded that. Many of them felt separated from God, for whatever reason. They said they wanted something more in their lives. Remember, these are monotheistic people, so we were never that far apart. They said they felt distanced from God and wanted to come closer. And then we'd talk about Jesus Christ. Here was the way, I said, the way to end that separation and come closer. And a lot of them said they weren't ready, but they would know when they were. Well, you're not going to be an idiot and press them under those circumstances. You went on being a friend. Some of them became Christians relatively early. Thousands of them waited."

For what?

Simonson and his colleagues were to make that discovery years later. The question of polygamy was never crucial in the process, but it's worth scrutiny to discover another and instructive face to the Christian mission movement. Call it the Pragmatic Mission, or "do whatever works."

Simonson: "When the Germans ran the missions years ago, they told the Africans they'd have to get rid of all their wives but one. Under the tribal system, the first wife is preeminent. The next wife is taken with the permission of the first because she can be a helper. What the Germans did was to allow the Maasai husband to choose the wife he wanted, and he invariably chose the youngest. The Germans, though, didn't get all that far in changing the system and, in trying to, they lost credibility with the people they were trying to change. Our people (American Lutheran missionaries) saw that polygamy was a violation of the law and explained that to the Maasai, since that was a way to create monogamous marriages. Some of the Maasai said they'd prefer to have one wife and put the rest aside, but they'd have to take care of the others and have huts for them. So what we do now is to say that monogamy is an ideal, but not an absolute. We said God allowed polygamy in the Old Testament days because there was something more important, which was the coming of the Messiah. God wasn't going to get hung up on the other stuff. Later, when Christianity came, a new ideal was set up, one man and one wife. We talked this through with the Maasai. We said in setting up these ideals, we had to understand what culture or lifestyle we're in. We said, you've got your wives and 25 children. If you become a Christian, you don't take another wife. If you've got six wives now, you're responsible to take care of all of them. They're yours. But the children of your marriages will not be permitted to take more than one wife and still worship in the Christian church. If you accept those things, we have no problems. Welcome to the church."

In other words, we're not going to cancel out your wives with any ex post facto rules, but you have to come part way by not adding to the harem and by telling the kids it's only one spouse each. Yet the issue is hardly settled and remains a spiky one for some missions. What the missions ought to do, Dean Peterson wrote, is to open their minds a little wider.

Many of these discussions about "plural wives" have been aired (in the mission movement) with great erudition. As far as I know, mainline Christian churches in Africa have not opted for polygamy as one of the normal ways of marriage. Polygamous households are often allowed into the church as an accommodation to pre-Christian society—but only for the first generation. The church makes it clear that its expects the second generation to be monogamous.

But—

I do not think that there is only one cultural form of marriage accept-able before God, nor do I expect that the "ideal" of monogamy will become the norm of Christian marriage in Africa without a great struggle and a good deal of time. I do suggest, however, that if the church chooses to continue upholding monogamy as the way of

Christian marriage, it must take more seriously its responsibility to engage in debate with traditional Africa's view that *true personhood depends on parenthood. Marriage without children is no marriage, and immortality depends on ritual remembrance by family members who are still living.* When Christian views on personhood, marriage and life after death become more significant to the believers than their traditional heritage is, the church will have begun attaining her goal of one-wife, one-husband in marriage.

Peterson's point is that the Christian advocates—which include both the evangelists and now the African pastors who have taken over the bulk of the ministerial work formerly performed by the Simonsons and Petersons—have to be serious about making Christianity more relevant. They can do that by laying the tenets of Christianity beside the traditions Africans grew up with. They can not only try to show where Christianity offers a better way, but also where Christianity can learn from the Africans, to redefine some of its own tenets in ways that weave credibly into the African's tradition. Take, for example, the tradition of offering sacrifices—sacrifices to please the higher being, sacrifices to mollify ancestral spirits, sacrifices to keep the cattle herds healthy. All kinds of sacrifices. They are a means to acquire protection and power and preserve the oneness of the community whose members share in the sacrifices. They are intended to purify the sacrificer and to make things right with those from whom the sacrificer is separated. If that culture (or cult) of sacrifice matters in the life of the candidate Christian, or has mattered, then it is not a long step to ask the African to see this: that his or her own sacrificial practices—and not only the sacrifices written so voluminously in the Old Testament—are fulfilled in the ultimate sacrifice, that of Jesus Christ.

None of that is easy, but it's reasonable, and at the core is the idea of a little more respect for the history of the candidate Christian's attitudes and the spiritual practices that surrounded him or her earlier in life. Simonson was among the quick learners, partly because the culture of one of those tribes in particular, the Maasai, fascinated him and eventually became threaded into his own life.

Like most of the Africans he befriended and tried to bring into Christianity, Simonson was engrossed by what the logical minds might describe—and sometimes not so tolerantly—as the supernatural. The tribal cultures in Africa were full of it, with spirits and demonology and the laying of curses and the hearing of voices. Simonson's ministry took cognizance of those traditional absorptions, but his acceptance of the "supernatural" leaned instead to belief in miracles and what he was sure were the handprints of God in events that were otherwise inexplicable. Nothing about the episode of a young Sonjo warrior paralyzed by a fall was explicable.

At the time, Simonson had been reunited with a friend he cherished almost above all others in the ministry, Peder Waldum. They were classmates at Concordia and later at Luther Seminary. Waldum was a few years older, having served in the military. After Simonson went to Africa, Waldum wrote from Livingston, Mont., asking how his congregation could assist Dave in his mission. Simonson responded with thanks and a suggestion that one of his most pressing needs was for a fund to enable the poor congregations of Africa to build churches they'd begun but couldn't finish because their money ran out. Waldum's congregation shortly afterward created an annual budget of $4,000 for church building in Africa and related needs. Eventually, at Simonson's invitation, Peder and his wife, Grace, flew to Tanzania to witness some of the results. They were in Loliondo when one of the Flying Doctors who'd been in the African Rift gave Simonson the news that a 19-year-old Sonjo warrior had fallen out of a tree gathering honey and suffered a broken neck. The victim's family asked if he could be flown to the hospital. The doctor said that any movement would kill the young man, and he could not in conscience fly him to the hospital. The parents mentioned Simonson's name and said he knew their son. A day later a group of Sonjo warriors came to the Simonson house in Loliondo, having walked the 26 miles from their village. They said the young man wanted to see the pastor before he died. Simonson asked Peder Waldum to ride with him in the Land Rover.

"The fellow was lying on a cow skin in front of his parents' house," Simonson said. "He couldn't move his hand to shake mine. He couldn't do much more than move his eyes. He was able to talk in a whisper. He said, 'Pastor, pray for me.' I looked at Pete. The medical people couldn't save this man with all their skills. He was asking us to pray for him. I said to myself, 'Yes, pray. But what if this doesn't work?' There are times when you ask yourself that question no matter how strong your faith. But the easiest thing in the world was what this man had asked us to do, to pray for him. I told Pete to join me in putting a hand on the young man's head, and we prayed. We then said goodbye to him and the other villagers. The two of us drove back to Loliondo before heading for Arusha with Eunice and Pete's wife. We spent ten days touring that part of the country, including time at one of the churches Pete's congregations had supported. Eunice and I got back to Loliondo after driving Pete and Grace to the airport at Nairobi, and we asked our cook what had happened to the young man with the broken neck in the Rift.

"Two days after you left for Arusha," the cook said, "he walked up here with a gourd of honey to say thank you."

He showed no effects of his accident. There was no evidence of a fracture. Simonson drove back to the village to confirm it. The young man was healthy. Inexplicably.

Or was it inexplicably? Several years later Simonson stopped again in the village in the midst of a fund-raising walk in which contributors from the

United States had joined him. They went to the home of the Sonjo warrior and found him the portrait of health. By then he was married and had three healthy daughters. "There's no question his neck had been broken," Simonson said. "When the doctor saw him and when Pete and I did, his nerves were gone. He was a few hours from dying. And two days later he was walking 26 miles with a gourd of honey as his gift to his friends."

So how do we account for it?

"You can tell that story to young students from today's seminaries," Simonson said, "and a lot of them are going to roll their eyes, practically telling you 'not the miracle business again.' So most people just raise that wall of logic when they hear something like this, and I've reached the conclusion that most of them aren't going to believe it until something like that happens in their own lives. I've seen it, and I believe. But I also believe, not seeing it. Something moved in that man's life and literally lifted him from a death bed. That something was our prayers."

He wrote to Peder Waldum with the good news. They stayed in contact, nourishing their friendship. A few years ago Simonson got letter from Montana telling of Peder Waldum's struggle with cancer and confiding that death was not far away. He flew to the United States and spent a week with his friend in Kalispell, Mont., reading, praying, sitting in silence, and then reminiscing. "We probably sang," Simonson said, "I don't know how I managed that. I may be the worst singer who ever entered the ministry, but I think Pete wanted that and we did. In the end we had communion together with Pastor Rick Nelson. Pete had only had a few days left. He knew he was going to die soon, and we both knew I would not be able to attend the funeral. We would never see each other again on earth, but we would meet again. He knew that, and he also knew how much we loved each other."

Not much later, back in Africa, Simonson received the news of Peder's death. It tore him up. He remembered their college years together, Peder's generosity and their shared faith, the day in the Rift village. Simonson sat and wrote from Africa at the time of the funeral. He doesn't call it a poem or essay or hymn. It was a message to a friend. It send in part:

> The Lord's command was to go, to preach and to teach,
> > one to the Maasai,
> > the other to all he could reach.
> So off we both went, surrounded by prayer,
> > to Sonjo, to Rheim, Livingston, Kalispell and elsewhere.
> We learned very soon that our people were proud,
> > and wanted His word preached clearly and loud . . .
> We'll share once again, the word, powerful and free,
> > "that where I am in glory,
> > > there also you'll be."

The Simonsons interlude in Loliondo lasted four years. It matured J. David's ministry profoundly and gave both of them a more intimate and meaningful understanding of Africa and the struggles of its people. When they returned to Arusha, Simonson was ready to plow into his ministry with renewed energy and without the distractions of his old struggles with Stefano Moshi. By the early 1970s, the oversized diocese of Moshi had been divided. The Moshi diocese was the one that aroused Simonson to mutinous urges to get a larger share of the diocesan funds for the Wa-arush people of Mt. Meru. The Evangelical Lutheran Church of Tanzania had worked out a geographical division that split the Moshi and Arusha areas and accommodated the interests of African Christians who lived around the Arusha, which was Simonson's argument all along. Out of this realignment grew the diocese of Arusha, which most of the missionaries agreed was accomplished without much strife despite the rancor of the Simonson–Bishop Moshi quarrel. It seemed a sensible way to put evangelism and parish work under more localized control. The new Arusha diocese was impressively vast. It stretched 220 miles from the Tanzania-Kenya border to the Maasailand of the south, where Simonson began his ministry nearly 20 years before, and 120 miles from east to west. If you were an itinerant pastor, as Simonson was as part of his charter, you were going to spend a lot of hours driving from parish to parish. He did, and he essentially loved it. The Arusha territory at the time had not absorbed much evangelism. There was teaching and conversion to do and aid to give, although the city of Arusha itself had become a center of international mission and services. In this, the government of the United States was not an ardent player. Tanzania's socialist government, and its chumminess with the Red Bloc at the time, made the country less than alluring to Washington or to corporate America. It didn't have much to sell, and its citizens were too poor to buy. Much of the help it got from the western world came from Canada and the Scandinavian countries and from the churches.

Simonson was revved up by the changes that greeted him on his return from Loliondo. The territory embraced by the new diocese was the part of Tanzania where he was comfortable and had been productive. It gave him access to hundreds of African friends and some savvy business connections among the Middle Easterners and the European nomads who worked the markets.

"All of what happened in the new alignment made sense," Simonson said. "In the Arusha diocese we had Maasai and Wa-arush, Sonjos and Chaggas who'd migrated from the Kilimanjaro area. The Moshi diocese was mostly Chaggas. So we were now separate but equal. At the time we had something like 200,000 baptized Christians in the Arusha diocese. It was thriving."

The figure by the late 1990s had grown to nearly 400,000 and 385 churches in a geographic area served by 71 pastors—only four of whom were from abroad—and 480 evangelists. The numbers of the Christian census in

Africa, though, are generally astonishing. It has to be remembered that they are unofficial and more a guess than a serious estimate. Still one of the more reliable recent estimates places the current figure at more than 350,000 million Christians, which would mean that approximately one out of six Africans is a Christian.

Simonson has no idea of the number of conversions his own ministry created in its more than 40 years nor did he bother to keep track. On that point he recalled the reflections of one of his professors at Luther Seminary, the late Dr. George Aas. "Conversion is a series of encounters, like the links of a chain," he said. "All of the links are equally important, not just the last one. You as an evangelist may be the one needed for link number four or number ten or whatever. It's not always the last one that's crucial."

At the time of the organization of Arusha diocese, however, Simonson was literally all over the map and at one time served as many as 13 congregations as the Maasailand version of the old prairie circuit-riders of his youth. And what else? A few dozen projects. Bootstrap was funding scores of schools. He'd built the foundation of a new expanded service to the Africans, the medical clinic of Selian near Arusha. He preached, counseled and taught the Bible in most of those parishes. With seed funding from the American Lutheran Church's United Mission Appeal, he and other missionaries distributed cattle to needy families in the country. The idea was for a family to qualify by building a shelter and growing an acre of grass. Each of 60 families got a heifer. The next year they distributed their firstborn heifers to 60 more families who'd met the requirements, and the heifer chain grew. This concept had the added virtue of restoring the dignity of the participating families, a goal so often demanded by the international aid organizations in exchange for their help. The project is now in the hands of the Heifer Project International, but the impetus essentially came from the restless brain of the reverend from Sisseton, S.D.

So did another in which packets of sunflower seeds were distributed to members of his parishes, with instructions on how to grow them. The sunflower farmers also got small hand presses to produce sunflower oil, which they sold. The sunflower farmers didn't revolutionize the Tanzanian economy. The opportunities were small. But it was a step, one that indelibly bore the print of Simonson's cowboy boots, which were now a part of his everyday, ministerial, walking around gear, along with the hard-brimmed rancher's hat and big-buckled belt.

He and Eunice and the kids, whenever they had a break from the boarding schools, had returned to live in the Ilboru section of Arusha, but by now they had some new and stirring architectural plans. In appreciation for the battles he'd fought for them, the lives he'd bettered with the services he'd invented and the ministry he'd given, the Maasai made a gift. On the upper reaches of Arusha, with a spectacular head-on view of Mt. Meru, is a plot of land the

Maasai owned. They set aside 4-1/2 acres of it, and told Simonson: "This is yours. You can do what you want with it."

There is almost no precedent, in that part of the world, for such a gift to a Westerner. "It was a very humbling thing," Simonson said. "After we'd given our thanks in the appropriate ceremonies, I remember Eunice and I sitting down to consider what kind of home we should build on the land, since that's what we'd decided to do. Do you page through the home-building magazines and find an award-winner? Do you build a Maasai-style hut out of mud and cow manure? Obviously you're not going to feel very comfortable building either one. So we finally came to the concept of a house that would express our respect for the Maasai and our appreciation for them."

What emerged was a kind of African-style hilltop manor which attempts to integrate the Maasai idea of community. The rooms of the living area and the dining and the cooking areas are open to each other so that those in the house or the guests move easily from one to the other and essentially know what's going on throughout the house except, of course, for the bedrooms. Simonson explains: "We took five different circles, each of which if completed would have been a house in itself. We interlaced them, so instead of dividing the space into rooms, we made them living areas connecting with other living areas. So what we call the kitchen and dining area flows into a lower living room and from there you can circle into other space for socializing or move back toward the dining area or simply to go out into the yard. There are no doors. A lot of this is Eunie's idea. If she's preparing food, she can be aware of everyone around her because she loves being a hostess, and I don't know anybody who could do it better."

It soon outdistanced it's nominal designation as a house. It became a reunion hall for American Lutherans in the middle of Africa. They would come dozens at a time, most of them presumably invited by David or Eunice. They'd come from Minnesota or the state of Washington or Wisconsin or Hawaii or South America; Lutherans on a photo safari or on church business or on their way to India. Somebody told them about the Simonson house, and they flocked in. The guest clans swelled over the years to include African plenipotentiaries, friends of Naomi, Steve, Nathan, Jonathan and Rebecca, Rotarians and Kiwanians and Lions (the ones with shorter tongues) who'd become involved in Simonson's fund-raising, and hundreds of people of miscellaneous faiths who happened to be on a photo safari and happened to have been customers of the Simonson family's lodge at Tarangire. Or they were customers of the tour company in Arusha and *might* be potential donors for the schools or clinic.

All of them got open-ended helpings of Eunice's breadcakes and African fruit mix. They also got a narrative from David Simonson about their African causes; the rules of hospitality precluded any hard-core salesmanship. However, volunteerism by the guests, once they got back to the states, was not discouraged.

"Actually, if I were living there alone," Simonson said, "I wouldn't see a whole lot of people. It's not that I'm not a social animal. It's just that I wouldn't be nearly the accomplished host that Eunie is in entertaining crowds, much as I find the visitors fascinating. It's a great way to get up to date on what's going on in the states. What I'd be without Eunie there is a kind of hermit. She's been just marvelous in running that house, mostly because the design is perfect for a person with Eunie's skills with people and her curiosities about them. If she's preparing food, she can be aware of everyone in the house and they of her, and she can respond. You can have five different groups in that house and right in the center is the lady of the house, and that's exactly why it was built that way. In the Maasai tradition, it's actually her house. In the Maasai culture, men don't have houses. They have wives. Each wife has a house. If a man has one wife, he stays in that house. If he's got two, he can stay in either house. If he's got more than two wives, he's got a logistics problem moving around, but the Maasai men don't really consider that a problem, it's a right and a privilege. While legally the house is in our name, the Maasai know it's Eunie's house and my land. That's the way it's supposed to work. With the Maasai, a house becomes the inheritance of the youngest son. The obligation of the oldest son is to marry first. The idea is that when the old man dies, somebody has to take care of the wife or wives. Whoever gets the house, when all of the traditions are figured in, gets it in exchange for taking care of the old woman."

Not many of these traditions are going to be faithfully observed when the Simonsons' hilltop manor passes on to the children, for which the lawyers—and the children—can probably give thanks. The small home in which Dave and Eunice lived while the manor was being built went through several incarnations as guest house and a residence for some of the Simonson children when they reached adulthood. But eventually all in the family lived in the house on the hill for an extended time while they were in transition. It's stood there for more than 25 years, the thatched conical roof lifting above the trees, the tropical flowers assiduously cultivated by Eunice and in the broad front yard, a small fleet of Land Rovers, belonging to Dave, Eunice and their random guests.

The acquisition of the gifted land and the construction house represented a roadmark in the Simonson mission and their personal journey in Africa. They were now landed people, recognized and prestigious figures in the Western community of northern Tanzania, their status considerably elevated from the years of exile.

Simonson mumbles when confronted with language like that.

"We're no elitists. We never aspired to that. We don't want to be looked at that way because it's a mortal cinch we don't feel that way. In mission work like anything else, sometime you make headway just by showing up every day, which we've tried to do. We came to Africa as servants. We're still servants. If the phone rings and somebody needs us, we're out of the door right now."

They are. That has not changed from 1956. It doesn't mean that Simonson can't stand there in the early morning and admire what's in front of him in the African sunrise, on the land given to him by the people he calls his brothers and sisters. Here is the great and mysterious pyramid of Mt. Meru, on whose slopes dwell the Wa-arush farmers, whose cause has been his most of his ministerial life. Around him are the bougainvillea and poinsettias that grow among African wildflowers, and above the flowering flame trees that light the landscape of the Arusha countryside.

"If you can't live on the Dakota prairie," he'd tell his friends, "this was not a bad substitute."

Well, yes. Poinsettias and egrets in the morning. But it was hardly a sanctuary of leisure. For years it served as the site of what friends of Eunice Simonson ultimately called "the Backdoor Clinic." It saved scores of lives, and it took the personal ministry of the nurse from Concordia to one more level of suspense and crack-of-dawn wakeups in the foothills of Mt. Meru.

CHAPTER 16

A doctor and a nurse flying in a light plane toward Monduli in Tanzania were confronted with a streaking flare a few hundred yards in front of them. The woman at the controls looked down for the source of the flare and recognized it immediately—a Tanzanian army base, one she had ridden past in her Land Rover dozens of times. She also recognized tardily that private planes had no business flying over the base.

Eunice Simonson made an abrupt left turn. While it lacked the polish of a professional pilot's maneuver, neither she nor the doctor sitting in the left seat much cared about aeronautical artistry at that point. They left the Tanzanian army's air space with all deliberate speed. Eunice Simonson, apprentice aviatrix, apologized to the licensed pilot-doctor with a blush. "I could have gotten us in a real mess," she said.

The pilot, Dr. Harold Houseman, a Mennonite from Lancaster, Pa., was undisturbed. He said she was doing fine. And in reality, she was. For a couple of weeks on their shuttling flights to provide medical services to Africans in the remote towns of northern Tanzania, Houseman had been turning over the controls to his nurse to familiarize her with fundamental flight procedure. They might run into an emergency. The pilot might have a stroke or a heart attack. She ought to know the basics of flying, i.e., how to get the plane back down on the ground. His objective in undertaking this flight training for Eunice wasn't entirely a case of crisis management. The doctor had piles of reports to write. When they got over terrain that presented no directional problems for the novice pilot on his right, Houseman would say, "She's all yours."

So this was one more stage in the shifting medical identities of the nurse from the prairie, now working in clinics in Arusha, educating families in sanitation and disease prevention out in the settlements and tending the needs of hundreds of ailing drop-ins each week at the Simonson house. And, when calls came from the Flying Doctors of Africa. She was flying to any one of 18 towns on their circuit, a partner with the doctor. She dispensed medicine, took blood pressure and pulses, applied bandages and gave immunization shots hours at a time. Between these chores she also learned how to fly an airplane. Her medical charts were full. The life excited her, and she seemed almost never to tire.

Houseman told her how to react if she heard the plane's stall warning horn: Get the nose down right now. He instructed her how to reduce power coming in for a landing, what the flaps were for and how to control them. He advised her on what kind of fields to look for if the plane lost power and she had to make an emergency landing: Stay away from the ones with tall corn and piles of boulders. If the fields don't look good, look for a road, but look first for utility lines, which you should try energetically to avoid. Also avoid giraffes and similar landing hazards. This was not facetious. Over the decades, hundreds of planes coming in for landings at a variety of airstrips from the Sudan to South Africa have had to pull up and do a 360 to avert a collision with lounging lions or ostriches skittering across the runway. Not all of those potential collisions were averted.

Eunice found flying a thrill. "When I didn't have to do anything with the controls except to hold the plane steady, going straight and level," she said, "it was wonderful to be flying above the changing African landscape, to realize what an enormous country this was, to look down on the Rift Valley with its alkaline lakes and great cliffs. You could get mesmerized, which might have happened when we flew over that Army base. Dr. Houseman had pointed out various mountains that I could use for markers in getting to this town or that. Those mountains would be my heading until he was ready to take the controls again. I must have lost my concentration on the flight to Monduli, because there's no way he would have given me a heading that would set off a warning flare from the Tanzanian army."

It could have been worse. It could have been a SAM rocket.

Her nursing venues for the next 20 years would range from hospital operating rooms to smoke-clogged mud huts, putting her face to face with a weeping mother whose child was dying in the mother's arms and with a Maasai warrior clawed by a lion. The episode with the wounded young Maasai gave her a glimpse of a tribal code in an unforgettable way. He and his companion had been looking after the cattle. A lion emerged from the bush and charged. The young warrior's companion threw his spear, missed and ran. The lion pursued him, killed him and then turned on the young warrior who had tried to rescue his companion. The lion had clamped his jaws on the young man's arm. The Maasai held onto his spear and, with the lion mangling his arm, drove the weapon hard into the lion's gut, killing him. Other Maasai found a way to get him to the hospital. "His arm was totally septic when he arrived," Eunice said. "We didn't have any anesthetic. It had to be cleaned. We poured antiseptic and antibiotics into him, and the doctors worked hard and long and saved him."

The hospital people expressed sympathy for the man who was slain. The warrior's response was blunt. "He ran. He deserved to die. People who run don't belong in the Maasai."

But her most profound service to the Africans with whom she and her husband chose to spend a lifetime was her daily, undramatic tending to a clientele that eventually numbered into the thousands. It came to be known among her admirers as "the Back Door Clinic," a charming description but essentially a misnomer. The back door was actually the front door of the Simonson's hilltop house, one of the few doors in a home laced with interfacing rooms. For years the queues of mothers and children would gather on the lawn, waiting for the woman they called "Mama" to look into a child's eyes or feel the child's stomach, and to work a cure. Her presence itself was a comfort. She had the carriage of an agreeable matron of a woman, her hair still brushed with a tint of brownish red, a handsome woman who seemed to inspire instant trust. Mama. They all called her that. It was a term both familial and respectful. She didn't look especially matronly belting down a dirt road behind the wheel of a Land Rover after one of the African runners brought word from a nearby village that she was needed. She had to tell them often that she wasn't a doctor and couldn't operate and sometimes she didn't have the right medicines. They knew that. But they couldn't find a doctor and she was, after all, Mama. When they came to her house in the morning the scene was not unlike the daily sick call in the army. The ailments were varied but mostly they belonged to the children. Usually she had something in her cabinets or kitchen counters that could relieve the pain or some advice that would ease the mother's anxiety. When she had no remedy, she always had an assurance and a kinship in her eyes that offered hope. None of them ever left Eunice Simonson's house without that.

Eunice explained the Back Door Clinic: "Wherever I went in Africa, I tried to be part of the community of women and children around me. When we lived in our first house in Ilboru, I taught health and did minor medical things for people in the neighborhood. When we moved into the house on the hill, it got around pretty quickly that I was a nurse and I'd help out in the neighborhood with whatever skills and supplies I had. I suppose it started when I'd go for walks in the neighborhood and people would come up to me and say their kids were sick. I'd invite them to come up to the house in the morning and I'd see if there was anything I could do. In a little while they started bringing their newborn babies, and the word circulated that Mama had some medicine, and it didn't cost anything. After a while it wasn't only medicine. People I knew in the states would send baby clothes. Well, I don't suppose that was an accident. I'd make appeals to church groups when we went back home on furloughs. I distributed those clothes to the African mothers to give to their kids. It got to be a practice that they'd come fairly early in the morning so that I could take care of them and do the rest of my chores the rest of the day. A lot of the problems were respiratory—kids coughing, kids with running noses or kids with more serious trouble like diarrhea and other intestinal disorders. I'd get medicines contributed by people in the states—pills and syrups and sprays, things like that. Often it was a matter of keeping the child supplied with plenty of fluids. I usually had milk for them. Sometimes I had only water. I kept a supply of bandages, Vaseline, gauze, cough medications and a lot of antibiotics for pneumonia and anti-diarrhea medicine. I didn't usually like to treat for malaria. I preferred to have blood slides done for that. Malaria can resemble a lot of other diseases.

"The most heartbreaking were the burn cases. For those I tried to do a lot of teaching. The mother would be cooking over an open fire and there'd be big pots of boiling water and boiling porridges, and the kids would crawl over the rocks and tip those pots. They'd get massive burns, ugly, excruciating burns. A lot of mothers put honey on them and one came with a rabbit skin. She'd spread the burn with honey and plastered it with the rabbit skin, thinking it would keep from wound from seeping. It prevented the seepage but I had to take the whole thing off because infections had spread underneath the rabbit skin. The whole concept of putting a burn immediately into cold water was something they just hadn't heard about. I treated for burns almost every day, and it was wrenching to see the pain those little children were in."

There were days when more than 40 people would fill Mama's yard. She maintained the little clinic for years, but eventually it began to be exploited by people for whom it wasn't intended.

"They were coming to the house in cars from the middle of Arusha, and not all of them were Africans. It was getting out of hand and draining my energies. I had to discontinue the services and look for a new approach. We wanted to be sure we took care of the people who were dependent on us, the ones from the immediate neighborhoods around us. So Dave had an idea, typical Dave. He'd taken the old German mission house in which we lived for eight years in Ilboru and converted it into a dental clinic. It had a very large yard, and the church people across the street agreed we could build a small dispensary there, where all of the mamas and babies in the nearby neighborhoods could come for medicine and advice. We had good people handling it. It was intended primarily for maternal child health care but eventually an outpatient component was added and it became a general dispensary for the public in those neighborhoods. The Maasai named it "Mama Naomi's Clinic" (in line with Maasai tradition linking the names of the mother and her firstborn daughter). The whole thing seemed almost like magic."

But it probably wasn't. Mostly it was David and Eunice. While she'd become a kind of full-service healer of the African bush, scrub nurse, anesthesiologist, immunizer, all the rest, Eunice Simonson never had much trouble understanding her limitations in the medical world. She knew her skills well. She knew of her capacities to reach people and to win their confidence, which she found out early is part of healing. But she never lost a kind of workaday humility that some friends found becoming and others found mystifying, in view of her immense achievement. Maybe that humility flowed out of the day in a hospital in Northfield, Minn., back in the 1960s, when she and her husband were home on leave, staying at a mission house. With David off on his inevitable fund-raising tours, Eunice volunteered at the hospital to get back into a hospital setting and bring herself up to date with advances in it. Until then, most of her hospital nursing had been done on medical and surgical floors, and she was interested in getting involved with intensive care and in coronary units.

"They had a wonderful staff of night nurses, who'd cover for me if I needed any special instruction or help," she said. "I was eased into some work in their small coronary care unit, which was usually staffed with specialists in that line. On that night there was a patient in the coronary unit, and one of the nurses asked if I'd stay in the room with him because they had to attend a meeting that had been called rather suddenly. The patient was a sweet old man who was on a drip that had been set up for him. The other nurses said nothing drastic had to be done in this man's case and no problems were foreseen. They said all I needed to do was to observe the overhead monitor, watching the sequence of drips. If I needed help, there was always someone out in the hallway who could call in the regular unit nurses. Everything went fine. The sweet old man opened his eyes after a few minutes and said, 'Oh, Lucy, we've had such wonderful years together, haven't we?' It seemed obvious that this little man was identifying me with the woman in his life, so I said, 'Yes, surely we have,' playing along with the illusion. He kind of sighed and said, 'Would you hold my hand?' I put my hand in his and suddenly he made a sound, threw his arms up and sank back into his pillow. I looked up at the monitor. It had gone blank. All it showed was a straight line. My first thought was, 'Oh, my, why did this happen to me?' Then I thought of this poor man. I called for the night supervisor and then put the man's hands together and quickly began reciting what I remembered of the 23rd Psalm and then I went into the Lord's Prayer, also thanking God for nursing and all the great things it had brought into my life and recognizing there were also times of death in it like this. The nurses rushed in to look at the old man—who then opened his eyes and gave me the most beautiful smile. He said, 'That's the nicest thing you've ever done for me,' and I almost fainted. The head nurse smiled. What had happened was that in throwing up his hands, the man disconnected the instruments on his chest. That disconnected the monitor. What I'd done was to look only at the monitor. I hadn't checked his pulse or looked for the other signs of life. I don't have to tell you that I became famous overnight in that hospital."

Nor does she have to explain that not many others would tell that story of professional embarrassment with so much gusto and absence of ego as Eunice Simonson. Her nursing service, most of it volunteer, didn't really allow for any towering ego. She dealt daily with the pain and grief of people who lived in mud huts and town shanties. She felt humble seeing the gratitude and the renewed hope in their eyes for her simplest service.

It had enormous time burdens, that kind of nursing. But she did have recreational outlets in her life. She became an excellent painter and also an actress, for which she could thank her ventures into amateur theater and her piano strumming back at Concordia. With other women from the English-speaking expatriate colony in Arusha, she got involved in a community drama enterprise which used an old theater on Arusha's main street as its forum. They'd take a stock English-speaking play, story or poem and invest the script with local situations and humor, some of it on the edge of raucous. "For instance, we did a version of *Snow White and the Seven Dwarfs*, only we made it 14 dwarfs because the witch didn't understand Swahili very well and decided she had to deal with 14 dwarfs. Eventually I was branded as a comedienne, because I played the part of the mayor's goofy wife in *The Music Man* and, according to the missionary critics, I played it goofier than they had ever heard. When I'd tell people about some of my roles I mentioned Noel Coward's *Nude With Violin*, which horrified them until I explained the nude wasn't me but a portrait. We also had a music group which was dominated by six Baptists, but it was flexible enough to play everything from Bach to *Fiddler on the Roof*. My favorite was the theater, though, and my favorite role probably was one of the nutty and murderous old aunties in *Arsenic and Old Lace*, the ones who kept welcoming people to the house and putting them away. Then I played the role of *Dolly*, one year when our great friend David Preus, who became head of the American Lutheran Church, was in town. We were walking down a street in Arusha one day and people kept running up to me and yelling "Hello, Dolly," and David nearly fell over laughing."

She ultimately directed and did some serious plays, one of them written by a Ugandan woman who'd become one of her good friends, a woman of faith and a history of much pain and suffering. She became a Christian during her ordeal and credited Christ with her survival. Her play was a series of episodes, called *He Touched Me*, in which she recounted in dramatic form the healing and exorcism performed by Christ in his ministry. Eunie's ultimate fate in the amateur theater of Arusha, the one that usually befalls all of the battle-tried veterans, was to become a "character actor." At Concordia, when she was young and beautiful, she'd played the femme fatale role in an Ayn Rand play, *The Night of January 16th*. It was also her last play in Arusha before the theater closed. "I played," she said, "a Swedish charwoman who testified against the star. So it had come to this. From ravishing beauty to funny old scrub woman. It's one reason I never had much trouble with humility in Africa."

Neither did she have much trouble understanding where and why she was needed.

By the early 1980s her work had expanded to include the role of nurse for the American community living in and around the city of Arusha. More immunization shots, malaria prevention, treatment for fever and care for pregnant women. The Canadians, who were in Tanzania in force to operate an experimental wheat program, inevitably learned about her and retained her to perform the same function for the Canadian colony. The Canadians set up three clinics to help them stay healthy. Eventually Eunice got acquainted with all of them, to which she had no objection because she found the Canadians uniformly easy to deal with. But it wasn't all roll-up-your-sleeve-please nursing. Sometimes it involved violence and trauma. A Canadian woman entering the gate to her yard after a shopping trip was shot five times by a robber. She'd been bending down to unlatch the gate and was struck in the thigh and buttocks. The Canadians called Eunice. When she arrived the woman was bleeding and in hysterics. Eunice drove her to the Mt. Meru hospital, where the situation was in disarray until one of the Canadians who came to the hospital with them volunteered to donate blood as a Type O or universal donor. Doctors administered a direct transfusion and stopped the bleeding, after which the woman was evacuated to the Kilimanjaro Christian Medical Center in Moshi.

"I stayed with her for three weeks," Eunice said. "It was one of the most stressful times of my life. She was in severe pain and shock, and she was terrified. I spent much of the time holding her, singing with her and praying with and for her. Each time I entered the room I found in her in hysterics. She had a fearful time when they removed pieces of the bullets. Some had passed through her thigh and buttocks and caused nerve damage in her legs. Some of the Canadians wanted her flown to Canada, and I put that proposal to the doctor. He said no, it wasn't a good idea in her present state. I found myself under harsh criticism by the woman's Canadian friends, who evidently thought I was part of the decision to keep her in the Moshi hospital. I wasn't, and their indignation hurt me. But she and I became close friends during this grievous time in her life and worked through her fears. We stayed in touch after she left the hospital, and she eventually was able to return to normal life."

In her wisps of idle time (she was also managing the hilltop house and catering to those intermittent swarms of guests it attracted), she got involved in clinical work for the Selian hospital that Dave Simonson and later Dr. Mark Jacobson of Stillwater, Minn., were enlarging each year for the primary care of Tanzanians who could afford no other hospital.

Plus—

She and the volunteers she recruited put together educational clinics for the Africans, gave immunization shots and distributed food. It was strictly a matter of, "African friends, we can help." Some of those volunteer American and Canadian women had been spending their spare time playing golf or bridge or tennis. This, they said, was better. The gave hundreds of hours. Eventually some of the recruits were able to take over Eunice's work, freeing her for the personal, in-house attention she was able to give troubled folks in what became the Back Door Clinic, which she still describes as some of the most satisfying years of her nursing in Africa. "It was a way of serving the neighborhoods first hand, with better facilities for it. The Tanzanian mamas would come in not only as patients or with children who were patients, but as neighbors. It gave them a chance to share their frustrations. Many of them were abused women. Some of them had been abandoned by the men and left to raise the children alone, with practically no means of support. It was a time when I truly was able to be a friend to these people. If they needed medical treatment, we were able to get a start on it. When I now look back on those years, I thank God I became a nurse. I don't how life could offer more enrichment than what it gave me in those daily gatherings at our door."

The new dispensaries, the rapid expansion of the Selian hospital and the development of the pediatrics ward there meant that Eunice Simonson—in the years beyond her middle age—could retire from her personal nursing agendas. It didn't mean she wouldn't answer random calls. And it didn't mean that she would turn people away from her door if one of the local ladies failed to get the message about the dispensary down the road and showed up at the Simonson's house with a wailing kid in her arms. It did mean that Eunice had more time for Africa.

Visiting nurses in later years would pump her with the usual clinical questions and those sessions went on for hours, but the nurses invariably got around to Africa. What, they'd asked, is the hold it has on you? You and your husband have served for years and you seem just as motivated today as you must have been in years ago. Why do most of the children of the Americans who spent a lifetime here find reasons to stay?

"It's not easy to define the belonging I feel here," she'd say. "I think it's the same one that pulls at men and women who grow up here as the children of missionaries or doctors or the other specialists who made Africa their home. You know, living here seems to give you a wider vision of the world and of the humanity in it. It takes you out of yourself. Here, for example, is Dr. Steve Friberg of the clinic at Selian, who grew up in Africa. His parents, Dr. Dan and Ruth Friberg, carried on mission work in Africa for more than 45 years and became two of the most revered figures in East Africa. Dan Friberg was an evangelist, a theological professor, a pastor, known to thousands through Radio Voice of the Gospel in his programs beamed from Ethiopia. Ruth was a nurse. There is no way to estimate the thousands of people whose lives they touched. Steve Friberg, one of their sons, moved to the states but had to get back and felt that medicine was the best way. He became a pediatrician and an indispensable part of Selian.

"What's the draw for these people in Africa? Well, you very early put a lower value on material things than you would if you lived in a prosperous country, as we did when we were young. You see that the fulfillment people can get out of life doesn't depend on having money and things. When you have each other, that's a lot. When you are part of a community that knows you and values you, that's a lot. None of our children, for example, could care much if they didn't have a roof over their heads. What I see in the part of Africa where I live is a more honest life, for some reason. A less selfish life, I think, than some of what I've seen in America and, more often, a freer life even without some of the material things. I think I can be relatively free in our house in the country near Fergus Falls, Minn., when we go back there. But when I'm in the city, the phones are ringing, there are pressures to do the social things, and one way or another you're sucked into a competition and bombarded with information, advertising, trends, all of that. Sometimes it's wonderful. But it's dizzying. And then there's Africa. I remember in the years when our kids were small and we couldn't afford to stay in safari lodges. When we'd go out to look at the wildlife, we'd drive to Tarangire and put up tents. And we'd look down into that marvelous acacia forest beneath the Tarangire slopes and see elephants trudging to the river and those giraffes, which always seemed so dignified and imperial to me, strolling through those umbrella trees. It seemed so other-worldly and a reversion of time. And we were the witnesses to it, our family, and it was just the most precious time. Before dawn you'd hear the doves and that distant grunting of the lions, and how on earth could you have an experience like that in the middle of Minneapolis?"

Well, no. The giraffes are going to be ticketed for jaywalking in the middle of Minneapolis. Eunice Simonson was saying that the friends who visited from the hothouse cultural climate in America were fascinated by those scenes themselves, and by the rhythms of life they felt in a place like Africa. "And they'd tell me, 'I'm not going to fall back into that frantic pace when I get back to the states. I don't want to change my wardrobe every season. I'm not going to do it.' And I'd allow myself an inward smile because I knew what was going to happen. In a year they'd tell me that they'd welched on that vow, that they had gone back to the old lifestyle, reluctantly, but they did in self-defense to stay up with everyone else. I didn't make any judgment about that. Why would I? I found myself doing the same things when I'd go back. When the Africans laughingly refer to us as '*wazungu*,' the ones who run around in circles, isn't that image true? When Dave says we've learned a lot more from the Africans than they've learned from us, there's so much truth in that. Sometimes the little things are the most profound. One thing I've always found special is the African way of greeting people. We'll barge into a situation and say what the shopping plan is for this afternoon or where we're traveling next. Or I just got off the freeway, and it was absolute gridlock. We lump all of that stuff together and that often passes for conversation. The Africans I know will look you in the eyes warmly and say, 'How is your home?' or 'How is your husband and how are your children?' and then 'How are things with you?' You know, even after nearly 45 years in Africa and being exposed to that pace and tone of conversation, I still find myself preoccupied some days with 'agendas.' How am I going to get all of this stuff done?' The African way is that it will get done and don't worry that much about it. Or one of my little helping girls will come in and, instead of taking a few minutes to ask her about her life and going through the social litany as the Africans do, I'll say, 'Good morning, it's good to see you. Would you please see that we get some water?'

"We've lost so much of the kindness of reaching out into the lives of others to show concern and courtesy and awareness. And these people from ancient and poor cultures can show us, if we're willing to see and to hear, how much better we could live with each other. And we're tempted to call these *primitive* cultures. It seems to me they're the sensitive ones. One word I've learned to use with great fondness, because it makes me feel so good to say it, is *salaam*, the Arabic word which conveys, 'happiness to you,' or 'good health to you' or simply 'peace.'

"Isn't that a wonderful way to say hello?"

It is, and there may be no one in East Africa more convincing with that testimony than Eunice Simonson. But finally, if her conversation is with visiting nurses, her listeners want her to remember one of her nursing stories that connected her irreversibly with the African experience. And Eunice will often remember the night a frightened husband reached her with the news that his wife's baby was coming and he didn't know what to do.

Eunice: "Normally I would have driven the Land Rover because most of the roads are just trails through the hills. But Dave was out in Maasailand with it. We also had a Volvo, which was a first-rate vehicle under most circumstances, but this family lived well out of town and the terrain was terribly rough. I got the car up the trail, and the husband ran in to get his wife. We just got her into the back seat of the car and she was telling us that the baby was coming. By the overhead light in the Volvo, I delivered this huge baby. I said we have to get something to tie the cord and cut the cord. There were other people there by now, relatives or friends, and they ran into the house and came out with a razor blade and some rags. We ripped them up and I tied the cord and cut it. It was mama's eighth or ninth baby, so it wasn't such a big deal for her. Her mother came with a clean cloth, and I delivered the placenta and cleaned her daughter as best as I could. Then I took stock of my own situation. There were hedges behind the house and I'd gotten my backside wedged into them and it was a turmoil trying to get myself dislodged. I finally managed and asked the father if he wanted to take his wife and baby to the hospital, but he said no, it was fine. I drove back home, and the next morning here was the father with this baby. He was so proud. He put the baby in my arms and said, "Mama, you brought this baby to us, and we want to give him a name that reminds us of you. We are going to call him Volvo."

Which meant, in the Maasai tradition, that in addition to being Mama Naomi she was now Mama Volvo.

There are people in Arusha who still call Eunice Simonson, Mama Volvo. She thinks that is charming. And in view of what it might have been, she's grateful she wasn't driving a Toyoto Corolla.

CHAPTER 17

Simonson learned biology and comparative religion the conventional ways, in the classrooms of Concordia College on the Red River of the North. He learned theology in the usual way, in the ceaseless dialogues with the professors of Luther Seminary in St. Paul.

But his instructors in economics in East Africa sported no academic pedigrees. Their expertise was the rough-and-tumble of Third World finance in the scruffy street markets of Arusha and Loliondo. They were crafty traders from the Middle East and India and southern Europe who made their living in the backwaters of international commerce, peddling, bartering and cutting deals. A number of them had encountered Simonson in his hustlings for brick, lumber, salt and maize as the de facto agent for the African settlements. They liked him. They liked his boldness and candor, and they approved his own developing skills in the bargaining pits. They found his gusto and his stylized appearance attractive and fascinating. Here he was, big-brimmed hat, western boots, big belt buckle, measured but unmistakable swagger coming down the street. This was a man of God with big and sometimes dirty hands from the smoke of the bomas. He seemed to know what he wanted and where he was going, and above all they trusted him. He promised money in December, he delivered money in December. He said he'd drive them 200 miles in his Land Rover, he did.

Which means it shouldn't have surprised the real estate folks in Tanzania in the early 1980s to learn that the family of the Rev. J. David Simonson was going into the safari lodge business. In addition, J. David was doing it in partnership with a polished Norwegian-born businessman from Minneapolis in a deal negotiated with one of those canny Asian entrepreneurs who trusted nobody to make the deal but David Simonson.

The cast of players might have been drawn from the era of the black-and-white film epics in which Humphrey Bogart and Claude Raines worked their private poker games, deal-cutting in the little side parlors, making up the rules and changing the stakes by the hour on whims and wit. Here was Simonson, visited one day by some of his pals from the European colony in Arusha and asked to broker the sale of an old hunting safari lodge on the shores of Lake Ndutu on the road to the Serengeti Plain. Here was an English woman, Margaret Gibbs, the esteemed third-generational proprietor of an old coffee plantation-cum-tourist lodge called Gibbs Farm in the highlands beyond the African Rift. With her was Per Kullander, a Norwegian who owned adjacent property. They had both lost their spouses recently and were planning to marry and to join their proprieties. With them also was Bjorn Figenschou, an engineer in the sugar business, a friend of Margaret Gibbs, Kullander and Dave Simonson, a man ready for a career shift into tourism. In absentia there was another one of Margaret's friends, Aadje Geertsema, an attractive Dutchwoman and wildlife researcher who had spent some time at Lake Ndutu, had fallen in love with its frontier loneliness, its wildlife and nature, and wanted to build a life there. All of them, through their own or family resources, wanted to acquire the remote and underfurnished little lodge built at Ndutu by an English hunter named George Dove, whose pith helmet and waxed mustache seemed to blend perfectly with the impala horns and buffalo skins that adorned the walls. But Dove was gone, and the owner of Ndutu was now one Chimen Patel, a Tanzanian whose origins were in Pakistan and whose safari lodge holdings were in a state of unease. The tourist business in Tanzania, never as healthy as Kenya's because of Tanzania's relative pauperdom, was worse than ever. Disputes between Kenya and Tanzania had forced a border closing in 1977. That barrier came down a few years later, but Patel's business was suffering, especially at Tarangire National Park, where he'd met Simonson at a missionary meeting and was favorably impressed. Patel owned the safari lodge at Tarangire. It was a chronic loser. The lodge was located within the park, which meant taxes and other obligations to the socialist government. The lodge at Ndutu, despite its more primitive flavor, was still running in the black. So the little alliance headed by Gibbs farm contacted Patel for the purpose of making a bid on Ndutu.

Simonson recalls it: "Jon and I were at the house one Sunday afternoon when they came up and said they had approached Chimen to sell Ndutu to their group. He said no way, that the only person in Arusha with whom he would discuss a deal for Ndutu was Simonson. The Gibbs group said they'd called on me to negotiate for Ndutu in their behalf. I said that's not my job at all. They said Chimen wouldn't talk to anybody else. So I went to see him. I was a little cagey. I wanted to talk outside. So we talked in the Land Rover. 'They'd like to buy Ndutu,' I said. He said, 'Sorry, it's not for sale. It's outside the park so I don't have to pay the park anything. It's the only safari lodge out there. Anybody coming through there (to or from the Serengeti) has to stay there.'

"Ndutu was spinning off some money for him and what he really wanted to sell was Tarangire, which was a couple of hours from Arusha by highway and a lot closer than Ndutu. That was a place Eunice and I loved from the first time we saw it, not the lodge so much as the setting. We'd go there with our family to camp. We couldn't afford to stay in the lodges in our early years, but we couldn't get enough of the animals, the scenery and just the gracefulness of the place. But the lodge was out of the way. The property was run down. Chimen wanted out of there. But I had to tell him I was authorized to negotiate for Ndutu, not Tarangire. 'No way you're going to get Ndutu,' he said."

The cards were starting to lay themselves out. The game was on. Simonson plunged in with both of his snakeskin boots, suddenly excited by the action.

There was a way, he decided. Margaret Gibbs, Per Kullander, Bjorn and Aadje and her family sponsors (with resources in Austrian banks) might be able to land Ndutu if they paired it with Tarangire. One of those, Ndutu, looked like a winner and the other was a turkey. Get what you want by buying them both. That was what he'd propose to them. He asked Chimen about it. Chimen crunched the numbers and arrived at a number that seemed, he said, fair, sensible and kind to his Pakistani heritage. A package deal: both lodges or none.

Simonson called the buyers together. "You've got Ndutu and you've got Tarangire," he said.

"We don't want Tarangire," they said.

Simonson shuffled the cards again. He proposed a company in which the Simonsons—J. David, Eunice and Jon—would be part of the lodge ownership.

It suddenly got more familial.

"They said if I was bringing Jon in, they'd want their own children in their deal for Ndutu."

Impasse II.

Right about here, Simonson decided, it might be time to take a look at the honored old proposition of (a) opportunity meeting (b) chance to create (c) the future. Most of their children wanted to stay in Africa. Jon did at all costs. So did Steve and Nathan. But all of them were going to have trouble getting work permits whatever permanent occupations they chose. That was the reality of life in the developing African countries. One of the emerging priorities of Simonson's life as it reached middle age was to give the Simonson children a lift in securing their futures in Africa. They had strong educations and ambition, although their resources were limited. But now here was a door opening, unexpectedly and almost accidentally, for Jon Simonson, a young man unsure about where he was going with his life in Africa and how he was getting there. He could run a safari lodge. J. David Simonson had no doubt of it. It would motivate him and give him stability, something he was still groping for in the infant little business the Simonsons had already launched in Arusha, the Serengeti Select Safari tour agency.

All that Jon Simonson needed was a safari lodge to run, and here was Chimen Patel offering to sell Tarangire, which was of no interest to the reverend's small clump of buyers. Eventually, Margaret, Per, et al, did acquire Ndutu, of which Aadje became the highly competent manager. "We'll buy Tarangire," Simonson announced to Chimen.

But how?

The price was beyond their means. J. David and Eunice had lived frugally. They'd made some investments but were hardly plutocrats. The kids all had meager savings, but the eventual Simonson share of the initial purchase price was something the reverend himself would have to come up with, largely borrowed from friends in business. Ultimately, the Simonson assets in

Tarangire were transferred in toto to the children. Jonathan became part of the Simonson combine at a relatively earlier stage and later Steve and Nathan. But there was no mathematics in the world that would stretch the Simonson resources to cover the full purchase price.

Another buyer would have to be found. Dave first consulted two or three of the business people who had taken an interest in his schoolroom and Selian projects and had become friends. It was an investment that seemed relatively far afield from their range of enterprise, and they declined.

Several years before, Simonson and Kjell Bergh had met. Their eventual partnership seemed, at least on the surface, to be a rare match of common interest and personal commitments. Kjell Bergh was a bright young Norwegian native who migrated to the United States as a free-lance writer for a Norwegian newspaper, but with arts and drives that went well beyond journalism. He settled in Minneapolis and became the operator of one of the world's most successful Volvo dealerships. In time he broadened his business to include a travel agency. Earlier he'd met a young woman from Tanga in northern Tanzania who'd come to America as an exchange student and was working as a teacher of French at Regina High School in Minneapolis. He and Maria were married in 1968. They presented a striking couple, the debonair, multilingual young industrialist from Norway and the artistic young woman from East Africa who eventually moved into her own business of instruction in African dance, fitness programs and, eventually, as the star of a home fitness video series.

She also introduced Africa to her husband, who was entranced by it and began looking for a home where he and his wife could spend months at a time visiting and touring. He met Simonson at a meeting of the Bootstrap organization, of which Maria was then a director. The couple were guests of the Simonsons in Arusha for several months in the early 1980s during an extended tour of Africa. Bergh asked the preacher if he could help locate a home for him, but nothing acceptable turned up. Simonson told Bergh he might have better luck investing in a safari lodge. The idea intrigued Kjell. His first choice was the remote property of the Lobo lodge on the north side of the Serengeti in Tanzania, a favorite of experienced African travelers. Lobo wasn't available.

But, several years after his initial interest in Lobo, Tarangire was available.

By this time, Simonson had assembled his deal for Tarangire, but to come together it needed a substantial investment by a party outside the Simonson family.

Bergh would have preferred Ndutu, but that, too, was unavailable. Simonson pitched the case for Tarangire. The road to Ndutu was often a horror, he said. From just west of Arusha to the African settlement at Mosquito River, it was chronically torn up, often submerged and a killer for all machines except the most stubborn Land Rovers. In some seasons, driving the road to Mosquito River meant trying to muscle up and down dirt moguls ten to twelve feet high in the road. Tarangire, on the other hand, offered no special supply problems and was immensely more generous to the duffs of commuting tourists.

Bergh assessed the case for Tarangire: "I was interested. I thought it had good possibilities. It had a marvelous location overlooking this acacia forest far below, where the animals were on view at all times of the day, moving to and from the waterholes and the rivers. I don't know of another place in Africa where the viewer can look on in comfort and safety and see such a huge diversity of wild animals."

With those advantages, Bergh thought the property could be upgraded and successful. He wanted to come in as an equal partner or as majority owner, but Simonson balked at that. Bergh agreed to put up 40 percent of the purchase price. Despite its later profitability, he second-guesses that decision today, because, he said, his role as a relative outsider led to disagreements with the Simonsons on management of the business.

Eventually some of those disagreements deepened and grew into random annoyances, although Simonson and Bergh had no trouble keeping up a surface appearance of cordiality. While the Simonson family and Bergh both had investments in the Land Rover company, Serengeti Select Safaris, they weren't always on the same page in computing what percentage each of them owned. The problem, at least for Bergh, was how the African business was run. As an executive operating a multimillion dollar car dealership and travel agency in the United States, he would have preferred a more sophisticated operation on the African end, although it's probably true that the Africa of the late 19th century was not all that far removed commercially from the days of the jungle telegraph. What he could do, and did, was to develop income for his travel agency by booking safarians from the U.S.A. into the Tarangire lodge and using the machines of Serengeti Select Safari. Both the lodge and machines, of course, were jointly owned by Bergh and the Simonson family.

The partnership sometimes took on the appearance of an expanding soap opera of mixed egos and interests. Remarkably, most of the time it's worked out, one way or another. At Bootstrap meetings, the Berghs and the Simonsons are profuse in their expressions of mutual love and admiration. At Tarangire, Jonathan Simonson and his wife, Annette, managed a series of overhauls and renovations in their operation of the lodge. Those renovations, mostly underwritten by additional money Simonson borrowed from corporate friends, included an outdoor swimming pool and a striking observation terrace serving customers who spend their nights in tidy two-cot tent houses outfitted with showers, toilets and sturdy canvas walls and concrete floors. The improvements and the global captivation over Africa fueled by the film, *Out of Africa*, produced a surge of new business for Tarangire in the late 1980s and 1990s. Kjell Bergh may have considered his acceptance of 40 percent ownership a bad business decision (compounded by the possible difficulty of selling a minority ownership to prospective buyers), but the lodge prospered and its value appreciated dramatically. Bergh himself delivered hundreds of customers annually through the marketing of his Borton travel agency, and annually led one or two tours himself, sometimes joined by his wife. Most of those guests were introduced at tour's end to the schools and medical clinic at Selian supported by Simonson's Bootstrap efforts, or they were introduced to Eunice's matronly charm and to J. David's description of the changes in the lives of thousands of people wrought by the schools and clinics. They were also introduced, of course, to the continuing need for contributed money. And the number of converts to those causes increased. So there were benefits all around. The Simonson family's interests in Tarangire were enhanced; the children and the vulnerable of Tanzania found new hope and friends.

Kjell and Maria Bergh were as committed to that end as the Simonsons. Both involved themselves in dozens of fund-raisers in Minnesota and elsewhere. And while Bergh occasionally found J. David Simonson confounding as a partner, he was and is full of admiration for the works performed by the ministry of Dave and Eunice Simonson over the years.

"The impact Dave has had in Tanzania is enormous," he said. "If you take the number of classrooms built there on his initiative; if you take the thousands of kids who have benefited from it, if you take 35,000 outpatient visits at Selian every year and calculated how that has impacted on the patients and their families; if you take the number of lives Eunie has saved or healed through her voluntary homegrown clinic as well as in her professional services; if you take the number of young people whose higher educations they've financed—the impact exponentially runs into the hundreds of thousands. In my experience, I don't know that there is any one person, or a couple, who have achieved that kind of human service."

Simonson is occasionally confronted with this kind of tribute. Make that more than occasionally. When it happens publicly, at a testimonial or gathering of Bootstrap clans at an annual banquet, Simonson will wryly pretend to blow off those endorsements with, "They want to pin a medal on me. The one they should pin the medal on is Eunie, for putting up with me."

But he will hardly deny the achievements. Why would he? He has made them happen. He would also hardly deny that he was telling the truth about Eunice putting up with some of his streaks of brusqueness and demanding habits. Why should he? She has.

"With much love and gratitude," she will add.

And with a high tolerance of suspense.

Kjell Bergh's occasional critique of Dave Simonson's imperial methods of running his operations doesn't dull his fascination with what drives the zealous reverend.

"Dave is powered by the need to excel," he said. "He's driven by challenges. With him, I think, the larger the challenge the more extraordinary his performance. He's one of those guys who sees the big picture and finds a way to turn it into reality. Some leaders see both the larger possibilities and the details that come with them. David just decided long ago that he wouldn't be intimidated by details, which he figures will more or less get swept along by the force of his ideas and convictions. The larger picture when you look at a man like Dave Simonson is that he is totally motivated by the principle of doing good for his fellow man, especially for that huge fellowship of the underprivileged and the powerless. He also happens to be competitive, wanting to know that he can do it, being reinforced when he sees he can. That kind of nature brings with it a sizable ego. A sense of theater isn't exactly unknown in personalities of Dave's type, people who stake out large events to create and to manage. He's done that much of his life, and he's done it well."

That has the look of a sensible picture of the reverend-dynamo, drawn by a sometimes exasperated business associate, a man of finesse in the board rooms and the diplomatic parlors but one who also understands and respects the visceral energies, the big views and the willingness-to-risk of the Dave Simonsons. The fact is that theirs has been a fruitful partnership, if you consider Tarangire's present estimated market value of approximately 15 times the original Simonson-Bergh investment. Shrewdly managed it has blended an appreciation for the early-century safari tradition (unhurried afternoons on the terrace for the guests, congenial service and evening campfires) with up-to-date marketing on the American end. Tarangire had thus become one of the more popular wildlife lodges in northern Tanzania.

And yet the episodes of soap opera in the Simonson-Bergh partnership hardly vanished in the bubbles of Tarangire's rising assets. The administration of Serengeti Select Safaris operations (the wheels of the Simonson-Bergh operations) changed sporadically. Some time after Bergh entered the Serengeti partnership, he nominated Naomi Simonson for the role of managing Serengeti Select. That responsibility coupled with her personal ones as a single parent eventually wore on her, and Kjell stepped in with a solution. She could join his travel agency in Minneapolis as a specialist on African travel. The new scenery might be a boon to both the mother and the boy. Steve Simonson took over the management of Serengeti Select, and Naomi and Seth moved to Minneapolis. But neither adapted to the change over the long haul. The tumult and speed of America, the often violent culture remained a mystery to Seth and was almost as difficult for Naomi, for whom Africa was still the country she understood most intimately. She left the job that Kjell Bergh had opened for her in his Borton Travel agency two years earlier, and moved to another travel company in Minneapolis, Bishop Travel, in which her father had a small share. He eventually expanded it and got it involved, not surprisingly, in African tours. This put the Simonsons' Bishop Travel in the position of writing African tour business in competition with the company owned by Kjell Bergh, one of the partners in the family business in Africa.

The melodrama got a little more congested not long afterward. Mismanagement of its assets under its previous operators had put the Bishop Travel company on the brink of dissolution. One of companies to which it owed money was Serengeti Select. Under court order, Bishop's remaining assets were placed in the hands of a Minneapolis bank. "The company was about to lose its license and go under," Simonson said. This meant that the monies owed Serengeti were going to disappear forever. So the lion-hunting, rugby-playing entrepreneur proposed a solution to the bank. The Simonson interests—essentially J. David and Eunice—would buy control of the ailing company. The money it owed Serengeti Select for safaris in Africa, Simonson said, would be paid by Bishop as soon as the company got back on sound footing under the new management. Later on, Simonson removed himself from the Tarangire and Serengeti Select ownership and transferred his shares to his children, his intention all along in his commercial ventures. The bank concurred in the purchase of Bishop Travel with Simonson as the new owner. Bishop was thus disinterred to write bookings once more under its new management.

A puzzled witness to these transactions was Kjell Bergh, who now found himself in a fascinating new commercial environment. He and the Simonsons were not only partners in the African safari business but, as the operators of rival travel agencies in America, competitors for the tourist dollars that supported their joint enterprise.

It may be the ultimate tribute to God's wisdom and discretion that he chose not to intervene in the expanding soap opera. No blows have been struck or are likely to be. Apart from an occasional stinging e-mail between Minneapolis and Arusha, peace has generally reigned. Friends of both found the picture entertaining. Here was Dave Simonson, admired by thousands for four decades of missionary work in Africa. And here was Kjell Bergh, whose superb performance in the pressure cooker of car sales competition had lifted him to the chairmanship of the American car dealers' association. They had been partners for years in Africa. Both were acknowledged humanitarians and participants in love feasts in which they publicly extolled one another. Yet here they were, competing head to head in the Midwest travel business. The centerpieces of their competition were their bookings to Africa and to a safari lodge in which they'd both held an interest for years.

It might be argued that only two Norwegians could subject two colliding wills and egos to so much creative stress and still come out of it talking to each other. Not only talking to each other, but speaking of each other in public with utter civility and endearment, and apparent sincerity.

On the other hand, it might not have been so amazing. Kjell Bergh didn't get to be the nation's number one car dealer and a candidate for two ambassadorships in the same year by being a lout at public relations.

And David Simonson didn't become the confidante of Sikhs and Maasai elders by being a political chowderhead.

CHAPTER 18

In midstream of his ministry in Tanzania, David Simonson was about to lead a small group of visitors into their last stop on a tour of the meager facilities of the Selian Lutheran Hospital in the village of Ngaramtoni outside Arusha. The hospital had begun as a one-room dispensary in the late 1940s and over the years had been slowly upgraded piecemeal whenever money was available, which wasn't often. Dave and Eunice Simonson had gotten personally involved in its services and funding in the 1970s, but it still lacked electricity and the fundamental needs of a working hospital.

As Simonson was about to escort his visitors into the children's ward, a Maasai woman emerged, holding her head and sobbing. Oblivious of the bystanders, she screamed and threw herself to the ground. It was the shrillest and most piercing cry of despair Simonson had ever heard. It left him inert and powerless. He knew the cause of the woman's anguish without asking. Her child had just died. Crazed by grief, the woman rolled on the ground, clutching her head and wailing. Simonson had found himself in the presence of death dozens of times, but he had rarely experienced a scene of such sudden and unbearable loss. He wanted to walk to the stricken woman, embrace and comfort her. But he knew also that at this moment the mother was inconsolable. At this moment, in her screams of abandonment and pain, she was beyond comfort. The privacy of her grief, the wrenching and violent expression of it, needed the silence of the bystanders more than it needed their awkward gestures of sympathy. Simonson bowed his head and prayed and, after a few minutes, finished his walk-through of the clinic with his visitors. No further talk seemed supportable in the aftermath of the woman's agony, and they finished without a word.

"God," he told himself, "we're not doing enough."

When the visitors had left he walked through the half-finished carpentry of one of the clinic's new buildings, unable to ignore the echoes of the mother's wails. From a cement sack he tore off a layer of paper and wrote his thoughts. They were a plea and a confession. The confession might have been ironic. Simonson had energized his lifetime and in some ways ennobled it by serving the powerless. He was now writing to God, telling God that he had fallen short and had to do more. It was a quiet cry of humility from a strong man,

overcome by the sight he'd witnessed and accepting guilt for what he believed
were his shortcomings as a caregiver.

A child died, today, Lord
    and I was there.
I didn't see it.
    You have already shown me hundreds of others.
This time you forced me to stand there and
listen to the wail of despair from its mother,
and you got what you wanted.
You have become impatient with me.
    You have seen me lose my zeal.
You have been disappointed with me
    when I've agreed to delays.
But you haven't given up on me—
    So, I heard her cry and recognized your voice.
It wasn't something so spectacular as an event,
    only one of the ten thousand children who
    will die today—needlessly
because of me and those that I call mine.
And so, right now, Lord, all I need is forgiveness.
    The rest can come later. I wasn't alone.
My friends were with me.
We came to see if what we heard was true—
and you convinced us, Lord.
A child died today, Lord, and you were there.
I was not alone. We were not alone. Our families were there
    because all of humanity was there.
We were one and we heard.
    We heard the cry which you hear ten thousand times a day.
    The cry of mothers whose children have been taken from them,
        WHILE WE WERE THERE.
May we be as responsive, Lord, as you were.
    May we become human as you did, giving ourselves as you gave.
In order that these cries of despair might become hymns of joy,
    let your humanity become our humanity and let us be like you.
    We would like to ask that what happened this morning
        might never happen again.
    We know that would be wishful thinking.
We would rather ask that what happened this morning
    might never again happen because of us.
May we be known amongst your people as
    those who serve, as those who share,
    as those who respond, but above all
        as those who love.
            Amen.

The day after sharing his prayer with his wife, Simonson got up an hour earlier than normal, drove to the Selian clinic, and took out a memo pad. He wrote down new goals and new numbers, and ended them with an exclamation mark. It meant: "New urgency. Let's get something done. Now."

Later, he talked about the transformation of Selian.

"I thought it was a shame that what we had for years at Selian was this dumpy little pill house sitting up there on the hill. What it was then was a primary dispensary unit, which may have served its purpose, but now so much more was needed. At least it was a beginning, a medical facility. But it didn't have any beds. It had an examining room and a waiting room and some museum piece medical instruments. For a time Eunie did volunteer work in a maternity ward that was on the outside porch of an adjoining building. We needed new buildings, a maternal child health care ward, all kinds of things. In other words, a hospital. There was no doctrine from anyplace that we **had** to have a hospital, but in the last half of the 20th century to me it was a semi-disgrace for a church (the Lutheran church in all of its alphabetical identities in the U.S.A. and Tanzania) as big as ours and as old as ours not to have something better."

David Simonson, of course, did not run the American Lutheran Church, to the relief of the directors of the mission board. Those were folk with whom he often clashed in his bullheaded quests in the service of humanity and God, AAD (Agendas According to David). The church had budgetary problems galore, problems that needed priorities, and the little pill house on the hill had to take its place in the interminable queues of fund supplicants. In the mind of David Simonson, the situation clearly demanded original thinking and a flanking movement to escape the budgetary vises of the wardens of church money. He sometimes admitted the church did have mounting stresses in allocating money. But he also had come in contact with some United Nations' statistics of global child death that confirmed the evidence of his eyes in Tanzania and explained that jarring scene he'd witnessed, the mother's devastation outside the Selian hospital.

"More than 10,000 children die each day in the world from diarrhea alone," he said. "Between 25,000 and 50,000 children die each day from all diseases. The biggest killers are diarrhea, pneumonia, measles and malaria. Those are figures almost impossible to fathom, but they are heartbreaking. If you took a minuscule part of the federal arms budget you could practically eliminate one of the biggest causes of child death, malaria. I try to reach the congregations with that message when I speak in the states. But in the meantime, you have to try to get something going where you are, in what you do. We were in Tanzania. Here was this struggling little clinic which started out by being able to give practically no care and just a small amount of medicine that it got as hand-me-downs from hospitals in the states. We were trying to build it up, but it was going slowly."

And then Dave Simonson met Mark Jacobson.

"He was a winner," Simonson called him, in the parlance of the rugby field. "He was a winner with stamina. He came in for the long haul and he was going to save hundreds of lives, which he has."

Mark Jacobson was an authentic medical missionary, a practicing young doctor specializing in public health, a native of Stillwater, Minn. and a committed Christian. He was a man who, with his family, was ready to dedicate a lifetime in the service of medicine for Africans who needed it to stay alive, who couldn't afford it and who didn't know how to protect themselves.

His credentials for that work could not have been more impressive. He was a graduate of Harvard and the medical school at the University of Minnesota, with a master's degree in public health from Johns Hopkins. Credentials don't save lives. To save lives in Africa, a doctor needs more than to intern for six months as a community service. He or she needs to lay down roots for the duration. The doctor needs to learn the languages and understand the fears, the superstitions and the ignorance. But the doctor also has to understand the laughter and worth of the people being served. Jacobson's ultimate destination was Tanzania. As a community health consultant for Johns Hopkins, he worked earlier in Nairobi, Kenya, training more than 600 community health workers.

Then Jacobson moved to Tanzania and eventually to Selian in the mid-1980s. The Lutheran Church in Tanzania gave him a title: director for the Maasai Health Services project in the Arusha diocese. Among the responsibilities of the Arusha diocese of the Tanzanian Lutheran church was to operate that little pill house. By the time Jacobson arrived there it had grown by a few buildings and by a few more rudimentary services, most of them directed to saving ailing children or healthy children vulnerable to pneumonia, diarrhea and a dozen other ailments. Until then, Dave Simonson was the de facto director of Selian, in charge of drumming up money to keep it going and to expand it. He got some money from the organized church and also from his pitches to congregations in Minnesota and elsewhere in the states. But what the little hospital desperately needed was a medical man who knew how to administrate, who knew how to treat and above all to teach, and a man with a vision and a fund-raising urgency to match Simonson's.

"Mark Jacobson had all that," Simonson said. "Under the regulations of the time the hospital was allowed only one medical missionary. But as it grew, we needed more. Steve Friberg was available. He wanted to come. The church (the ALC in the states) couldn't or wouldn't send him. Something about money. We had to be creative. The Order of Lutheran Discipleship in the states bailed us out. They funded Steve, and we were rolling."

Lurching forward aggressively might have been a more accurate description of the pace of the hospital's progress at that point. Money was always the dragon threatening the goal of a bigger and better Selian. Jacobson laid out plans. They needed reliable electricity. They eventually needed a surgical theater and they sorely needed more beds. They needed an expanded well-baby clinic, which David and Eunice had originated. And while they were always going to fundamentally serve the poor, they eventually could broaden to the point where people of means would recognize the quality of Selian's services and be billed ability-to-pay hospital costs for private rooms and services. The patients who were better off could help make the hospital self-sufficient.

All of this came. It came in increments and in ways that didn't appear on the flow charts of progress. One of Mark Jacobson's earlier patients was an African child who'd suffered third degree burns over much of his body when a cow kicked over a pot of boiling water in the family's hut. Jacobson tenderly removed a blanket from the child's ravaged body. A year before, the child would have died. There was no pediatric clinic near the family's village. But on this day he'd been driven to Selian. Mark began the treatment. The boy was hospitalized. The treatment continued. And a few weeks later the boy was discharged from Selian, without permanent injury.

Jacobson brought to Selian a blend of good, hard American medical training with the horizons of an idealist. They were quieter horizons than David's, but they were just as high and broad. Apart from the immediate caring for patients, the hospital's biggest priorities were preventive medicine for the Africans it could reach—mostly education—and hard cash.

Somewhere, Simonson had heard the name of Jim Buchanan, a lawyer in Denver, Colo. He was working on an estate plan familiar to Simonson when a mutual acquaintance of both, Arthur Vikse, told Simonson: "You need to get things done? Bring Buchanan into the mix."

Buchanan was coaxed into the mix. He arrived as a guest of the Simonsons and was sitting at the dining room table when some of Eunice's Back Door Clinic patients arrived. Among them were some ailing kids Eunice wasn't equipped to handle. She had to send them to a government hospital in Arusha where sometimes three or four children at a time were forced to occupy the same bed because of the overcrowded facilities. "Sometimes," Simonson told Buchanan, "those kids will die of a disease they didn't bring into the hospital with them."

Buchanan, not a hard man to motivate, needed no further persuasion. He began noodling with numbers and names. Coloradans headed the list. But eventually people from other parts of America—donors, corporate figures and professional people, such as Dr. Jack McAllister of Stephenson, Va.; Dr. Verce Fuglestad of Fridley, Minn., Rich Voelbel of Hopkins, Minn. and many others—joined in Buchanan's initiative. What emerged was an organization called C-6, the Consortium for Community-Centered Comprehensive Child Care, based in Denver. It became the stateside board of the hospital, although the hospital was also overseen by the Lutheran Church of Tanzania and the government's ministry of health. The goal of C-6 was to raise decisive money for the expansion and modernization of the Selian hospital, which would give Jacobson and his aids clear-cut budgetary underpinnings for a building plan that made sense and had predictable funding.

And why was that so critical?

Simonson: "It became obvious to us when Mark and I met one day after I'd come back from a leave. I could tell he was burdened. He said three children at the hospital had died. They'd been connected to a respirator, and the electricity went off. It was a terrible thing. I said, 'Mark, we have to get going. We have to do something.'"

Simonson's impulse was to solve the problem and to avert future tragedies now. This afternoon. Solving problems right now doesn't always work. With the Simonsons of the world, however, strategic planning to solve problems more often is freighted with delay rather than buoyed by wisdom. David Simonson put in a telephone call to Duane Tollefson, the pastor of First Lutheran Church in Fergus Falls, where the Simonsons were connected. "We've got a problem, Duane," he said, "and we need help right now." The time was 5 p.m. in Africa. It was early morning in Minnesota. Tollefson might have been surprised at being rousted out of bed at that hour by any other caller than J. David Simonson. "We need thousands of dollars right now to keep kids alive," Simonson said. He explained what the money was needed for. He remembers citing the figure of $40,000, which with J. David's casual recollection of numbers may have been the one he used. In any case, it's approximately what he estimated as the cost of a new state-of-the art generator that would automatically kick in if Selian's erratic electricity failed. Simonson gave the name of somebody he thought could produce the money. The pastor said he probably wouldn't be home because of his work schedules. "Call a few members of the church," Simonson suggested.

Four hours later, Simonson got a call from Fergus Falls: "You've got the money."

Simonson remembers looking at the clock which read 9 p.m. He also remembers a passage in the Bible. "God is speaking to his people," the reverend recalled. "He says, 'Before you asked, I answered.' We asked at 5 in the afternoon and we got an answer (Minnesota time) before noon of the same day."

God was clearly at work in the Scriptures and equally in Fergus Falls.

In a day or so, Deana Miller at the Bootstrap office sent an order and a check for $15,000 to the English corporation that then produced some of the world's best generators. It was installed at Selian not long afterward and is still there, working on both Tanzanian and Minnesota time.

Only a Simonson, perhaps, would have had the brass and credibility with his brothers-and-sisters in Christ on the Minnesota prairie to deliver that kind of money so fast, standing on the razor's edge. Both he and Jacobson knew there had to be a less frenetic way to do it. C-6 was the way. Buchanan and his associates over the years raised hundreds of thousands of dollars. The buildings advanced. But while they did, Jacobson, with other staff members at Selian and with volunteers, but often Jacobson alone, traveled the dust and mud of Tanzania, educating and counseling. No statistics would ever reveal how many lives that kind of undramatic medicine saved or rehabilitated. What do you do about sanitation? About diarrhea and pneumonia and malaria.

And then, what do you do to avoid AIDS?

It wasn't always a matter of traveling the dirt roads into the Maasai villages. Sometimes Selian invited the Maasai to come to Selian to become deputy health workers. It had to be resourceful in this because the hospital served a northern Tanzania population of some 150,000 people, most of them small landholders or roving Maasai, the large majority of them Maasai or their tribal cousins, the Wa-arush. And what were the resources available?

"One evolving emphasis at Selian," Simonson said, "was not only to provide immediate health care but to prepare people from the Maasai villages to become caregivers themselves. Coming out of public health service, Mark immediately embraced that idea and organized the process. Prevention was going to save a lot more lives in Africa than the surgical room, much as that was needed. So the Maasai came in. They stayed in boarding facilities while they were learning about things like how to keep drinking water clean, about getting the sewage downstream from the drinking sources, how germs are transmitted, how flies carry bacteria, how kids can pick up parasites at play, the need for basic good nutrition, things like that."

At Selian and when Mark Jacobson and his people took their counseling on the road, they quietly but emphatically had to squelch some of the traditional remedies for children's disease. "Too many of the Africans grew up thinking that if the kid has diarrhea," Simonson said, "you don't put anything into the kid's mouth, that the way to make them better was to dry them up. Which meant that the child was going to die of dehydration. So the Selian people bore down on oral rehydration. They told the villagers about the needs for getting fluids into the child's system, about putting sugar and salt in the water."

Hundreds of health workers in Africa were delivering the same message, and eventually and slowly the infant mortality rate began to decline. But child deaths were only part of the ravages to health afflicting Africa. By the 1980s, AIDS had become a major killer of adults in Africa. Unlike the spread of the disease in parts of the Western world, much of the epidemic in Tanzania and elsewhere in Africa was caused by heterosexual transmission. Promiscuity, a behavior pattern that began with early and accepted sex in the tribes, made millions vulnerable to the virus.

"Promiscuity is hardly a culture pattern unique to Africa," Jacobson said. "But because most of the Africans lacked the basic knowledge of how AIDS could be transmitted, of their vulnerability to it, and the protections available to them, they were open targets. You couldn't go into the field and expect to change behavior overnight. You couldn't change it this year or next year. But you *could* make people aware of the lethal power of AIDs. You could make them aware that their life was in their hands and they had to deal with their sexuality accordingly. You could direct them to information from the government, and you could tell them about how condoms could give them some protection, although it could hardly give them any guarantees."

Dozens of days, Mark Jacobson stocked his Land Rover with information packets and drove the dirt roads, some days hundreds of miles of them, and gathered clusters of villagers around him at tiny clinics or in community buildings. He was the *daktari,* the Doctor-in-Charge of a growing hospital, but he came to the villages with no pretensions He didn't preach. He made no judgments. He told his listeners that their lives were at risk, and what they could do to avoid infection. He saw people in the communities dying of AIDS. And when he did, it was then that he brought in his God, who was also their God, because Christian or not, these people mostly believed in one benevolent God. He comforted and prayed. He nurtured and did what he could medically.

He was a medical missionary, utterly committed and compassionate, at work in the Africans' valleys of fear, where he and his family lived among the people they served.

The money raised by the C-6 organization in Colorado kept Selian growing, but Simonson and Jacobson saw more needs. Why not? If no general has enough soldiers, no doctor in the bush has enough instruments or enough nurses or enough beds. They had to strengthen the professionalism of the care Selian gave and modernize its equipment. Early in the 1990s Simonson asked the Bootstrap board to diversify its fund-raising beyond school building and to make money available to Selian when it was so designated by the donors. This had the effect of bringing hundreds of small contributors into a Selian support campaign that until then was essentially underwritten by big corporate and professional donors attracted by C-6.

A few years later, the Arusha diocese of the Lutheran Church of Tanzania turned over financial control of the hospital to the hospital itself. It was an act that freed its administrators and its godfathers to perform an overhaul on its budget and to make it self-sufficient after all of its years of grubbing along. By 1996, the money Selian received from its patients increased by nearly 100 percent. The nominal new patient fees it was able to impose sent the total income from the patients themselves soaring by 64 percent, and still the average African patient had to pay the equivalent of only $3 for a day at the hospital or per visit as an outpatient. For the first time in its nearly 50-year history, Selian balanced its budget.

And today: The once-dumpy little pill house outside Arusha has become the most respected medical facility in the whole of the Arusha locale, a full-service hospital with 100 beds offering outpatient, inpatient, obstetrical, surgical, pediatric, maternal and child health services. Its staff grew to 139 people, including four medical doctors, an assistant medical officer and nine medical assistants, a nutritionist, a physiotherapist, some 40 nurse/midwives and nursing assistants. With its new operating theater in place, it was able to handle nearly 2,000 surgical cases. It treated more than 21,000 outpatients, 9,000 children and 6, 000 mothers in its maternal and child health services. It examined and treated hundreds of AIDS victims and thousands for malaria, pneumonia and diarrhea. Medical students from around the world came to visit and help. It expanded its laboratory and x-ray services. It found financial and material support not only from C-6 and Bootstrap but from more than a dozen human service agencies that included the Lutheran World Federation, Global Health Ministries, Rotary International, the Lutheran Coordinating Services, the Christian Council of Tanzania, the Deutsche Institute fuer Aerztliche Mission, the Rouner Center, individual churches in Minnesota, California and elsewhere and from thousands of individual contributors.

The little pill house had became a consortium of lifesaving.

Yet it could not spare its first architects, Dave and Eunice Simonson, from finding their own lives threatened by illness that one way or another rose from their lifelong stewardship in Africa.

CHAPTER 19

There were dozens of times when they could have died in Africa, Dave and Eunice Simonson. They could have died from accidents on the road or from the frenzy of a wild animal. They were vulnerable to diseases with which they were almost in daily contact and to the body's erosion from the peculiar stresses imposed on mission life in Africa. The ones not peculiar to the bush, such as coronaries and cancer, came later in life.

After all of those struck, Simonson was still standing and digging back into the African dirt and into the Maasai's souls. He was never especially fearful about the possibility of death in Africa. In fact, he felt himself insulated in a way explainable only by those who are convinced they are on a mission directed by a power larger than themselves.

"It's not going to happen before our work is finished," he said.

On the face of it, David Simonson's assertion that God called him to serve in Africa might cast off the faint whiff of megalomania. Does God truly direct our affairs in this way? Is there is a divinely ordained purpose in all of our lives or in *some* of our lives; and when the call comes or the direction is staked out, will we recognize it, or should we recognize it?

Millions believe there is such purpose and direction. Others, perhaps lukewarm believers or skeptics, might offer the view that God does not run our lives around the clock; that one of God's supreme gifts takes the form of the choices and the will that he grants to people; and that ennobling one's work by describing it as the will of God is impressive but fanciful. Or, as the lawyer might say, it presumes facts not in evidence.

But this is fundamentally the stuff of theological debates. Whether Dave and Eunice Simonson were impelled to Africa by Dave and Eunice Simonson, or by God, or by the three working in partnership, is not a question that seriously concerns the thousands of Africans who were touched by their stewardship. With David and Eunice, it is not a question at all. They believe they were called. They believe it without equivocation. It is a conviction that carried them to Africa more than 40 years ago and which buoyed and nourished them in the face of their personal and professional trials through all of those years. They were years that included physical and emotional risks, family crises and the demands for endless energy and ingenuity in dealing with the massive needs they saw around them in their shared ministry. They were years that dealt them as many reverses as successes; the times of Simonson's conflicts with adversaries that ranged from lions to bishops. They had to handle the demoralization of not having enough hands or money to save more lives. But deciding that God intended them to plow ahead, not only believing that but *knowing* it, somehow put them beyond defeat. They were going to make it happen because it was intended that way.

Simonson's conviction that he was working with an angel on his shoulder and God in the backseat will amuse the cynic. But cynics don't spend much time in the African acacia forests and hacking a runway out of lava ledge in the Rift Valley. And when you looked hard at their lives and work in East Africa, you had to ask these questions: How *did* these people survive it all, and if it wasn't an angel draped on Simonson's shoulders, what was?

The lion and the leopard could have brought an abrupt end to the reverend's career, but they didn't. Neither did the wild trajectory of the work truck in which Simonson fell asleep and left the road.

What about malaria?

"I faced the same health hazards that most missionaries do," Simonson said. "What made mine a little longer on the medical sheets was the fact that I hung around so long and got exposed to practically all of it. Eunie and I hadn't been in Africa very long when I took the first hit. We went to a movie in Arusha one night and had to sit apart because almost all of the seats were taken when we got there. About an hour through the movie I started to have trouble breathing. It got worse by the minute. I was sitting in the front row, and I knew I had to get out of there. Eunie was sitting in the back. When she saw me reeling toward the door she thought I was drunk. She followed me out, and we got to the Land Rover. I lay down in the seat and just passed out. It was my first real attack of malaria. We drove to a friend's house, and they put me in a bed. By the next day I must have lost 15 pounds in sweat. The blankets and sheets and mattress were totally waterlogged. I'd heard all kinds of stories about malaria and its possible effects, how you could be affected mentally if you stayed for more than two years, that kind of talk. You also heard malaria was something you just had to wait for and let the body set up its defenses. And then there were all of the cures and preventions. I got over it after a while, but there were more malaria attacks in the future. Before those came I was down with anthrax, which the world now knows comes from being around cattle or around people who work with cattle. When you live with the Maasai, you're going to be around people who work with cattle every day and everywhere. I was told later that of those who get serious anthrax, not many survive unless they get treated in a hurry. I wasn't treated in a hurry. And I have to admit I almost died. It was pretty brutal. I still have scars on my legs from it. One thing that first anthrax attack did was to get me introduced to part of the British medical apparatus in the old Tanganyika. The Brits, for all you want to love them, had some oddities in Tanganyika."

That first bout of anthrax turned into a psychological scrimmage between the hairy-chested evangelist and a hardboiled ward matron who let the patient know with looks and body language that she would enter no objection if he dropped dead on the spot. No points were scored in this match and no verdict rendered, which might have been a favor to Anglo-American relations.

"In some parts of the British medical system the head matron was more visible than the doctors. I had one who must have had a bad love affair some-place in her recent history. She was one of those drill sergeants of a head matron, tough as nails with the patients. I don't spend a lot of time wearing pajamas when I go to bed, so my upper half was usually uncovered in the hospital. She couldn't stand that, which made no difference to me. I'm not sure why she was worried about appearances, because she was about as round as they come. She wore a nursing belt, which made her look like one of those Kung Fu or Sumo wrestlers.

"But I did survive both the matron and the anthrax, although I think it was close in both cases. The orthodox wisdom in the mission stations and the Maasai bomas was that once you had anthrax, you weren't going to get it again. I thought that was great news, until. . . ."

A few years ago Simonson was struck by anthrax again, and it nearly killed him.

Medical people in Kenya somehow worked a cure. In part this surprised the medical people but not the patient.

"The simple fact was that my work wasn't done in Africa," he said. "I look at it this way: I'm not singled out with any kind of bulletproof vest against potentially fatal diseases. But I also am convinced that the Lord brought me to Africa for a reason, and the Lord is going to allow me to run this course. No way was something like anthrax going to remove me from the action."

That is more than faith. It is the affirmation of what Simonson truly believes is a contract between heaven and earth. Step aside, anthrax.

Whether you accept the idea of a contract or offer some logical doubts about it, nobody has been able to adequately calculate the odds against Simonson's double escape from an illness as grave as anthrax with the limited medical remedies available where it happened. Nor can they explain the results of the medical tests in America after Eunice Simonson's struggle with hepatitis.

The Simonsons' mission community had been battered by a hepatitis epidemic. Eunice cared for many of the victims, working with doctors to bring them back to health. The disease eventually infected her, and she became seriously ill. She was hospitalized for six weeks in Arusha and returned home severely weakened.

"My liver had become nearly comatose and I was told the damage was permanent," she said. "I was grateful to be alive but saddened to know that my serving days might be over or severely limited. The women in the community had prayed continuously for me and helped care for our children and Dave while I was in the hospital and later while I was convalescing. And then one day Mama Mesiaki walked into my bedroom. Mama Mesiaki was the wife of one of Dave's African co-pastors. She was a wise and tender woman who became a sort of prophet to her own community. We'd worked together in Bible and health classes and became close friends. On this day she walked into my room and said, "God told me to come to you this morning to offer healing."

"We prayed together, and she spread some ointment on me. She had to leave to make another call, but when she was gone, that peace that had settled over me while we were praying remained with me."

On their furlough to the states the next year, Eunice underwent liver function tests in a completely modern hospital in British Columbia in Canada, where she was visiting relatives.

A doctor who'd become familiar with the background of her case came in with the report. "It's hard to believe," he said. "You have a totally healthy liver."

The report on her husband's heart years later was not so benign. By now Simonson was into his 60s, building wider and higher at Selian, building his classrooms, preaching his sermons and flying from New York to Minneapolis to Denver to Seattle raising money when he visited the states. He was also up to his ears in the commerce at Tarangire and with Serengeti Select Safari. He was still rushing around the savannah in his Land Rover expanding his congregations and doing pastoral work. It was a venting of energy that needed calories. It probably needed less than Simonson took in. He took his three sizable meals, indulged a beer here and there and rarely saw a chocolate bar he didn't admire. Heading into his 60s he was overweight and grappling eagerly with the daily strain of his schedules and commitments. He knew he had to curb some of that velocity and the juggling. He knew it because the health expert in the bedroom, Eunice, kept reminding him. He was also aware that he had an enlarged heart, which he attributed to the athletic exertions of his younger days. What he didn't know was that his heart and the clogged arteries that were trying to sustain it constituted a ticking bomb. He'd never seriously considered himself an obvious target of a heart attack or of the coronary disorders that precede it. He hadn't sat down to make the simple analysis that evades most people with the same medical resume. He was overweight and his cholesterol levels were high; he was a male in his 60s and inviting stress into his life every day with his high-octane work schedules and pursuit of goals. A cardiologist would have looked at that rap sheet and shuddered. The cardiologist also would not have been surprised by the scene at the Simonson's home away from Africa in Fergus Falls, Minn., in 1993.

They had finished their packing for their return to Tanzania when their daughter, Becky, arrived from North Dakota to accompany them on their flight from Minneapolis to Africa. Simonson was about to get into the car when he felt faint. His color changed, and he felt powerless.

A few minutes later a doctor in the Fergus Falls hospital made a preliminary examination and ordered a hospital ambulance to drive him to the Unity Hospital in Coon Rapids, a Minneapolis suburb. It was obvious to the doctor that Simonson was experiencing a potentially fatal cardiac condition, a diagnosis quickly confirmed at the Twin Cities hospital. He'd need surgery for widespread arterial blockages. It was an operation now relatively routine, especially in the sophisticated medical citadel of the Twin Cities. But its success wasn't guaranteed. The news left him in a mood of foreboding. He might not get out of this. The heart condition might finish him. Or it might disable him and foreclose what he regarded as the signature project of his mission career in Africa, the secondary school for Maasai girls in Monduli. The plan for it was ready. All authorizations were in place. It was time to get out the hammers. He was just a few years away from mandatory retirement from mission work under the regulations of the Evangelical Lutheran Church in America. And now he was stuck with catheters and a morass of tubes in a hospital thousands of miles away.

"I was disappearing from the scene and not able to carry all of that out," Simonson mourned. "I had to do something."

What he did probably cannot be documented in the hospital dossiers, or in anybody's dossiers for that matter.

"I decided to have a sort of discourse with God," Simonson said

It should be noted that Simonson did not say he was petitioning God or making a plea. He said he was having a talk with God. The purpose of this talk was to jog God's memory. "I reminded him," Simonson said later, "of the obligation we had to the Maasai girls to build that school."

The outsider might suggest that God's well-celebrated omniscience did not require reminders from his flock. But this was David Simonson, who'd never doubted from the first day in Tanganyika that God had brought him there with plans for missions in mind; and that God was the de facto senior partner and enabler in the good works for which Simonson was a designated rainmaker on the scene. These things being true, Dave Simonson could talk to God frankly. "Your servant needs time, God. Five or six more years to do the work at Monduli."

He might have added, "We're in this together." He didn't. What he said was, "If it is your will."

The partners were evidently on the same page. The operation succeeded. Simonson returned to Africa with Eunice under directions from the doctors and his wife to slow down. This he did, unevenly, but with reasonable sincerity. He was conscious now of the impermanence of the human body. The close escape in Minnesota had shaken him. He began to observe a schedule of medical checkups at the Mayo Clinic in Rochester, Minn., and elsewhere. One of them produced a higher than normal reading in one of the markers for prostate cancer. A biopsy revealed the presence of malignant cells. Of the optional treatments, he chose radiation, 30 days of it in St. Paul. His PSA reading, an indicator of cancerous cells, dropped to acceptable levels. In the midst of these treatments and examinations, he was found to be diabetic.

They ordered insulin injections, which he began taking. While grateful for the discovery and treatment, he nonetheless began looking for an escape hatch from the regimen of insulin treatments. Some medical person had told him that in his time at the hospital, he was aware of four or five patients who'd been able to free themselves from the need for insulin. "My idea," Simonson said, "was that I could wedge my way into that small group."

This was undiluted Simonson; if not the indestructible Simonson, then the irrepressible Simonson. In time, he *was* able to reduce the amount of insulin he needed. He removed 30 to 40 pounds and, by the mid-1990s, in his mid-60s, he looked younger and healthier than he had in years.

So what was the moral there?

A man who preached in Africa for years offered a suggestion: "Most people in our business talk about having some kind of spiritual contract with God, acting at God's unspoken direction. A lot of us truly believe that. But Simonson—when you look at his career, what he survived, and the course he stayed on—maybe he really *did* have that kind of commission, and it really was God's will that he be allowed to finish."

To which David Simonson might respond, "What do you mean 'maybe?'"

For whatever brashness his personality needed as an outlet for his man-of-action urges, Simonson was a man of uncompromising faith. God was not only in his heaven but at Dave Simonson's side, at his family's side and at the side of anybody who prayed to him. He had seen his prayers answered a hundred times. Realists said his schemes for thousands of schoolrooms for African kids couldn't fly because the money wasn't there, nor was it there for the hospital at Selian or the school at Monduli. But he prayed and talked to God and sometimes in his spells of depression when it appeared he might have to leave Africa in retirement, he cried. And always, he said, he was heard.

His family and particularly Eunice shared his convictions and never more so than when Becky Simonson Weinreis, the second of their daughters, lay stricken with a brain tumor. The events in its aftermath are not easily explained on medical grounds and the explanation, in truth, might go beyond medicine.

Becky was the gentle child of the Simonson menage, one who seemed to attuned to the world of nature and its animals in an extraordinary way. She would find little animals which seemed to be suffering, or which simply looked lovable and needed attention, and haul them to the family home in Arusha. Animals, whether in a zoo or the back yards or on the Serengeti, seemed to respond to her calls or her touch. At school in Africa and later in the states she became an athlete. She retained a fondness for Africa. But it was not the indispensable part of her life that it was for the other Simonson children, and when she married Jim Weinreis, the young North Dakota rancher, she settled comfortably into life on the western range as the mother of four children. The family had visited in Tanzania for the Christmas of 1995 and was preparing to leave when Becky was struck by a grand mal seizure. When she appeared to stabilize, she and her family flew back to the states. A short time later she suffered another seizure. Doctors at North Memorial Health Center in Minneapolis discovered that a large and malignant tumor had invaded much of her brain. Her mother received the news while escorting friends and family on safari in Zanzibar.

"I flew back to be with her in Minneapolis," Eunice said, "but by this time she was having other symptoms that deepened the crisis. I telephoned Dave in Tanzania to tell him of the gravity of Becky's condition. If anything, it was worse on Dave than on me. I was at her side. Dave couldn't be."

From Africa, Simonson telephoned Rev. Jim Nestingen of Luther Seminary in St. Paul. The two had become friends during one of Nestingen's visits to Tarangire with a ministerial group. Together they had organized the Order for Lutheran Discipleship, which began as a small network of friends in the ministry who wished to deepen their spiritual fellowship. It also gave moral and financial support to some of Simonson's causes for which he could not extract aid from the mainline church organizations because of their budget crunches. Jim Nestingen wasn't totally in love with Simonson's elephant-in-the-parlor style of making headway with his projects, but he admired the missionary's unsinkable spirit and his lofty goals.

"Jim," Simonson said, "I can't be in Minnesota with Becky and Eunice. I can't be her father when she needs one. Will you be her father for me? Can you hold her and pray with her?"

In Jim Nestingen's mind at that moment, the thousands of miles between the two men dissolved. He felt joined with the troubled father, as powerfully as though they had physically embraced. They were united by their faith and their fear and by their prayer. Nestingen said simply, "Of course I will."

With her friends and closest relatives present, Nestingen conducted a healing service for the stricken young woman just days before her scheduled surgery at North Memorial. Afterward, he talked again to Dave Simonson in Africa, bringing him up to date. Simonson asked about the prayer service. Nestingen described it. "Did you use the oils and do the anointments," Simonson asked. Nestingen said no, it wasn't that kind of service but it was full of hope and shared faith. Nestingen could feel the rising agitation and despair on the other end of the phone line. Simonson made no effort to conceal it. His daughter was facing surgery for a brain tumor that might be inoperable. He was thousands of miles away, unable to hug her and pray with her. He also couldn't talk to the doctors first hand or comfort Eunice and Becky's husband. In all of his years of invoking God's power to save a life or to ease a pain or to build a church, he had never felt as helpless as he did at this hour. In all the years of managing the events of his life or bulldozing his way, he had never felt so out of it. He had also never felt the cold hands of dread that he did now. What he didn't allow himself was futility. There had to be hope for Becky. If God was in his heaven, God was also going to be in the operating room. God and medicine. For Simonson, that became his invocation. It reached back into the centuries, into the mists of the very beginnings of worship, when tribal ritual merged with petitions, anointments with prayer, belief with healing. He talked to Nestingen again. "The laying on of hands and the oils, Jim," he said. "Will you do that?"

Nestingen said he would.

They gathered at the home of Verce Fuglestad, 18 people surrounding the young woman, hand-in-hand, praying and singing. Jim Nestingen led. He had first told Becky he believed in confession and absolution, and that he practiced it. He heard her confession and gave absolution

While the others prayed and sang communally, he touched her body with olive oil and placed his hands on her head. They closed their eyes.

On the morning of surgery at North, they all walked to the operating room at Becky's side, singing hymns. She seemed almost buoyant, thanking them and waving her hand. "It's going to be all right," she said. The door to the operating room opened, into the deepest unknown of Eunice Simonson's life.

"The prayer service had been tremendously intense," Eunice said later. "But when it was over, I don't think I've ever felt the sense of peace I did then. On the morning of the operation we had the feeling that whatever lay down the road for Becky, she was in God's hands, whether she was be healed at least partially, or whether her child could be saved (she was three months pregnant) or whether Becky's time was here and she would go to meet God. We felt at peace although the diagnosis was bad. The doctors felt that they would have to remove much of the motor area of the brain to save her, which would leave her severely paralyzed. We continued to pray. It was the hardest on her husband, who kept pressing the medical people for options that would give Becky some chance to lead a meaningful life.

"The doctors had suggested that she might want to consider aborting the child because the anesthetic she'd need and the other treatment might leave the child permanently damaged. Becky refused that. She said she wanted to have the child. And when the hour for surgery came, she waved to us with a truly brave smile, and I felt so full of love for her, but also so fearful.

"I was praying in the chapel when the doctor came in. He said simply, 'You've had your miracle.'

"Somehow the invasion of the brain by the tumor had been reversed. They were able to peel the tumor off the cortex of the brain rather than cutting it off. There was a strong hope that Becky would regain some of the use of her left side. When she regained consciousness she tried to be cheerful, and I was filled with this deep wave of thankfulness. The people at North Memorial allowed me to stay in Becky's room and to care for her while her husband had to go back to North Dakota to be with the children. Jim Nestingen came to visit her for 60 straight days, and on the day she left the hospital not long afterward, she practically forced him to do a dance of celebration with her on the hospital floor.

"In the time that followed, life was full of struggle for Becky, learning how to walk again, how to do things with her hands, but she worked hard to overcome her disabilities, and she has. And when she gave birth in a hospital in Dickinson, N.D., to a beautiful and perfectly health baby named Anthony, the miracle was complete."

Nobody who was in the operating room on that day of surgery is going to argue the point.

CHAPTER 20

He was a medicine man. Ole-Ntokote. He was full of flashing eyes and fervor and fury, loosing his wisdom and premonitions on his clients and his brethren of the Maasai plain. His face was lean and animated and practically announced that here was a very bright guy and a substantial character not easily flim-flammed. It was a face laced with middle-age creases that reflected both his authority and his invitation to a good laugh. But Ole-Ntokote was usually serious and often mysterious, and when he was, he spoke with an orator's lyrical voice that could captivate the hyena.

But one day Ole-Ntokote the non-Christian himself heard a voice, which in time led to a phenomenon of mass Christian conversion seldom witnessed in the East African steppes.

No medicine man on the plains of Kenya and Tanzania commanded the respect that the Maasai accorded Ole-Ntokote. Like doctors and parsons, there are good medicine men and bad ones and mediocre ones. The bad ones are the crooks and impostors of the trade, masquerading as sorcerers and fortune tellers, dabbling in curses and trying to enrich themselves by exploiting superstition and myths. The good ones, the missionaries learned quickly, are both priests and healers in their communities. They may not be doctors but they *are* psychologists; and sometimes they are visionaries, touched by a gift of prophecy. Like Ole-Ntokote, they are credited by their people with inexplicable powers to dig out the roots of their pain or their fear or to lead them in directions away from death. What have you done to offend the spirits of those who have died? How have you misbehaved? Make amends to those you have injured. Being a medicine man could be profitable. Even the good ones were not exactly coy about that. It could mean payoffs in cattle or goats or beer for working a cure or the appearance of a cure. Being a medicine man could also mean facing the potential competition from Christian missionaries, who were preaching salvation to those who were willing to clean up their lives. In this competition, the medicine men were laps ahead. The Maasai were traditionalists. They believed in a God who was linked to the earth and governed the nature and the pastures around them and who had conferred special privileges on the Maasai. Because all of the world's cattle belonged to the Maasai, they had a divinely-ordained license to heist the next tribe's cattle. The Christian missionaries weren't overwhelmingly sympathetic to the virtues of cattle theft, and they had to say so to the Maasai. They also weren't crazy about drinking orgies and polygamy, customs to which the Maasai macho society felt partial. But well beyond those impediments to the conversion of the Maasai to Christianity was their self-designated status of elitehood. They were Maasai. They were independent and fearless and masters of themselves and they already had their spirits, the God of their childhood and their brotherhood.

While other clans around them turned to Christianity in droves in the 20th century, the Maasai did so only in isolated dribbles that scarcely registered on the census tables of Christian evangelism. Even the popular and admired missionaries like David Simonson produced no stampedes of Maasai to the baptismal founts. Simonson never regarded this as a failure of his or anybody else's ministry. It didn't alter his fondness for the Maasai. It didn't influence his eagerness to work with them and to build for them.

"They'd tell me that they were interested in what we had to say about Jesus Christ," he said. "They'd tell me that there might be a time in the future when they were ready. The time wasn't now, but we'd know when it came."

Ole-Ntokote roamed the Maasai Mara of Kenya and the Maasai plain of northern Tanzania in the 1980s and 1990s as a kind of itinerant prophet and healer, domestically content with his three wives and flourishing in the esteem of his peers and his patients. Other medicine men came to him asking him to share some of his craft. Some in the Christian community (Simonson among them) would later call him the most powerful religious figure in East Africa, more powerful than Christian bishops. But until the 1990s, he knew nothing about this improbable person the missionaries called Jesus Christ, knew nothing much about the religion they were espousing and had no interest in it.

He was tending his goats and sheep on a grass knoll one day when rain began to fall. To the Maasai, rain is the sign of God coming to earth. Rain nurtures and replenishes. It is the source of goodness. It is the accompaniment of God, but it is more. God *is* the rain. While the rain was falling, Ole-Ntokote saw a white stone lying on the ground. He picked it up and noticed that the stone was shaped like a human ear. As he stood there, fascinated by the configuration of the stone, Ole-Ntokote heard a voice from above. It said, "Feed my sheep."

That was the story he later told to the Maasai.

Does Simonson believe this episode occurred, that Ole-Ntokote actually heard a voice from heaven?

"Absolutely," he said. "He was known among the Maasai as a man who could communicate with God. Why should we scoff at that? We've had prophets who said the same. It's in the Scriptures, and we believe. I believe what this man later told his people because of those historic events that took place several years afterward, and we were there to witness them."

En route to those events, Ole-Ntokote admitted his bewilderment about the scene in the rain.

"He didn't have a clue to what those words meant, 'Feed my sheep,'" Simonson said. "He just kept herding his goats and sheep until later, again in the midst of the rain, he heard the voice again. He told me the voice said, 'I want you to go to my people, the Maasai. The time for them to come into the kingdom has arrived. They will come under the name of the one who is called Jesus.' He turned to go and then said to the voice. 'I've heard you before. I didn't know what you meant when you said, feed my sheep.'"

So Ole-Ntokote was now narrating a dialogue with God. Simonson, with his off-the-cuff impulses to impart his own punchy language to the scene, explained what happened next.

"Ole-Ntokote told the voice that what he wanted to know is what happens if he didn't do anything."

"The voice told him either you do it or die."

This sounded convincing to Ole-Ntokote. From that point he began carrying the message to all of the medicine men he knew to prepare their people to enter the kingdom of God and this Jesus Christ.

By the early 1990s, he was actively working the ranks of the Maasai medicine men, urging them to abandon their deceptive ways if they'd been practicing cheating and sorcery. He told them to burn the props they'd been using to divine the future or pretending to divine the future. He was, his peers affirmed, powerful, persuasive and practically irresistible in the force of his evangelism. From one Maasai boma to another in southern Kenya and northern Tanzania, Ole-Ntokote carried his one-man mission. He'd heard God, and now was the time. We will go together into the kingdom, he said. We will start sending our children to schools so they have a chance to improve their lives. We should send them to school instead of being selfish and making them herd the cattle and goats. We have to stop stealing cattle. The book of God doesn't give us the right to do that. We can't take any more wives than we already have when we come into the kingdom. God has spoken to us, the Maasai. He is telling us to look out for each other. We will. We will be baptized into the kingdom together."

The Maasai listened and followed.

"They listened," Simonson said, "because this man was a genuine prophet in the Maasai's eyes. They were being shown the way by one of their own priests, who stood above all the others. He's one of the most extraordinary men I've ever met. He'd never received any formal education. But during the time he was learning about Christianity after that episode of the voice in the

193

rain, he actually memorized the Bible in the Maasai language. He'd get up to preach to the Maasai like he'd seen the evangelists do, holding the Bible. He was holding it upside down because he didn't know how to read. But he'd quote from it flawlessly and as eloquently as anyone I've heard. Until the time of his own baptism he'd never heard of Jesus Christ. Now he'd taken the name of Isaiah to go with his Maasai name. In one preaching session he was joined by a native evangelist, who'd misquoted the Bible in his haste to get over a message to his audience. Isaiah corrected him. By 1992, the Maasai who followed Ole-Ntokote were ready to be baptized. They'd received some basic instruction in Christianity, which had to be done or baptism is a travesty. They were ready."

But Dave Simonson, who'd spent a lifetime in African mission sweating and preaching and praying for this hour, was thousands of miles away.

The head of the Arusha diocese, Bishop Thomas Laiser, himself a Maasai and a onetime student of Simonson's, had heard about the Maasai phenomenon up north and had prepared a scenario for a mass baptism of the Maasai. Somebody discovered that J. David Simonson, who more than any other in the clerical clan deserved and wanted to be on the scene of this great feast, was on leave in America, probably raising more cash for his Maasai causes.

The mass baptism was delayed. It was delayed again when Ole-Ntokote was summoned by Kenya's President Daniel Moi to intervene in some intertribal political dispute. "Ole-Ntokote commanded that kind of power and prestige," Simonson said. "I don't want to labor the point, but those things had a way of happening in our work in Africa, and I have to believe that if God was going to point the way to a mass baptism of the people who'd been at the center of my life in Africa for 40 years, he wasn't going to put me on the sidelines now."

The designated sites for the ceremonies in the late summer of 1992 were places like Maninowa and Esoit Sambu in northern Tanzania. One was on a grassy hillock under a candelabra tree to which the Maasai walked from as many as 10 or 15 miles one way. The evangelists had laid out the schedule to accommodate some of the Maasai women, who had to do the early morning milking, walk for miles to the baptismal site, and then get back in time for the evening milkings. The Maasai came in their red robes and their beaded collars and their staffs. They came by the hundreds, escorted by wind bands of Maasai musicians who joined them as they neared the ceremonial sites. Some of them knew the Maasai words for the Christian hymns, and they sang robustly or reverently or curiously. Some of them looked and felt awkward, because this was a total unknown for them, so unknown, in fact, that some of the pilgrims from the remotest Maasai bomas had never seen human beings with white skins. But the awkwardness disappeared when Ole-Ntokote appeared among the celebrants of the service. Ole-Ntokote with his elegant hands spread before them in welcome and blessing. He was their priest, their medicine man and their prophet, and now he was walking hand in hand with them into the place the Christians called the kingdom. Even those who didn't know the words sang.

Nor had they ever seen the contraptions which some of the white skins were training on the ceremonies, small boxes with a red eye at the end. Television. The Lutheran church, whether in Tanzania or Minneapolis or Ashland, Wis., has rarely been accused of flamboyance in its self-promotion. But here were swarms of Maasai men, women and children being baptized into the church, and if that doesn't constitute a media event, Martin Luther himself might have bellowed from the grave: "Don't be bashful, folks. This is something else."

It was all of that. Here were the pastors and evangelists in their shoulders-to-the-toes clerical garments, almost all of them Africans, gently placing their fingers about the heads of the new Christians, cleansing them with the waters of baptism and touching them with the mark of Jesus Christ.

Here were random scenes of colliding cultures. Two of the Maasai who had never seen the white-skinned creatures before approached Dr. Mark Jacobson of the Selian Clinic in Arusha, himself a missionary and a longtime friend and healer to the Maasai. They felt his skin and worked his eyelashes to convince themselves that this wasn't some kind of costume Jacobson was wearing.

A bush version of masquerade ball? It might have been, except that the Maasai were slightly more astonished when Jacobson spoke to them in their own language and welcomed them into the church in which they were now brothers and sisters. And here was the Rev. J. David Simonson in his white-as-ivory alb whose hem was dappled with maroon splotches from the clay of the Maasai plain where he'd come to baptize. He was one of the few white ministers in the queue of evangelists who were performing the rites, which vividly reflected the passage of the Christian movement from the hands of the foreign missions into those of the Africans. Simonson moved massively but tenderly among the Maasai with whom he'd lived for 40 years and who'd told him so many times, "when we're ready, we will come." They came for three days to that knoll near the acacias and candelabras, because they couldn't all be baptized in a day. There were more than a thousand of them, and that figure mounted in additional mass ceremonies in the years that immediately followed.

To the detached onlooker with some passable knowledge of Maasai history and of the plodding but mostly fruitless attempts by Christian missionaries to convert them over the decades, the events in the acacias had to produce puzzlement. What or who was going on here?

Apart from the voices from heaven and the white ears, African seminary students of that time had their own explanations. Some of them said it was time because people in the tribes were ready for a God of the whole world instead of one limited by tribal traditions; in other words, as one missionary phrased it, the tribal God seemed too local. Others wanted to free themselves from tribal taboos and the cult sacrifices, and were deeply impressed by the picture of a supreme sacrifice by Jesus Christ.

Eunice Simonson's recollection of those three days on the northern Tanzanian knolls might have cleared up some of the puzzlement of why it was happening. This assumes that the onlooker is as prepared as Eunice Simonson to see something in the rain beside the raindrops and the pools of water in the African clay.

So where was this rain?

"It may have been the most incredible part of the baptisms," she said. "Each morning the sky was blue. Each day as the baptisms got under way, clouds appeared. And then it rained. Each day delivered showers in the afternoon."

A coincidence?

"Oh, no. Each time the showers came we remembered what rain showers mean to the Maasai. Rain, the Maasai believe, means God is present."

And what else?

"Well, I don't know what else would be necessary," David Simonson said. "But it's been part of our creed, hasn't it, that God works through us, through certain people God has chosen. These people become the channel of God's will and goodness. Here was Ole-Ntokote, possibly the one man in all of East Africa who could lead the Maasai in accepting Jesus Christ, a man who until he heard a voice in the rain had no knowledge of the teachings of Jesus Christ. It's been part of the Maasai's spiritual dilemmas that somehow and somewhere in their past they got separated from God, had offended God and needed something to bring them back. Mark Jacobson said it at the baptismals. They have been seeking reconciliation for a long time. Here was the voice of one of their own telling them that he had been shown the way, and now the way was open for them. They entered the gate, and they were reconciled."

And perhaps this would be the culmination of Dave Simonson's stewardship in Africa. He was now a few years away from mandatory retirement as a missionary of the Evangelical Lutheran Church in America. Approaching his mid-60s, he was facing some medical issues that eventually would be resolved but which seemed to point to a farewell to Africa for the two of them in a year or two.

If that's the way the compass appeared to be pointing, the magnets were all wrong. There was one more mission for David Simonson, one that history and the odds seemed to consign to the museums of lost causes.

Simonson decided that what East Africa needed was a high school for young Maasai women. The Maasai elders frowned. Some of them laughed. It was an offense to their tradition. Young Maasai women didn't need school. They needed strong hands, good backs and enough milk for their babies.

The church itself squirmed. Where would the money come from? How would you get the girls out of the bomas? Who's going to build it?

Simonson viewed these questions with no special fright. He, Dave Simonson, would build the school. He didn't know how but he would build it. What scared him was retirement. When the church said it was time to come home and live on your pension and spruce up the house in Fergus Falls, how was he going to answer?

He didn't have to. His old protege, now Bishop Thomas Laiser of Arusha, had the answer.

The answer was that it was not time for David and Eunice Simonson to leave Africa.

CHAPTER 21

Traditionally for the young woman in the Maasai bomas, premarital sex is not only permitted but virtually required. When the Maasai girl marries, having babies is not an option. It is mandatory. Second to owning cattle, having children is a mark of prestige and prosperity for the Maasai male.

Traditionally for a young woman in the Maasai bomas, sharing her husband with his other wives is part of her charter of womanhood. So is doing the tribal grunt work—building the hut with dung and mud, hauling water from the river, milking the cows and cooking in the dark and steamy innards of the family kitchen. It also means keeping the children away from the boiling pots, looking after the other wives' children, washing the clothes, enduring her husband's drinking sieges and eating separately with the other women whenever the men hold their council sessions around their goat feasts. It is traditional for the women to stay out of eyesight on those occasions so as not to contaminate the scene, since they are lower members of the family and therefore not privileged.

What is this for the women of the Maasai? Family life or something closer to a no-parole sentence to a penal colony?

It is, Mama Ruthie said, the way Maasai women are supposed to live; the way they have been forced to live for centuries. It is a backbending, demeaning life understood by millions of other women in the tribal societies of Africa and the rest of the world. We will meet Mama Ruthie again soon, an almost legendary female maverick among the Tanzanian Maasai, a human bombshell. It ought first to be noted here that there was one more condition of womanhood that was traditional among the Maasai: Girls and women didn't need an education, according to this tradition. They *shouldn't* have it.

So they didn't get it. Have your babies. Tend more cows in your husband's *kraal* for the privilege of marrying him. Don't quarrel with his other wives. Wash the clothes. Shut up. Boys were increasingly allowed to attend primary schools, but in one year of the 1990s, only 26 Maasai girls graduated from primary schools, out of a Maasai population variously estimated from 200,000 to 400,000.

"It was pretty hideous when you looked at it," Simonson said. "There was and is so much about the Maasai that I've admired, their bravery and independence and their real belief in the mystical strength of the community of the Maasai; the idea that you are an empty person without that community. But when you look at the future of the Maasai heading into the next millennium, you get to a conclusion fast: something dramatic has to change in the way these people live if they're going to survive as Maasai. They used to drive their cattle where they wanted; they said it was their right as a nomadic people. They can't any more. If something got in their way, they fought. They can't do that any more. They can't very well run around stealing cattle, either. They're being squeezed. They don't have the land they used to, and they don't have the water they used to. They're a very colorful and engaging people, very proud, but clinging to the past is going to make the squeeze ever worse. What they need is new vitality in their leadership, people to speak for them and to do a better job of fighting their battles with the politicians, to find a way to deal with the new worlds around them—and that includes the infighting of the new native governments of Africa."

They have a resource that might save them, Simonson said, a resource buried under centuries of macho privilege in the Maasai culture. The young women of the Maasai, Simonson argued, could send them into the 21st century with new ideas, new drive and new hope. Before he joined the bishop, Thomas Laiser, in floating the scheme before the Maasai elders, Simonson tried it out on some of his friends. Privately, they scratched their heads. Here was Dave Simonson. Whenever the missionary clans gathered in their parlors in Arusha, he was popularly accused of advancing the agendas of male chauvinism. Here was Dave Simonson, lion-hunter and rugby player, the prototypical "man's man" who had rarely been seen brandishing a liberator's sword in behalf of the female clergy in the Lutheran church. This same Dave Simonson was now embarked on a crusade to elevate women in the society of the Maasai—the Maasai, who without argument belonged in the world class of male-dominated societies. His idea was a high school–college for the Massai women. Was the reverend transformed somewhere on the road to Monduli?

Simonson today looks on this question with some pain and some amusement.

"The business of chauvinism is some sort of kangaroo court judgment," he said. "Maybe I did walk to a different drummer than some of my colleagues. I've never had any doubts about the power of some women to lead, just as I've never had any doubts about the lack of spine and vision in some of the men with whom I've worked or with whom I've dealt. That's humanity. In our house, my mother was the leader, all 5-foot-4 of her. When I got into missionary work and funds were needed for what we were doing in Africa, I could always count on the Lutheran Women's Missionary Federation being the backbone of mission contribution, and over the years they raised millions. I have seen or worked with women in the clergy who were absolutely first rate."

All of which sounds like a ringing endorsement by the reverend for some kind of affirmative action to boost the cause of women. If so, where does this chauvinist reputation come from?

"I've always held that the test for going into a calling like the ministry or missionary work ought to be deep spiritual faith and willingness to serve. That's one thing. Men have no monopoly on those attributes. But if you move from there into the idea that one priority of ordaining to the ministry should be advancing the causes of women or any other group, then the priorities, I think, are getting tilted. That would mean putting the advance of women ahead of the needs of the church or the sanctity of a genuine calling, and I don't think that's a direction that meets the highest need. I'm not sure how you can call that attitude male chauvinism, but it's been done and I get stung all the time with that charge. As long as we're on the subject, I don't know who could have done a better job of launching the school at Monduli than the women of the teaching staff who came there and built that curriculum and did it creatively and unselfishly and I think will eventually be credited with turning around the lives of scores of Maasai women who were looking at a dead end."

How smothering was that dead end?

"Until the school at Monduli was started," Jane Tellekson, its first headmistress, said, "nobody looked into the eyes of the girls to search for the mind behind them. Nobody asked them about hope. Nobody got beyond that voiceless attitude of submission that afflicts most of the Maasai young women. They do have spirit and fire if you liberate them from the their mental and spiritual straitjacket. It was just almost impossible to crack the tradition."

It wasn't that the Maasai women didn't harbor some strong attitudes about their own lives, their children's and the community's. They hadn't been beaten into brainlessness and apathy. Far from that. People who'd dealt with them on any level approaching equality could vouch for their shrewdness and their resourcefulness, if given the chance. What they didn't have was the privilege of speaking out and getting involved in the boma's business.

Shut up, woman.

Jane Tellekson is one of those volunteer women Simonson salutes as pioneers in the launching of the school at Monduli. She had no such ambition a couple of years before when, as a recent graduate from St. Olaf College in Northfield, Minn., with a headful of ambitions to become a corporate powerhouse, she scoffed at a relative's suggestion that she spend a few years in Africa. "Africa for me was snakes and scorpions and steamy jungles," she said "Take it away. I wanted no part of Africa." Still, the relative's quiet lobbying and her own curiosities led her to Africa and eventually to Monduli. In a few months she was full of ardor for the project, plotting a hundred ideas to bring the Maasai girls out of their manacles. Simonson was the primary although by no means the exclusive architect of the plan. It was an idea advanced years ago in different venues by Simonson, the late Tanzanian prime minister, Edward M. Sokoine, and some of the Tanzanian church people. Foremost among these was Laiser, then the newly-installed bishop of the Arusha diocese. His relationship with Simonson had undergone some ironic changes in form but never in their mutual fondness. Laiser first was Simonson's student, then his peer in the ministry and now his superior as the diocesan bishop. In the early 1990s, Simonson reduced his work load for the Evangelical Lutheran Church in America to halftime, opening up work time for the remaining special projects of his stewardship in Africa, projects for which he could not expect to log on church time.

"In the eyes of a lot of people Monduli wasn't a special project," he said. "It was a pipe dream."

It wasn't a pipe dream for Thomas Laiser, who as a Maasai had intimate knowledge of the devaluation of women in the Maasai culture and of the stagnation facing the entire tribe. Simonson didn't have to apologize to Laiser for dreams, pipe or otherwise. Laiser knew Simonson as a guy who usually delivered, who looked further and higher than most of the evangelists Laiser knew and who pursued those goals with more common sense and elbow grease than most idealists he knew. Simonson and his allies envisioned a six-year course for Maasai girls, beginning when they were 14 and had graduated from a primary school. Competitive examinations and interviews would be conducted to recruit the brightest young women in the Maasai lands. They would study in the traditional disciplines, but they would also get deeply into public health and hygiene, would learn languages, would keep themselves fit in accordance with the Maasai holistic tenets of living and would learn the arts of leadership. They would advance in classes of 45 or so, and when they were finished they would go back into their communities as educated people, capable of leading and teaching. They would be knowledgeable in disease prevention and assertive enough to get into the politics of their communities and of the country. None of the school's advocates needed to be told that one more and nearly transcending of its virtues stemmed from the hard statistics of infant mortality among the Maasai. The children of educated women, even women of the barest education, lived longer.

Simonson eventually gave the school the energy and the funding it needed to get it started. He also gave it charisma and the kind of ingenuity for which Simonson was now renowned (or notorious) throughout church circles in Tanzania. He had no corner on the perception of hazards facing the Maasai in their aimless drift into the 21st century. The traditional Maasai councils of elders were going nowhere. The Maasai commissioner of the Monduli district warned about that in a proposal supporting the school Simonson was ready to build. The commissioner was blunt about a solution: Start educating the women.

And why? The commissioner made it clear with italics:

The women are capable of bringing to the "strategy for survival" discussion their rich gifts of *solidarity* amongst themselves, *an uncompromising understanding* of their cultural values and their inborn *tenacity* when cattle, children and food are involved. These are the ingredients required in the (Maasai's) present dilemma and they are best expressed by the women, because they are *different.* This difference must be recognized, accepted, appreciated and utilized for the benefit of the entire community.

It was one of those late-century discoveries by the bureaucracy. Maasai women are important. They are educable and, by God, we may need them to save us.

By the late 1980s and early 1990s, Simonson and Laiser were ready with plans.

"Lets get it in front of the elders for their reaction," Simonson suggested.

The bishop and the reverend went into the bomas to lobby their notions about the school. The reception fell considerably short of exuberance. What the Maasai seemed to be saying about the bishop was "take a few years to learn about the world and then maybe we'll listen." What they seemed to be saying about the white-bearded missionary was "wait a few more years and then maybe you'll give up this crazy idea."

One of the problems was that some of the Maasai had already received the bride price (usually in heads of cattle) for their daughters. The bishop's relative inexperience gave them a further excuse for grumbling. They were also unsure about Simonson's status as he neared church retirement. "What they told us between the lines was that when the bishop has worked a little longer—and remember he was one of their boys—and done something noteworthy, they would listen harder. And they would also would listen harder when the pastor at Monduli (Dave Simonson) was no longer running the congregation and working for the American church but full time for the Maasai school. Well, the next time we approached them I'd officially retired. I was out of a job. And the bishop had assumed a position of involvement with the government representing Maasai issues, and he was now viewed as an outstanding elder. So the next time we met, we had them."

Simonson's stonecutters and carpenters had already begun work on the school at Monduli when the reverend scheduled an important meeting with his pal, Bishop Laiser.

"I'm retiring, bishop," Simonson said. "It's mandatory for me as a missionary. They can't fund me any more with mission money in America at my age (65). I may have to leave Africa."

It was a kind of pro forma statement to which neither party attached any serious credibility.

Simonson would leave Africa only in a body bag if he had his preferences. The bishop knew that and had other plans.

"Retirement," the bishop said, "is a Western concept. We don't recognize it around here. You came to Africa, David Simonson, believing you were answering a call, and God had given you direction. I believe that, also. It follows that if you're going to leave Africa before you've finished your work, you can only do that at God's direction. Have you heard anything like that from God?"

"Nothing like that," Simonson acknowledged.

"Then God has decided your work isn't done."

"It looks that way."

"Then the issue is decided."

Simonson stayed. Monduli was just about to get going if the Maasai elders broke down and approved. He had to formally retire as a missionary sent by the Evangelical Lutheran Church in America (ELCA), with full pension rights. Those, combined with the Simonsons investments and his business interests made David and Eunice relatively secure financially. The school at Monduli was going to be run under the auspices of the Evangelical Lutheran Church of Tanzania and operate under the regulations of the Tanzanian Ministry of Education. Simonson was now free to act as an ex-officio employee of the Tanzanian church and to concentrate on the school. It was a role that did not foreclose him from preaching and building more churches and more classrooms for the primary school kids of Africa. In other words, nothing much had changed except that he was now off the ELCA payrolls and free to moan more openly about the parent church's "retreat" from mission work.

But he and Laiser now had what amounted to official backing for the Monduli experiment. They went back into the elder councils with an almost unbeatable hand, and the Maasai reconsidered. In Mama Ruthie's community, the elders still refused to listen to women as equals, although they did give them permission to talk. Mama was a large, robust woman, free-swinging in the tribal society. Her face was round and open. It was a face vibrant and compelling when she talked, so compelling as to silence the bossiest of the elders. When Simonson came shopping his plans for a school in Monduli, to give the Maasai women some knowledge of the world and some decent self-esteem, Mama Ruthie got into the thick of the tribal arguments. The rules of the council debate barred her from standing before the elders to argue for the school. Her answer when this rule was invoked was the Maasai equivalent of "to hell with the rules." She said she didn't have to stand. She could talk from her knees. She did. Her speech scorched the ears of the crustiest elders. When it was over, one of Simonson's Maasai pals who was in the meeting gave him a synopsis of the action.

"You people call her Mama Ruthie," he told Simonson. "After she talked, we're going to call her BaRuthie." Simonson erupted in laughs. He knew

Mama Ruthie and he now knew the seismic impact of her speech. In the Maasai language, *baruthie* means "dynamite."

The elders ran up the flag. All right, they said, let's try *it*. We'll let you take the ones you think you can educate, and we'll see if you're right."

The answer won't be available for several years, when the inaugural class graduates and the graduates face a proving ground.

But all of the auguries are good approaching the 21st century, a time Simonson had been telling the Maasai was the time for them to start creating their new world.

The school needed a campus, a place. For Simonson, Monduli was the place from the beginning. It was a community some 20 miles from the Arusha, which was the administrative center for northern Tanzania and the source of most of the human services available for that part of the country. He'd built a church in Monduli. The territory was amenable to church people and to schools. In addition, there was a lovely coffee plantation sitting out there ready to welcome a new school as its neighbor. The Maasai owned part of the plantation. Simonson and Laiser asked the Maasai elders whether they wouldn't consider it an excellent gesture of gratitude to offer part of their coffee acreage to the Evangelical Lutheran Church of Tanzania in exchange for six years of quality education for their young women. The elders thought this seemed reasonable and, by 1994, the carpentry had begun.

Simonson gave his own evaluation four years later: "Our first call class was 45 girls. We were going to have six forms or school years, 45 new students coming in each year. We were going to require them to spend four months in a preliminary class when they first came in, learning English, Swahili and math. In the first year they were going to study physics, chemistry, biology, math, English, Swahili, civics, history, religion, geography, home economics and agriculture.

"All of this has happened and is happening.

"Completing Form Six is the equivalent of finishing the first year of college in the states. By 1998, we'd introduced four 45-girl classes into the school, with two more to go. When all of them are in, and the girls have gone up the ladder through all of the forms, we expect them to have an education equal to what they could get in some of the best American colleges. You ought to see the progress, not only in academics but the rest. You put running shoes on them in the recreational periods, you've got track stars. By the first years of the 21st century, we expect to see a couple of them in the Olympics and a couple of them running for national office."

Simonson long ago decided that there were only minimal virtues in re-straint. That attitude lifted him into an architectural plan for the school which, with quality and attractive materials, would still replicate the features of a Maasai village. "We wanted it to be something Africans would understand—

the concept, the school campus. We wanted the classrooms to be in the shape of a Maasai house, bigger and neater, of course, and with modern facilities. We began with good stone and concrete blocks for the walls and corrugated iron for the roofs and we painted those buildings attractively, and we haven't deviated as we expanded. The whole design was to make the girls feel as though this was an enlarged Maasai boma but where they didn't get their lungs filled with smoke and where they'd come to study instead of haul water. We didn't put in a thornbush fence to keep the lions out the way they do in the bomas. We did build a barbed wire fence. The elders told us why we should. 'The lions we're worried about coming over the fence are the two-footed ones,' they said. They were worried about the girls' protection. So we built that barbed wire fence high. But above all, in designing the campus as we did, we wanted the girls to know that while this was a modern and academic version of the places where they'd lived, the people who were building it respected their sense of place."

That was the concept, and four years after it began to take form at Monduli, the fulfillment of it was close to extraordinary. The chapel at the center of its concentric circles of buildings was all but complete. Dorms, classrooms and teacher's cottages formed the inner circle. The library and administration buildings and laboratories would go up on the outer rim. The coffee plantation, a "donation" to Thomas Laiser's diocese by the Maasai and the Monduli community, was in midstream of rehabilitation from the ratty condition into which it had fallen. Parts of it were planted to maize and beans, enough to meet most of the nutrition needs of the students. The coffee itself offered some prospect of becoming an important cash crop for the school. "The coffee is premium Blue Mountain stuff," Simonson said. "Highly exportable. We expect to be doing that by early in the next century." Being Simonson, he started promoting it long before that. In the early years of the school, he stocked his Land Rover with bags of "our own Blue Mountain" coffee, mercilessly shopping it to his guests and to tourists in Arusha.

Jane Tellekson drew no salary. There was no budget for Western teachers, although Tanzanian teachers did receive some wages from the church from whatever funds Simonson could scrounge in the earlier years. The Jane Telleksons were expected to raise money for their expenses from congregations and service groups back in the states. The prospect of teaching Maasai girls with her skimpy knowledge of Swahili and her ignorance of the Maasai language scared the young woman from Wayzata, Minn., in the early months. She couldn't be sure how they reacted to her. But one day she got sick and was confined to her room, and at midday the Maasai girls came to her place with a large bowl of soup, singing their songs in their lovely red uniforms, telling her how much they missed her and feeling so bad that she wasn't feeling well. Hearing that, she cried, and the relationship of Jane Tellekson to the school and the Maasai kids was locked for the rest of her days in Africa.

The eventual price tag that Simonson and his planners calculated for the completed school was nearly $2 million, a figure not exactly bashful even by Simonson's shoot-the-moon standards. It wasn't going to come falling out of the acacia trees. He got out his traveling bags. The new schedules gave Simonson and his wife time for six months home leave in the states, three months at a time, time that the most relentless fund-raiser ever to come out of Scobey, Mont., used for coast to coast arm twisting. He went to congregations and to the teakwood offices of corporate executives. He organized campaigns and went international. Money in the early years came from congregations and organizations in the United States, Denmark, Holland, Canada and Germany. Part of it was to confer the $350 annual scholarships needed for the students' expenses. Simonson's all-court press hardly was confined to the pulpits and board rooms. From the beginning of his mission in Africa, he scoured the landscapes for equipment and material with the shrewd eye of a junk dealer. Somebody in Fergus Falls called him to say the state Department of Transportation was getting rid of its old signposts on I-94 and putting in new ones. Simonson bought them at chicken feed prices and shipped them to Monduli for his barbed wire fences. And the buildings kept going up.

And finally, the Maasai students—were they overwhelmed by this revolution in their lifestyle? Were they really studying? Did they have to make some serious sacrifices of their own. The answer was a measured "yes" on all counts. A visitor who'd attended one of the first classes at Monduli found himself amused by the girls' welcoming chant, based on a nutty limerick they learned as part of their first English class: "I was eaten by a boa constrictor, and I didn't like it very much." The visitor returned two years later and was somewhat jarred to hear these same students speaking a very manageable English and discussing with the instructor when the word "shall" is grammatically correct and when "will" is correct. The visitor wasn't altogether sure he'd learned the difference himself.

For the Jane Telleksons, all illusions about the barriers they faced dissolved quickly. She and her colleagues would go into a Maasai primary school to find a few students who were ready or wanted to attend the school at Monduli. They were met with raw hostility in some of the communities. The big majority of Maasai girls were scarcely literate. Most of them wanted to grow up to have babies and had no interest in higher education at Monduli. But they found the girls they wanted and needed. Sometimes they had to be sure they weren't being victimized by forgers and impostors who pretended to be Maasai girls or who put in phantom qualifications that had to be rooted out by the interviewers.

But the ones who wanted to come and were motivated to come sometimes had to be incredibly brave just to come. One of the girls in the first class was told she had to leave school and come home. Her father said he'd already received 30 cattle for her from a Maasai warrior who planned to marry her. The district officer in Monduli heard about it and intervened, telling the father that if the girl wasn't allowed to go to school, he was going to be fined those 30 head of cattle. The warrior wasn't buying that deal. When the girl tried to sneak out of the boma, he caught her and raped her three times on the floor of the hut.

"She managed to escape after that," Simonson remembered, "and hid all day while he was looking for her. She traveled at night through the African Rift to get back to Monduli. To do that she had to walk beneath the volcano, Oldonyo Lengai, a place that's just swarming with snakes at night. But the girl made it back to the school; it meant that much to her, and she had that much guts."

The price of going to school in Africa.

But slowly, the Maasai are understanding what is happening and why. Many of them expressed pride in having their girls transformed into scholars. "They were told that when the girls went home on leave, they had to come back to school in better shape then they left," Simonson said. "So a lot of them got out the goats and the girls ate big meals and came back fat and sassy, which means that some of those elders, at least, are now totally convinced that this is the way to go."

Scores of them proved that by showing up for Jane Tellekson's wedding to a young builder from Duluth, Rob Juten, at the Monduli school. They came with their gifts of goats and fabrics. They joined the Monduli students in their songs of celebration and in their prayers at the chapel. There were close to 2,000 people thronged around the couple, and if there was any scene to anoint the more than 40 years of stewardship in Africa for David and Eunice Simonson, that gathering in Monduli might have been the scene. Hundreds of the Maasai people, to whom the Simonsons had dedicated their work in Africa, came as fellow Christians or simply as Maasai who wanted to pay their respects to the missionaries who became their friends and to the school teachers who had taught their children. It was an occasion filled with fellowship and thanksgiving, and it seemed to give a benediction to the couple from the prairie who had never lost their idealism or their belief.

And when the time came for Jane Tellekson to eat a piece of the half-cooked goat meat the Maasai ceremonially offered to the bride, she opened her mouth without a hint (all right, without barely a hint) of squeamishness.

"Man," Simonson said, "she had a mouthful and there was no way she wasn't going to swallow all of it."

Which she did, with a gulp and prayer and to cheers all around.

CHAPTER 22

For years Dave Simonson had dreaded the approach of the new millennium. He sulked about it, and he fought it. The prelude chords of the 21st century coming close were ominous sounds to the Simonson ear. They meant the preacher was on the verge of reaching the age of 70, which by most of the rules of the pulpit and the actuarial tables meant a civilized pasturing-out on the western Minnesota prairie. It would mean good-bye to Africa, the Maasai and those large bright eyes of trust he and Eunice saw each day in the faces of the African kids. They were faces that had welded them to Africa nearly 45 years ago.

And yet Simonson had never psychologically signed any of those rules of engagement that would end his stewardship in Africa in accordance with custom or, some of his doctors groused, in accordance with common sense. In the end he outfoxed the millennium. He decided to turn it into a celebration. Yes, he had to leave the employ of the big church organization in America that was his institutional godfather. That was a policy he couldn't dodge. But he'd then conspired with the bishop in Arusha to keep him in harness figuring out ways to save the Maasai by educating their young women. So with the year 2000 approaching, he was turning down all requiems and still wheeling his Land Rover the 20 miles to Monduli from his home in Arusha, often with Eunice in the passenger seat, both of them still admiring the grape-colored jacarandas and the flame trees that escorted them en route. Riding through that corridor of color as they had when they came to Africa, they were tantalized by the thought that nothing much had changed in their four decades there.

Yet when they recovered from the reverie, they knew almost everything had changed. The mission movement had changed drastically with the times. Tanzania was now a sovereign republic, the colonials long gone. When the century turned over, the Monduli school would be all but finished. The number of classrooms financed by his Operation Bootstrap Africa would be closing in on 2,500. The burgeoning medical clinic at Selian was self-sufficient, its budget approaching $400,000 and the number of lives it had saved was reaching into the thousands.

Most of the half-century of change in Tanzania, they felt, deserved applause. Which made Dave and Eunice Simonson content and reasonably at peace. So for the preacher, it didn't really matter how much longer he and Eunice would be able to handle the physical drain. If the time came when one or both of them couldn't, they'd be ready to move on. They had outlasted the bureaucracies, a four-year ostracism, life-threatening illness and the strains of a lifetime of building, healing and ministering. They had survived the restless demands they imposed on themselves to meet the human and spiritual needs with which they were surrounded each day. They had emerged as heroes to thousands whose lives were better for their presence. Simonson's work had been honored personally by each of the Tanzanian presidents—Julius Nyerere, Ali Hassan Mywini and Benjamin Mkapa—with all of whom the preacher had enjoyed a cordial relationship.

And now their souls, Simonson would say, were too deeply rooted in the earth of the Africa they knew best for them to worry about the time when they would actually have to go.

Maybe they never would. What they had now was the best of two worlds—Africa for six months, their home in Fergus Falls, Minn. for three or four months, time with Becky in North Dakota, time with Stephen, Naomi, Nathan and Jon and the grandchildren when they were in Africa. The reverend could still build his schools and Eunie could still dispense medicine to the African mamas here and there. And on Sunday mornings, Dave Simonson could once more slip his leather stole over his shoulders to preach to an African congregation. For the how-many-thousandth time? It was no ordinary stole, he told himself each Sunday morning. It was the stole made by the Maasai from the hide of one of the great hooved animals of the Serengeti, the oryx, and presented to Simonson as a gift.

The approaching millennium inspired at least one program chairman in the states to ask Simonson to summarize the events of his stewardship, to talk about what contributions he and Eunice had made to Africa that gave them the highest satisfaction. Simonson complied with the demands of courtesy and addressed the question, but only briefly. For the rest of his time on the podium he reached back to an earlier valedictory of his, when he'd asked his listeners not to dwell that night on the gifts they'd made to Africa, as important and as appreciated as they were. The gifts that might be more critical in their lives, he said, were those that the Maasai and the other Africans could make to them, if in America they were willing to open their eyes and their hearts.

"The first gift they are ready to offer you is the gift of identity," he said. "Who am I? Where do I belong? I have to remember that I don't even have my own name. I am the son of somebody or the brother or sister of somebody. What we call uncles they call brothers and sisters. Aunts for them become mothers. Cousins are brothers and sister. So for them, what we call our extended family is something far more intimate. For them, that relationship is also permanent and indivisible. The family is their identity, and it gives them their value. It is not limited by space. It can include you and include me, wherever we live. It is not limited by time. It includes those who are visible to them and those who have passed on but are still family. It includes those who live today and those who have lived before them in their family and those who will come later. Their identity, their family, their community are inseparable. It is the bedrock of their lives. If they are separated spiritually from their family or community, they are diminished and they will be lost unless they change their lives and those relationships. That is a gift they can give, if we want to receive it—being part of their family, they being part of ours. I think that is a beautiful thought and a beautiful gift.

"Another gift they are willing and ready to share with us is the gift of wholeness. In the midst of our brokenness, our loneliness, our isolation, our separation, are we aware of what it means to be whole? Our African family does, and they are offering it to us. Out of our relationships will come that wholeness. They don't distinguish between the spiritual, the physical and the emotional. All of these are there within the human personality. The African relationship is one of whole, based on human relationships—those we have with individuals, those we have with our community or family, and those we have with the earth and finally our relationship with God. If we keep those relationships healthy, if we build on them, if we ask forgiveness or give it when we have received or caused injury, if we help one another and if we keep God in the center of our lives, we will be healthy. Our lives will be blessed. What the Maasai are talking about, whether it is in relationship between you and your family and your community, or the relationships among nations—is reconciliation. They are asking us to keep up the possibility of reconciling, that no injury or sin is so great that we cannot reconcile with one another or with God."

If you will allow an intrusion by the writer here. I've traveled parts of Maasailand several times with Simonson, walked for 200 miles in the African Rift with him and traveled among the Maasai bomas independently. When I first heard Simonson deliver this eloquent homily on the gifts available to us from the Maasai, I'd think: "All right, Dave, all right. Working and living with these people, being their brother, is your lifetime mission and it ought to be blessed. But isn't this a romanticized view of how these people live and what the moral is in it for others? Isn't the reality of that life a long distance from the idealization in which their admirers wrap it?"

I thought so. The rational man. But the longer I've considered those siftings from the Maasai life by their white-bearded elder and brother from the American wheatfields, the more appealing they grow, not as an idealization but as an essential truth. You first have to discount some of the bad behavior, the sexism, the fondness for cattle theft and the other warts. Forms of them exist in any society. But deep in their history, as Simonson would know better than most, was this bonding force, community, their belonging to it. Their serious wages to pay if they separated from it.

Their history seems to be telling us that we *are* family, not only with our natural brothers and sisters but with those who are willing to accept their embrace and those who want or need ours. Once that commitment is made, our family grows, and we are better and stronger for it. When you think further about it, we are guilty of the rankest kind of arrogance if we tell ourselves this: These people we often call primitive can't be capable of seeing life more clearly than we do. Or trapping ourselves into the arrogance of thinking, as Dean Peterson wrote, that we have nothing to learn by looking at the Africans' traditional religion, when we might have so much to learn. Consider their belief, for example, that members of family who have died are still part of the family, the so-called living dead, whose interests should be considered in how the living behave. We prefer to talk about heaven and tell jokes about ghosts, but who is to say which of us is closer to understanding the mystery of afterlife?

From the first year he preached in Africa, Simonson's strong voice from the pulpit brought a summons to action in his audiences. It still does. It is a voice that has reached into the consciences of thousands of people across the United States and into the pockets of most. It has stirred giving that has reached into the tens of millions of dollars, giving that has brought school, medicine and hope into the lives of countless Africans.

Do numbers like that validly measure his ministry, and that of Eunice?

"The numbers themselves, the numbers of baptisms, patients and pupils are a pretty soulless way to define ministry," he said. "I think what the numbers mean is that we came here to Africa with the idea of bringing something into their lives, whatever seemed right, whether God or classrooms or a surgical room where we could save lives. The needs in Africa are so huge they're never going to be fully met or even met beyond the most minimal way. Babies are still dying by the thousands daily of starvation or disease. Both of those are preventable by the world if the world, the prosperous part that has so much to give, is willing to see and to make the smallest sacrifice. People get tired of hearing about the huge, obscene outlays we make for the machines of killing. They are tired of it because they know it's true and they don't know how to stop it. All that I've done, what people like me have done, is to try to sting that conscience, to appeal to the best of what is in the hearts of most people. If I've given it all the energy and love that was available to me, if Eunice has, then we don't need numbers to tell us if we have met the pledge with which we came to Africa. We will know that we have fulfilled our commitment. However imperfectly we've done it, I think we have. But you can say the same about so many of those who brought the same pledge to Africa—Dean Peterson, Elmer Danielson, Stan Benson, Bill Smith, Mark Jacobson, their wives, and so many more."

The verdict on the ministry of Dave and Eunice Simonson might better be pronounced in the eyes of the Africans who believed them. For whatever scuffles Simonson provoked with the hierarchies, the bruises he inflicted with his impatience and his occasional spurts of haughtiness, the sum of his ministry seems extraordinary in the lives it improved or saved and the global involvement of giving that it inspired. It was a ministry that did not substantially deviate from the straight-line course and simple statement of purpose with which it began: "See a need, and respond." It began with an avowal that this was a ministry and a lifelong mission that was for keeps. No alteration of that vow was ever made. None was considered. In many ways, Dave Simonson's ministry bridged the eras of mission in Africa. He arrived at a time when the concept of lifelong foreign service was a creed of those who enlisted in it. But the revolution in Africa in mid-century, the reach for independence among its poorest but most aroused peoples, changed mission forever. When the millennium approached, the boards of foreign mission in America had reset their course. The churches in Africa were now directed by African leaders, most of their work done by African evangelists, pastors and lay people. The truism in mission work, "eventually the good missionary works himself out of a job," was never more appropriate. The Simonsons, the roaring dinosaurs of the other era, railed against the gradual receding of American churches from the traditional missionary concepts. But in America, there was rising competition for church monies, more causes to support and shrinking treasuries when those causes were measured by per capita outlays. Better to devote the resources you had, the big church agencies had decided, to working *in relationship, in communion* with the churches in Africa that were now under African control. Better to devote those resources to educating underschooled people in creating their own resources, to give them technical support and technical advice, help them build their farms and their industries.

It made sense. Simonson had adopted those "teach a man to fish" ideas himself. He'd launched that sunflower seed program to encourage Tanzanians to start their own family oil products business; the heifer program, where he rounded up enough heifers to give one to each of scores of families, the theory being that when they reproduced, the owners could pass on the offspring to other families. In his calmer moments, Simonson might agree that independence in Africa and the autonomy it brought to African churches forced major shifts in the direction of foreign mission work by American churches. "But leave room," he seemed to be saying, "for some future Dave Simonson or Dean Peterson or Elmer Danielson."

It would be nice. God knows some of them are still needed, assuming they could be cloned or subsidized. But whatever direction mission work takes in the next century, its responsibilities will still be vast as measured by the massive increase in the Christian population in once-primitive countries. In 1800, the ELCA's Division of Global Mission noted, 23 percent of the world population was Christian. In the year 2000, that increases to 32 percent. Even more dramatic, however, has been the geographical shift in the world's Christian population. In 1900, 87 percent of the world's Christians lived in Europe and North America. Today, 60 percent of the world's Christians live in Latin America, Africa and Asia.

If any assessment has to be made of the zeal with which Christian mission has been advanced in the 20th century (for better or for worse, the owly skeptic might say) it is there in cosmic numbers.

Simonson is no owly skeptic. He is one of those who carried the cross into those primitive lands, lands now not so primitive because of those energies and willingness to risk. If that is the big picture of his ministry, Simonson prefers a more intimate picture, one that finally narrows to his relationship with his God.

"I can remember there were those who said that the times would come when you weren't sure whether you were carrying out God's will or yours, and those times did come. I knew that I wasn't going to be able to get a conference with God each morning to figure that out. When the doubts came about the direction you were going in, you just had to carry on and trust that sooner or later God would let you know. That happened. There were instances when he would appear, one way another, and there would be a Presence. I was aware of it. I can't define it. It was there. Sometimes the feeling was so intense that I don't think I could have survived if it weren't eased in some way, and it was. Those were the times when God was letting me know no matter the mistakes I made, I was doing what he wanted. I always came away strengthened and feeling peace. Some people will scoff at that. But then I bring up something like the school at Monduli, where almost every step of the way something happened or somebody came on to the scene to move that along when it seemed to reach a dead end. There was Thomas Laiser and Mama Ruthie and that coffee plantation and then there were these marvelous young women who volunteered to teach, and finally the Maasai girls who risked so much to come into the school. All of those things couldn't have happened without somebody arranging it, and I'm not talking about Dave Simonson. All of which means that we're looking into the new century in the Africa that has given us life and our reason for being. And I keep coming back to a question the Maasai asked so many times: 'Why are you doing this; you come from another place and you're doing this for us. Why?' And I'd give them the same answer. 'You would give help to me if I needed it. I did, and you gave, so we're brothers after all.'"

It finally it comes to the one constant. Africa. Africa elusive, Africa cruel, Africa that burns its way into the living soul of those who want to possess it but know they cannot. Africa of the Maasai and Dave Simonson, of the stately women in their striking orange and black saris, carrying gourds of water on their heads but moving into a new time when they may not have to; the plains of butter yellow grass waving in the wind; the desert and the great Nile; Lake Victoria and Kilimanjaro; of Karen Blixen and David Livingstone; idyllic and murderous; of hungry millions and sick kids and gorgeous landscapes and herds of wildebeest. Africa that Aadje Geertsema watches for hours from her chair beside the fire on the edge of the wildland at Lake Ndutu, transfixed as the daylight gives way to the spreading vermilion and indigo of the African twilight. There is no one Africa. There are hundreds of Africas, most of them still searching.

And, if you will forgive the writer's intrusion one last time, it might have been that searching and implausible Africa, so wild and so electric, that enfolded us in a walk in the Rift Valley with Simonson years ago. We got up in the darkness to walk that day's 20 miles out of the 200 from Loliondo to Arusha. It was one of Simonson's boxcar fund-raisers. Everybody put up $15,000 for the privilege of walking on lava rock baked by centuries of equatorial sun, and through lion country.

We heard the first lion at 5:30 a.m. It was a few hundred feet away. It was growling and bellowing. I couldn't resist the thought that it was lonely. The clue was the answering call from a second lion a few hundred feet on the other side of our trail. The lions had us straddled, and we could only guess at the significance of the grunts and roars they were exchanging across the tall grass of the Engaruku Basin. The reverend was carrying two Ruger Blackhawk .357 revolvers in his holster. They looked impressive, but if the reverend was going to save us from a charging lion with a .357 revolver, we had a better chance quoting from John 3:16. I will tell you this about the roar of a lion when it is close and all that stands between the two of you is a few yards of blowing grass and a $14 flashlight from Target: I have heard approaching freight trains when my car neared a crossing. I have heard 10-ton boulders falling from a mountain wall overhead and I have heard lightening bolts splitting trees in the Minnesota wilderness. I will take the freight train, boulders and lightning bolt light years before I will take the sound of a roaring lion in the African bush. It is a sound that cuts through your bones and spins your stomach. When it is truly close, it seems to shake the ground under you. But by sunrise the lions were gone and the reverend, never dazzled by long sermons, led a two-minute devotional before we were off for Sonjo country. There, the friends and parishioners of Simonson were scurrying through the forest with their bodies striped with white paint, with bows and poisoned arrows in their hands. They weren't looking for us, thank God. They were after some Maasai cattle thieves who'd just raided their pasture. Simonson introduced us to one of his favorites, a little guy with a huge bow and enough toxin in those arrows to paralyze a regiment.

I thought then: You aren't going to find many copies of David Simonson. wasn't sure Christendom is ready for it. He was beefy, gregarious and devout.

He was also a passable autocrat and showman, taking us through his East Africa, introducing us to the scores of natives who knew him, some of whom he'd baptized. And a few miles later we were immersed in something marvelously alien and primeval. Monkeys called down on us and seemed to be mocking us, unseen in branches so dense they sealed out the sun. Wild primrose crowded our trail. A family of guinea hens flitted for cover ahead of us.

I had a question for myself. This East African wilderness of the acacia and fever trees, its elephant grass and the purple escarpment of the great Rift, was it essentially any different from a thousand years ago?

Yes and no. The wilderness was almost the same. Those sounds in it, the screams of one animal yielding to the superior strength of another, were about the same. But the revolver-packing preacher up ahead, Simonson, was one part that made it different. He wore his white beard and the western boots and Outback hat. He had vast shoulders and a bountiful gut, and he waddled a little when he walked. We walked with him not only because his Africa was an irresistible Africa but because Simonson was a special kind of dreamer, with his Bible in his belt and Rugers on his hips, but a dreamer still. He saw African babies who deserved something more in their lives than malaria and lung disease. He saw children who needed hope as much as they needed food. So he built schools and clinics, where before nothing stood but clumps of beaten-down banana trees. We'd walked with this man and filled our heads with sensations to last the rest of our lives. And now the last palisades separating us from Arusha lifted before us. The walk had been demanding and overwhelming. In the final 24 hours, Africa gave us a mural of its startling geography, its pain, history and hypnotic force. We came to a Maasai village which was celebrating the victory of one of its warriors over a lion that had attacked their cattle. He had attended a university in England and spoke an English that could have been mistaken for Richard Burton's. Why was he back living in the African Rift? "I told these people I would," he said. "I'm not here because I have to be here. I'm here because I want to be here. It's where I belong."

We entered low scrubland as we came out of the Rift. The wind created spiraling dust rising hundreds of feet in the air, transforming itself into walls of silt that turned day into dirty brown. We lunched in the dust-filled classroom of a stone schoolhouse the Canadians built four years ago. A pupil's notebook was lying on a bare bench that served as a desk. In carefully crafted letters, the Maasai boy had made notes about how to write a letter in English. And now this same boy was somewhere on the great plain, standing watch over a herd of cattle as his ancestors had done for hundreds of years. With a Maasai school teacher acting as guide, we scaled the 800-foot escarpment and came out on a wide meadow where herds of goats and cattle grazed. Mountains rose in all directions. It was the kind of scene you might experience in central Montana, except that here there was the inferno of the desert gorge just behind us, the everlasting snows of Kilimanjaro to the east, thatched villages just above us and giraffe, gazelles, ostrich and hyena not many miles away. Add roaring lions. It was hard for the brain to hold all of that in one day, in one lifetime. But when we arrived on the outskirts of Arusha, 200 miles and eight days from where we started, we walked beneath groves of bougainvillea and flame trees. It was one more Africa. Simonson had been trying to explain it. If you dream enough, the beauty in Africa outlasts the pain.

And finally, there was one more Africa: an Africa made better by the lifetime of service by two dreamers from the plains of America.

In the midst of the hard times of the 1930s, the Nordbys of Portland, N.D., still managed their Sunday best on special days on the prairie. As a kid, Eunice (second from right) knew more about making angels in the snow than she did about Africa, but it didn't take her long to learn about the Maasai after she met Richard Reusch (below). Eunice's brother, Harold, later became a respected researcher in the field of citrus foods. Their father, Rev. Harold Nordby, was a circuit-riding preacher and their mother, Olga, taught school, kept the family fed and clothed and on time at church.

All of these little Simonson folks eventually became hard-muscled football players at Concordia College in Moorhead before entering notable careers that included the ministry (Dave, right, and Luther, second from left), business (Paul, left) and medicine (James, perched on the table at five months.

Richard Reusch emerged from the battlegrounds of the Bolshevik Revolution in Russia to build himself into a legend in East Africa as a Lutheran missionary, lion-hunter, mountain climber and all-around risk taker. When he moved later to Minnesota as a professor at Gustavus Adolphus, his wondrous tales of Africa motivated both Eunice and Dave to chart their lives in that direction.

After nearly ten years in Africa as a bush nurse, mother of five and wife of a roaming missionary, Eunice Simonson might still have won beauty contests, although no such events were ever part of the Simonson agenda in Tanzania. She and David returned to Minnesota in 1964 to live temporarily in Northfield on a year's leave from their work in Africa. Simonson was by then a highly visible figure in African mission work.

As a child growing up in Africa, Jonathan, the youngest of the Simonson boys, quickly made friends with the African kids in the villages around Arusha, where the Simonsons spent much of their ministry, and here in Loliondo, where they lived for four years. His early fascination for vehicles of any kind—wagons, Land Rovers, etc.—eventually turned him toward mechanics, engineering and lodge management.

By the 1970s, the Simonson family had moved into a hilltop manor on land given to them near Arusha by the appreciative Maasai. It was their tribute to the work done by David and Eunice in building schools and for healing and nourishing thousands of Africans. From the top, Stephen, Naomi, Nathan, Rebecca and Jonathan.

For four years, the Simonsons lived in this house during David's "exile" to Loliondo in far northern Tanzania on the edge of the great Serengeti Plain. Simonson was banished there after a dispute with the bishop of Moshi over the distribution of church funds. Despite that collision, the Simonsons performed some of their most notable work during those four years, Dave as a pastor and broker of the Maasai's needs, and Eunice as a nurse in the nearby village of Wasso. The house was somewhat nortorious. It had been built on specifications out of a magazine. The builder got some of the directions wrong, and the house was shakily lopsided until Simonson did some shoring-up.

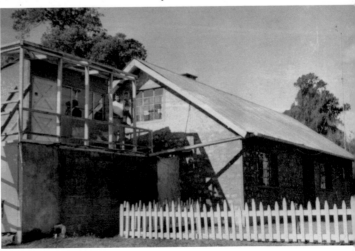

The robust reverend from the American wheatfields was ignorant about the arts and crafts of rugby football when he arrived in Africa. But Dave Simonson's American football experience, his powerful frame and his competitiveness quickly attracted rugby promoters. The team from Arusha for which he played became the champions of Tanzania. His success in rugby stimulated his sons to get involved and the whole Simonson clan, including Nate (left) and Steve, eventually played together. Eunice didn't play, but she did cheer a lot.

When her obligations as a nurse and mother allowed it, Eunice Simonson reconnected with the stage as a member of a lively troupe in Arusha, whose members included both Africans and men and women from the American and European colonies in the city. The cast of a spiritual play, "He Touched Me," written by one of Eunice's African friends, gathers here after curtain of one of the performances. Eunice is second from right, front row.

The American missionary community in Tanzania gathered as often as it could from the 1960s through the early 90s when it was more sizeable than it is today. The mission families came together to socialize and to talk mission matters. Gatherings such as this one near Arusha offered a change of pace and were valuable in the sharing of information and building solidarity.

Mothers with children would assemble in the Simonson yeard by 7 in the morning each day to wait for "Momma" to minister to their pains. Eunice operated her Back Door Clinic for years, tending to thousands of children and adults, giving what medicine she could, healing, counseling and generally loving those who came. Over that time her clinic performed an incalculable good.

One of the Simonson's renowned humanitarian efforts in Africa was what became known as Operation Bootstrap, a fund-raising project that eventually led to the construction of more than 2,000 classrooms in Africa. It was made possible by money contributed largely by American churchgoers and the work of African village men and women, who built the classrooms with material purchased with the donated money and with mud bricks they made themselves.

Pictured here are members of one of Bootstrap's earliest boards, from left, upper row: Oscar Husby, Don Sorensen, Art Dale (then executive director), Edgar F. Johnson, Richard Kvamme, Verce Fuglestad; first row from left: Dick Hefte, Dave Simonson (Bootstrap's founder), Lenore Madson and Dennis Sobolik.

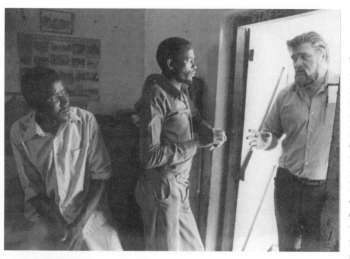

They are simple buildings, the more than 2,500 classrooms built in East Africa during the last 30 years under Dave Simonson's Operation Bootstrap. But they have brought school into the lives of hundreds of thousands of kids who would otherwise have been forced to study outdoors under the tropical sun, in smoke-filled huts or under rocks. It has been a landmark effort in mission work in Africa linking thousands of American contributors with the families of the African children, whose parents (two of them with Simonson, upper photo) made the mud brick that formed the walls of the schools and did the carpentry. Most of the buildings cost approximately $3,000, which paid for the corrugated roof and concrete, the door, the blackboard and the study tables, if tables were available. Over the years the Bootstrap program raised more than $7 million to build the schools, the great bulk of it contributed by church-goers in Minnesota and the Midwest. There were not many amenities in the classrooms, like this one near Arusha in Tanzania. But to those hundreds of thousands of children, it was school—the first one they ever had.

Baptism is the beginning. In the Christian tradition, it touches the newly baptized with the mark of Jesus Christ, the cross. It is administered joyously here by Isaac Landei, an African minister of the Lutheran church and by Stan Benson, a longtime missionary now living in retirement in St. Peter, Minn.

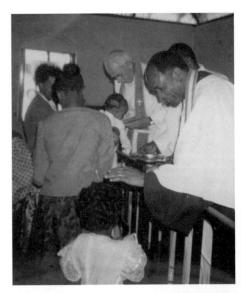

The compelling features and presence of Ole-Romo (below), a Maasai medicine man, were familiar to Lutheran missionaries of the late 1990s and particularly to Dave Simonson, whom he befriended. The tribal medicine men were powerful and influential figures who could both block the mission movements in their localities if they chose, or assist it if they respected people like Simonson. Ole-Romo chose to offer his friendship and helped to build a Lutheran chapel at Wasso in northern Tanzania, where the Simonsons lived for four years and where they served often thereafter.

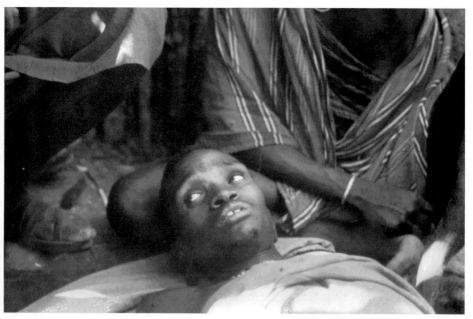

He was gathering honey in a tree, this 19-year-old Sonjo warrior who lived in northern Tanzania. A branch snapped, plunging him to the ground. He lay there paralyzed, his neck broken. Dave Simonson, who knew the family, received a visit the next day from the young man's friend. They'd walked 26 miles to tell him that Naguyani Muyuroso, the striken warror, wished to see the pastor before he died. Simonson and a friend, Peder Waldum, drove to the scene. The young man could move only his eyes and lips. "Pastor," he said, "pray for me." Simonson knelt over him and prayed. He tried to comfort him and then the family. Simonson and Waldum then drove back to Loliondo. And two days later—

Naguyani Muyuroso, paralyzed and dying with a broken neck when they last saw him, walked to the Simonson house with his brother, Petro (right), with a gourd of honey as an offering of thanks. He was perfectly healthy. It was God's will, Simonson said. There was no other explanation.

Joining hundreds of friends of Africa in Fergus Falls, Minn., their home away from Tanzania, Dave and Eunice walk hand-in-hand in the 11th annual Operation Bootstrap walk for funds for classrooms and for the secondary school for Maasai girls in Monduli, Tanzania.

Simonson's periodic fund-raising walks in the Rift Valley of Africa are somewhat more strenuous than the stateside project. Once every three years he invites friends to join him on the eight-day, 200-mile trek from Loliondo to Arusha. All are people who have solicited pledges in the states, the money being committed for construction of classrooms or the Maasai girls school. From left: Dick Hefte, Simonson, Kjell Bergh, Donna Reed and Jim Klobuchar.

He was roaming the plains of the Serengeti, herding his cattle, one of the most powerful of all Maasai medicine men, Ole-Ntokote. He knew nothing of Christianity and had no interest in learning about it. In a light rain, he later told Dave Simonson, he heard a voice from above. The voice said, "Feed my sheep." The words baffled him. He kept on walking until he heard the voice again, telling him to go to the Maasai, and to tell them, "It was time for the Maasai, my people, to enter the kingdom." The medicine man went to some missionaries, and finally met Simonson. Ultimately, Ole-Ntokote accepted Christianity, an act that led directly to the baptism of 3,000 to 4,000 Maasai into the Lutheran church, the most dramatic event of its kind in modern mission.

The Simonson home near Arusha. The land on which it was built was a gift from the Maasai.

Almost no congregations on earth are as colorful as the Maasai in celebration. They gather here under the acacias to dedicate their new Lutheran church on the outskirts of Arusha in Tanzania. What made it especially festive for them was the presence of Thomas Laiser (in green robes), the bishop of the Arusha diocese, as the presiding prelate. He was one of their own, a Maasai.

Years before he'd become the bishop of the Arusha diocese of the Evangelical Lutheran Church in Tanzania, Thomas Laiser was a student of David Simonson's. Because their friendship and trust were close, neither felt any awkwardness when Laiser became Simonson's superior. When Simonson came to his office in the 1990s to announce his formal retirement, the bishop ended the conversation quickly and amiably. "Retirement," he said, "is a Western concept. We don't recognize it here." Simonson stayed.

The ochre togas most of the young Maasai wear to ceremonies are traditional tribal dress, as are the earings and multi-colored beaded collars worn by many of the women. Historically, the Maasai have resisted conversion to Christianity, preferring their own tribal religion but professing interest if not enthusiasm for Christianity. The 1990s, however, witnessed a change in attitude among many of the Maasai, particularly under the leadership of Bishop Thomas Laiser of the Arusha diocese of the Lutheran church, himself a Maasai.

When a Maasai congregation comes together to celebrate, a songfest is one of the first and irresistible priorities. The director, with all of those marvelous bracelets on her wrists, leads and the young men and women harmonize. The songs are their own, sung in infectious cadence and syncopation, the lyrics based on biblical texts.

Women were traditionally subjugated in the Maasai culture, which was a hardcore patriarchy in which the men herded the cattle, fought the lions, stole cattle and ran the tribal councils. Women bore babies, cooked, hauled water and were supposed to keep their mouths shut. But as the Maasai culture deteriorated with the shrinkage of land available to the nomadic life, it became apparent that fresh ideas were needed to preserve the society. Some progressive Maasai bureaucrats plus Dave Simonson, Bishop Thomas Laiser and others had an idea: Train women to be new leaders. This was the origin of the Secondary School for Maasai Girls near Monduli.

At the Monduli school, the Maasai girls screened from primary grades are offered extensive courses in language, arts, mathematics, reading, writing, history and geography, accounting and graphics plus practical courses in hygiene and medicine. Instructors were volunteers from America in the early years but, increasingly, Maasai teachers are being hired and the school is generally under Maasai supervision.

When the Maasai tribal owners turned over the land for use by the Monduli school, part was a moribund coffee plantation that showed its neglect. But the Monduli builders reasoned that a revived coffee business could eventually be the primary source of operational money for the school. The plantation was overhauled, and its prime Blue Mountain coffee bgan growing again. A limited crop is now being processed. But coffee takes time, and the expectation is that by early in the next century, tons of coffee will be sold annually to keep Monduli solvent.

With their highly animated walls, decorated largely with original art by the Maasai girls, the Monduli school's dormitory rooms provide plenty of sociability for the students. Eventually the four and six-person dorm rooms will be replaced by rooms for two, allowing more space and privacy.

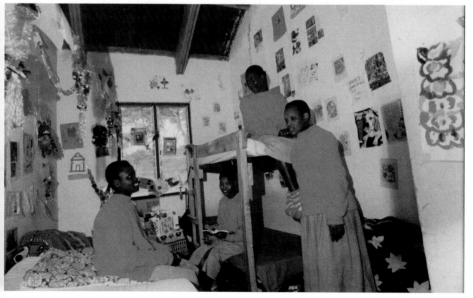

Holding a ceremonial shield of buffalo skin given to him by Maasai elders, Dave Simonson is surrounded by red-uniformed students at the Maasai girls school at Monduli on one more landmark day—the completion of the front wall of a school's chapel, designed by the reverend himself to represent the Maasai's values of community and kinship with the earth.

Visitors to East Africa often remark on the character in eyes and faces of the Maasai. It is a quality shared by both young and old, and is evident in the reunion of these two young friends near the village of Kitumbeini in northern Tanzania.

Although they are venturing into a different world with their classes at the Monduli school, home for the young women is still the tribal boma. Her friends and relatives turn out to welcome the student on the right on her return for vacation. The smoke and the darkness in those huts are familiar to her but not the most attractive part of communal living, something she might want to change in the years ahead.

The Maasai are historically hardy and tough, but that tradition doesn't mean they can't be affectionate. A student at the Maasai girls school admires her mother's beads, while her little sister looks quizically at that beaded cross the family scholar is wearing.

Eunice Simonson vigorously denies any pronounced skills as an artist. Her work offers a strong rebuttal. Her portrait of an African herdsman, sketched on the East Africa plain, hangs on the wall of the family home in Ilboru.